Advanced MySQL 8

Discover the full potential of MySQL and ensure high
performance of your database

Eric Vanier
Birju Shah
Tejaswi Malepati

BIRMINGHAM - MUMBAI

Advanced MySQL 8

Commissioning Editor: Pravin Dhandre
Acquisition Editor: Namrata Patil
Content Development Editor: Chris D'cruz
Technical Editor: Nilesh Sawakhande
Copy Editor: Safis Editing
Project Coordinator: Namrata Swetta
Proofreader: Safis Editing
Indexer: Mariammal Chettiyar
Graphics: Jisha Chirayil
Production Coordinator: Nilesh Mohite

First published: January 2019

Production reference: 1310119

Published by Packt Publishing Ltd.
Livery Place
35 Livery Street
Birmingham
B3 2PB, UK.

ISBN 978-1-78883-444-5

www.packtpub.com

`mapt.io`

Mapt is an online digital library that gives you full access to over 5,000 books and videos, as well as industry leading tools to help you plan your personal development and advance your career. For more information, please visit our website.

Why subscribe?

- Spend less time learning and more time coding with practical eBooks and Videos from over 4,000 industry professionals

- Improve your learning with Skill Plans built especially for you

- Get a free eBook or video every month

- Mapt is fully searchable

- Copy and paste, print, and bookmark content

Packt.com

Did you know that Packt offers eBook versions of every book published, with PDF and ePub files available? You can upgrade to the eBook version at `www.packt.com` and as a print book customer, you are entitled to a discount on the eBook copy. Get in touch with us at `customercare@packtpub.com` for more details.

At `www.packt.com`, you can also read a collection of free technical articles, sign up for a range of free newsletters, and receive exclusive discounts and offers on Packt books and eBooks.

Contributors

About the authors

Eric Vanier is one of the few DBAs worldwide specializing in MySQL performance, and is an expert with large architectures such as those for Air Miles, Cogeco, McGill University, Bombardier Aerospace, and many more. As a senior DBA and instructor for 18 years, he has a track record in performance and troubleshooting on dozens of high-profile MySQL systems, including complex cluster environments.

I want to thank my wife, Sia, who helped edit this book, and for her encouragement as well.

Birju Shah is the principal architect for Endurance International Group. He has a bachelor's degree in computer engineering from Gujarat University. He has the experience and expertise to build scalable products for hosting domains. He is passionate about the latest architectural patterns, tools, and technologies, and he helps organizations to follow best practices. He is also passionate about technical training and sessions.

I would like to thank my father, Bhupendra Shah; mother, Sheela Shah; my wife, Chiragi Shah; and my cutie pie, Dhanya Shah, for their help and continuous support. I would also like to thank my friends Jignesh Raval, Gopal Rohara, Rajeev Sahu, and Arnav Chaudhry for their support and guidance. Special thanks to Ali and Chris for their continuous support, and the Packt team for giving me the opportunity to contribute to a few chapters of my first ever book.

Tejaswi Malepati is the Cassandra Tech Lead for Target. He has been instrumental in designing and building custom Cassandra integrations, including a web-based SQL interface and data validation frameworks between Oracle and Cassandra. Tejaswi earned a master's degree in computer science from the University of New Mexico, and a bachelor's degree in electronics and communication from Jawaharlal Nehru Technological University in India. He is passionate about identifying and analyzing data patterns in datasets using R, Python, Spark, Cassandra, and MySQL.

I'd like to thank my family, friends, and team for their constant support and encouragement in completing my second book.

About the reviewer

Karthik P.R is the founder/CEO of Mydbops. He is a MySQL database consultant with solid experience in MySQL. He and his team provide MySQL consulting to some of the largest internet companies. Prior to building Mydbops, he worked with Yahoo! as lead MySQL DBA. Karthik is an active speaker in the MySQL community, and a blogger as well.

He has also reviewed *MariaDB High Performance* by Pierre Mavro and *Getting Started with MariaDB* by Daniel Bartholomew, which are both published by Packt Publishing.

Packt is searching for authors like you

If you're interested in becoming an author for Packt, please visit `authors.packtpub.com` and apply today. We have worked with thousands of developers and tech professionals, just like you, to help them share their insight with the global tech community. You can make a general application, apply for a specific hot topic that we are recruiting an author for, or submit your own idea.

Table of Contents

Preface   1

Chapter 1: Introduction   5
  Why MySQL 8?   6
  Why is MySQL 8.0 the next generation?   6
  Why it is so important to have a good MySQL architecture design   7
  Summary   8

Chapter 2: MySQL 8's New Features   9
  Global data dictionary   9
  MySQL 8's support roles and history   12
  **MySQL 8 supports the creation and management of resource groups
  and permissions**   13
  InnoDB enhancements   17
  JSON enhancements functionalities   18
  Invisible indexes from MySQL optimizer   21
  Features deprecated in MySQL 8.0   24
  A quick look at the features removed from MySQL 8.0   24
  Summary   26

Chapter 3: Indexing Your Data for High Performance   27
  How does MySQL optimizer think in MySQL 8.0?   28
  What kind of data type should I consider indexing first and why?   30
  Why should I have a good index strategy?   32
  What impact does an index have on MySQL performance?   33
  How to display and analyze a table structure   35
  How to efficiently read MySQL query execution plans   41
    How to effectively read the EXPLAIN results   41
      id (JSON name: select_id)   44
      select_type (JSON name: none)   44
      table (JSON name: table_name)   45
      partitions (JSON name: partitions)   45
      type (JSON name: access_type)   45
    EXPLAIN extra information   46
  How to know when to create an index   48
  Multiple column index versus multiple indexes   49
  How to organize your columns in an index for good performance   54
    Case study 1 – how to use the EXPLAIN plan tool in MySQL 8.0   57
      EXPLAIN options   58

Case study 2 – how to display and analyze a table structure versus the
EXPLAIN plan tool 60
Case study 3 – how to organize your columns in an index efficiently 62
Creating a missing index 65
Tips and techniques 67
The five general rules for your indexes 67
Tip 2 – the five general rules to optimize your queries 67
Tip 3 – understand your material resources 68
Tip 4 – the configuration is not the only thing to take into consideration 69
Tip 5 – recommendations on the performance of the MySQL architecture 70
A technical case study 70
Summary 72

Chapter 4: Advanced Data Techniques for Large Queries 73
The most important variables are full-scan indicators 74
Partitioning a table 76
An overview of partitioning in MySQL 8.0 76
Available partitioning type 77
Horizontally partitioning your data 77
Managing partitions 77
RANGE partitioning 78
LIST partitioning 80
HASH partitioning 82
KEY partitioning 83
Using partitions 84
Partition pruning 84
Getting rid of unused and duplicate indexes 86
Unused indexes 86
Duplicate indexes 87
Bonus – potentially missing indexes 88
The most important query optimizations 90
Optimizing a query with the WHERE clause 90
Optimizing a query with a GROUP BY clause 94
Optimizing a query with the ORDER BY clause 96
Temporary tables 98
Case study 1 – an example of how to optimize a complex query 101
Case study 2 – how to optimize sort indexes 105
Tips and techniques 107
Partitions 107
Optimization 108
Techniques 108
A typical use case: time series data 108
Example of a mass DELETE 111
Summary 112

Chapter 5: MySQL Data Dictionary in MySQL 8.0 115

MySQL data dictionary structure in MySQL 8.0   115
Dictionary object cache   117
Transactional storage of the data dictionary   118
Applications of the data dictionary   119
Removal of file-based storage metadata   119
Serialized Dictionary Information (SDI)   120
Limitations of the data dictionary   121
Tips and techniques   121
Summary   122

Chapter 6: MySQL Server Settings   123
  Getting started with the most significant variables   123
  MySQL server optimization   125
    Control the types of data change operations   125
    Enabling the adaptive hash indexing function   125
    Set a limit on the number of concurrent threads   126
    Controlling the amount of InnoDB preloading   126
    Increasing the number of background threads   126
    Controlling InnoDB input/output performance in the background   127
    Taking advantage of multicore processors   127
    Preventing punctual operations   127
    Configuring the number and size of instances   127
    The InnoDB buffer pool   128
  The thread cache   129
    Case study 1 – when MySQL uses more than 100% of a CPU   130
      How to detect high usage of the MySQL processor   131
      Correcting the use of the MySQL CPU   132
      How to prevent MySQL from using high CPUs   132
    Case study 2 – when MySQL swaps on disk   132
  Tips and techniques   133
  Summary   134

Chapter 7: Group Replication in MySQL 8.0   135
  High availability and requirements   136
    Scaling   136
  Replication   137
  Group replication   138
    Use cases for group replication   140
      Elastic replication   140
      Highly available shards   141
      Alternative to master – slave replication   142
      Autonomic systems   142
  An overview of MySQL's database replication   142
    Asynchronous replication   144
    Semi-synchronous replication   144
    Delayed replication   145

Global transaction identifier-based replication	145
Multi-source replication	146
MySQL's group replication architecture	**147**
Group	148
Writeset	148
How group communication works	149
Certification process	151
Total order delivery	151
Detecting failure	152
Network partitioning	153
Traditional locking versus optimistic locking	154
Distributed first commit wins rule	154
Drawbacks of optimistic locking	155
Modes of group replication	155
Single primary mode	156
Multi-primary	157
Group replication requirements	157
Configuring the server	158
Configuring group replication	158
Monitoring group replication	166
Replication_group_members	166
replication_group_member_stats	166
Replication_connection_status	167
Replication_applier_status	167
Server state	167
Limitations of group replication	**168**
Group replication security	**169**
IP address whitelist	169
SSL	170
VPN	171
Operations on an online group	**171**
Changing the group mode	172
Tuning recovery	172
Combining group replication versions	173
Performance tuning	174
Message compression	174
Flow control	175
Summary	**178**
Chapter 8: InnoDB Cluster in MySQL 8.0	**181**
What is InnoDB cluster?	**182**
InnoDB cluster requirements	184
Installing MySQL Shell	184
How to use MySQL Shell	185
Installing an InnoDB cluster	188
MySQL InnoDB cluster for a sandbox environment	188
InnoDB cluster in a production environment	195
Configuring the router configuration	199

Managing clusters   201
    Getting details of a cluster   202
    Removing instances from a cluster   202
    Adding instances to a cluster   202
    Restoring a cluster after quorum loss   202
    Rebooting a cluster after a major outage   202
    Rescanning a cluster   202
    Checking instance states   203
    Dissolving an InnoDB cluster   203
InnoDB cluster limitations   203

Storage engines   204
Setting a storage engine   205
    MyISAM storage engine   205
    The MEMORY storage engine   206
    The CSV storage engine   206
    The ARCHIVE storage engine   207
    The BLACKHOLE storage engine   207
    The MERGE storage engine   207
    The FEDERATED storage engine   208
    InnoDB engine   208

Migrating from master-slave replication to MySQL InnoDB cluster   209
Summary   215

Chapter 9: Monitoring Your Large Distributed Databases   217
MONyog   218
Pros   219
Cons   220
Conclusion   221
Datadog   222
Getting started   222
Pros   224
Cons   225
Conclusion   225
Navicat   225
Pros   227
Cons   228
Conclusion   228
Comparison between monitoring tools   229
The price   229
Pros   229
Cons   230
Top clients   230
Tips and techniques   231
Summary   232

Chapter 10: Authentication and Security Management with MySQL 8.0 233
MySQL 8.0 security features   233

Privileges provided by MySQL 8.0   234
Where are privileges stored in MySQL 8.0?   235
The differences between dynamic and static privileges   236
Creating roles and users in MySQL 8.0   237
Displaying assigned roles using SHOW GRANTS   239
Troubleshooting connection problems   240
Tips and techniques   241
 Restricting or disabling remote access to the server   241
 Disabling LOCAL INFILE usage   241
 Changing the username and password for root   242
Summary   242

Chapter 11: Advanced MySQL Performance Tips and Techniques   243
Tips/best practices   243
 Optimizing your queries for the query cache   244
 EXPLAIN your SELECT queries   245
 LIMIT 1 when getting a unique row   247
 Indexing for search fields   248
 Indexing strategy for Joins   249
 Avoiding SELECT * and COUNT *   250
 Almost always have an ID field   253
 Using ENUM over VARCHAR   255
 Using prepared statements if and when possible   256
 Splitting the big DELETE or INSERT queries   257
 Avoiding the delete trigger   259
Techniques   260
 Can MySQL perform queries on billions of rows?   260
 Is InnoDB the right choice for multi-billion rows?   261
 How big can a MySQL database get before the performance starts to
 degrade?   261
 Why MySQL could be slow with large tables   261
 Is MySQL the best solution for handling blobs?   261
Summary   262

Other Books You May Enjoy   263

Index   267

Preface

Businesses, whether small or large, use MySQL to access and manipulate their enterprise databases across the world. *Advanced MySQL 8* will be your one-stop guide to implementing and managing large-scale MySQL distributed clusters to run high-volume websites, enterprise systems, and packaged software.

Who this book is for

This book will appeal to database administrators, data architects, and all those who want to advance in developing database applications in the MySQL environment.

What this book covers

Chapter 1, *Introduction*, walks through the changes that took place in MySQL 8, compared to the previous versions. We also study what makes MySQL 8 a next-generation database, and also cover its architectural design.

Chapter 2, *MySQL 8 – New Features*, not only covers all the new, exciting features of MySQL 8.0, but also reviews the deprecated and removed features as well.

Chapter 3, *Indexing Your Data for High Performance*, explains how to optimize MySQL performance by using indexes and Query Execution plans with examples. Optimization involves a good understanding of MySQL Optimizer, index strategies, and a solid knowledge of how indexes and queries work together.

Chapter 4, *Advanced Data Techniques for Large Queries*, explains how to analyze and optimize large MySQL queries and covers various tips and techniques. We will take a look at the concept of partitioning your data and deep dive into it.

Chapter 5, *MySQL Data Dictionary in MySQL 8.0*, explains how to get optimal MySQL Server 8.0 settings and how to work with MySQL's data dictionary, and also covers the data dictionary's limitations.

Chapter 6, *MySQL Server Settings*, explains how to get optimal MySQL Server 8.0 settings. We will also work on two case studies, which will focus on scenarios when MySQL uses more than 100% of a CPU and when MySQL swaps on disk.

Chapter 7, *Group Replication in MySQL 8.0*, focuses on an important topic: high availability. With this feature, we will be able to create a very powerful, reliable, and highly available replication infrastructure.

Chapter 8, *InnoDB Cluster in MySQL 8.0*, explains what InnoDB cluster is and its requirements. We will learn how to create one and manage it. We shall study the limitations of InnoDB and learn about its storage engines.

Chapter 9, *Monitoring Your Large Distributed Databases*, explores and compares the top three monitoring tools for large distributed databases, which are MONYOG, Datadog, and Navicat.

Chapter 10, *Authentication and Security Management with MySQL 8.0*, goes through the differences between dynamic and static security privileges, along with an overview of the grant table. We will see also how to troubleshoot a connection problem and share some tips and techniques.

Chapter 11, *Advanced MySQL Performance Tips and Techniques*, covers pattern and anti-pattern use cases for MySQL and different ways to enhance and optimize the performance of a database, followed by solutions to commonly asked questions.

To get the most out of this book

A genuine interest in SQL is required, which will help in mastering MySQL 8. If you're passionate about data analysis, optimization, and advanced queries, it will be so much easier for you to get you to the next level!

Some examples shown in this book use data sets that could not be publicly distributed. In those cases, you can replicate the examples using similar types of data sets

Download the color images

We also provide a PDF file that has color images of the screenshots/diagrams used in this book. You can download it here: http://www.packtpub.com/sites/default/files/downloads/9781788834445_ColorImages.pdf.

Conventions used

There are a number of text conventions used throughout this book.

`CodeInText`: Indicates code words in text, database table names, folder names, filenames, file extensions, pathnames, dummy URLs, user input, and Twitter handles. Here is an example: "Mount the downloaded `WebStorm-10*.dmg` disk image file as another disk in your system."

A block of code is set as follows:

```
# server configuration
datadir=C:/mysql-8.0.13/data/server1
basedir=C:/mysql-8.0.13/
```

Any command-line input or output is written as follows:

```
mysql> select * from mysql.plugin;
```

Bold: Indicates a new term, an important word, or words that you see onscreen. For example, words in menus or dialog boxes appear in the text like this. Here is an example: "Select **System info** from the **Administration** panel."

Warnings or important notes appear like this.

Tips and tricks appear like this.

Get in touch

Feedback from our readers is always welcome.

General feedback: If you have questions about any aspect of this book, mention the book title in the subject of your message and email us at `customercare@packtpub.com`.

Errata: Although we have taken every care to ensure the accuracy of our content, mistakes do happen. If you have found a mistake in this book, we would be grateful if you would report this to us. Please visit `www.packt.com/submit-errata`, selecting your book, clicking on the Errata Submission Form link, and entering the details.

Piracy: If you come across any illegal copies of our works in any form on the Internet, we would be grateful if you would provide us with the location address or website name. Please contact us at copyright@packt.com with a link to the material.

If you are interested in becoming an author: If there is a topic that you have expertise in and you are interested in either writing or contributing to a book, please visit authors.packtpub.com.

Reviews

Please leave a review. Once you have read and used this book, why not leave a review on the site that you purchased it from? Potential readers can then see and use your unbiased opinion to make purchase decisions, we at Packt can understand what you think about our products, and our authors can see your feedback on their book. Thank you!

For more information about Packt, please visit packt.com.

1
Introduction

MySQL is the most popular open- source database system on the market and has been around since 1995. Oracle has owned MySQL since 2010, and MySQL is distributed in two versions: The Community Edition (open source), and the Enterprise Edition, which you must pay for and of course it comes with a series of enhanced features not available in the free version.

It should be mentioned that the Community Edition version (open source) is more popular than the Enterprise version, and can be downloaded from the MySQL website (`https://www.mysql.com/`). This edition has all the features you need for safe web applications that are reliable and secure. Websites such as Google, Wikipedia, Facebook, YouTube, and so on, are some of the biggest users of MySQL.

I'm curious whether you know what *MySQL* means.

MySQL is a combination of *My* (the name of the daughter of co-founder Michael Widenius) and *SQL* stands for Structured Query Language.

This book is an excellent choice if you want to learn advanced concepts at the performance level. Also, you will learn how to analyze and optimize complex queries with different techniques. You will learn to configure and optimize MySQL servers and then I will teach you how to secure your database, using back-up strategies.

We will also go through all the new features of MySQL 8.0 including the Group Replication and InnoDB cluster. Together, we will look at the best surveillance tools that exist on the market today. Throughout this book, I will share my experiences and techniques to help you better manage MySQL in its everyday management and to have a better understanding of its complex and broad architectures. Finally, I will share some techniques with you, which will allow you to make more efficient MySQL 8.0 databases and which I use with Fortune 500 customers.

In this chapter, we will cover the following topics:

- Why Oracle decided to go with MySQL 8.0
- Why MySQL 8.0 is the next generation
- Why it is so important to have a good architecture design
- A review of the chapter

Why MySQL 8?

In short, Oracle has decided to create a new version of MySQL with the number 8 simply because MySQL 6 already existed in 2007 but was then abandoned.

So why isn't is called *MySQL 7*, then? Because Oracle already has a version 7, called *MySQL Cluster*, and this version is 7.5 (GA). So, the next number that is available is 8. At the moment, MySQL version 8.0 is in DMR, which means it is in development and not available for production. However, I encourage you to download and test the new features.

Why is MySQL 8.0 the next generation?

As you can guess, MySQL 8.0 will be the next generation of databases because it will include the traditional side of SQL and NoSQL with JSON. The new features are not just those that I just mentioned; you will also find the following:

- **Common table expression (CTE)**: A type of temporary table associated with a query that will allow you to use the WITH command for recursion.
- **Invisible indexes**: These are invisible to the MySQL optimizer; that is, they are maintained by the optimizer but not used by it. This has the big advantage of being able to test the behavior of the MySQL 8.0 server during evaluation and not the index.
  - Oracle has also added to MySQL 8.0 what are called **persisting configuration variables**, and this new feature has the ability to make persistent changes to the MySQL configuration online.
  - The data dictionary has been optimized, a very good improvement.
  - Great features have been added for replication as well.

Let's not forget the new roles that will facilitate user management—and many other surprises besides.

## Chapter 1

Why it is so important to have a good MySQL architecture design

It must be said that MySQL is easy to use and its operation is very fast. MySQL requires at first a general knowledge of SQL to work effectively with it. MySQL does not require much more knowledge, but a little knowledge of common **relational database management system (RDBMS)** is helpful.

However, despite the fact that MySQL comes with a minimal configuration to help your database launch and perform well, MySQL needs more attention to maintain optimal performance, and in general a good understanding of MySQL's configuration becomes more important.

The fact is that the more your database grows with time and demands more hardware resources such as memory, processors, and disk speed, the slower response times will be; this is a sign that your data model need to be revised and adjusted to meet growing and critical demands. The better your data model is at the beginning, the easier it will be to re-adjust your configuration along the way.

The more your business or website grows the more you need a good solid MySQL architecture. During this growth phase, you will notice that you will be asking yourself questions such as the following ones:

- Do I need to completely rethink my MySQL architecture?
- Should I start thinking about having a large MySQL infrastructure?
- Do I need to review my queries?
- Do I need to create indexes?

Imagine the questions and doubts when we are in the phase where MySQL is likely to under-perform. That's when you desperately start looking at your options on Google and YouTube to see how you can improve your architecture.

This is what I call the *critical* or *gray-zone* phase. You will try to make all kinds of changes with the hope of solving your performance problems when the solution was simply to have a good architecture and a logical structure of your data right from the start.

Fortunately, MySQL 8.0 will provide a detailed understanding of high availability with InnoDB Cluster, Global Replication, and all the other features that have been added or improved. I must mention that I have been so far pleasantly surprised by the new performance of MySQL 8.0.

Summary

The objective of this book is to progressively give you a detailed understanding of advanced MySQL concepts and how they can be applied to complex situations, such as the following:

- How to optimize complex queries
- How to improve your architecture for large databases
- How to manage complex high availability more effectively
- The best tips and techniques for complex situations
- The new features of MySQL 8.0 that can help you make your large databases even more efficient

Do not forget to explore the monitoring tools that let you identify queries that are the slowest and most complex.

I will also share my favorite tips that I use every day to help Fortune 500 companies, and finally I will guide you in this book through the most complex situations that you may face on a daily basis.

MySQL 8's New Features

2

In this chapter, we will not only cover all the new exciting features of MySQL 8.0, but we will also review its deprecated or removed features as well, and learn about its functionality.

The following are the topics that we will discuss:

- Global data dictionary
- MySQL support roles and history
- Creation and management of resource groups and permissions
- InnoDB enhancements
- JSON functionality enhancements
- Invisible indexes from MySQL optimizer
- Features deprecated in MySQL 8.0
- A quick look at the features removed from MySQL 8.0
- A review of the chapter

Now let's take a look at the main reasons Oracle has gone so far with its development of the **global data dictionary** in MySQL 8.0.

Global data dictionary

In an optimization strategy, to be able to obtain an ideal optimization of MySQL, it is essential to have an understanding of the operation in the backend, to be able to make the right adjustments.

It's like when you bring your vehicle to the garage to check an abnormal sound. A competent mechanic will be able to give you good recommendations and do the right thing to correct the situation because he knows how the engine works, and it is the same with MySQL and optimization.

MySQL, like any other database, needs somewhere to store its schema names, table definitions, and other metadata; these are most commonly stored in a combination of different locations, including .FRL, .PAR, .OPT, .TRN, and .TRG files. This has gradually become a bottleneck in various contexts over time.

A visual example of files external to MySQL tables can be seen in the following diagram:

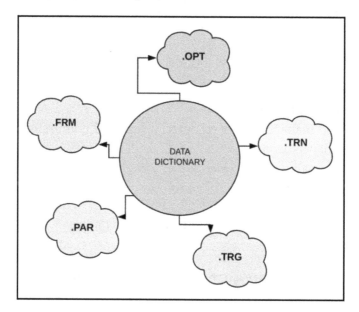

To push MySQL further and provide users with more features, more reliability, and better performance with the INFORMATION_SCHEMA schema, Oracle has created a new enhanced transactional data dictionary in MySQL 8, which we will explore next; we'll also discuss why Oracle has been motivated to push its development in MySQL 8.0:

- **INFORMATION_SCHEMA**: MySQL users have complained for years about the implementation of the INFORMATION_SCHEMA, mainly at the performance level, because of the fact that disk access requires additional disk I/O. In MySQL 8.0, it is implemented as a view over dictionary tables and avoids temporary table creation.

- **Desynchronized dictionaries**: Prior to MySQL 8.0, in MySQL versions such as MySQL 5.7 or 5.6, the data dictionary was oriented as a **shared center**, where the server and InnoDB had their own separate data dictionary, however, some information was doubled. This duplicated information in the MySQL dictionary and the InnoDB dictionary may no longer be synchronized, and we need a common **reliable source** for the dictionary information.
- **Standard inexistant**: Standardization is completely non-existent in the data dictionary (for example: storage in MyISAM tables, .FRM, .PAR, .OPT, .TRN, and .TRG files) and this makes it very difficult to maintain. Having so many different files, and no standardization, forces code to handle more dictionary information, and makes it more difficult to use for programmers who require MySQL access metadata:

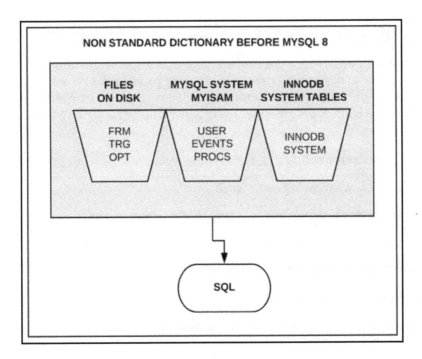

- **No atomic data dictionary**: Saving the data dictionary in **non-transactional** tables and files types means that your data dictionary will not be safe for replicas, because they will not be considered as **atomic**, and of course **non-transactional**. In other words, maintenance is very difficult, because performance is affected and the risk of having an unstable architecture is high.

- **Difficult recovery**: As stated earlier, because the data dictionary is not atomic, it will be very difficult for you to recover your data from the data dictionary, and it will be problematic for replication.
- **Improvement**: The good news is that in MySQL 8, the data dictionary has a version table. This will allow automatic updating from Version 8.0 and later. One of the new features we will find in MySQL 8 is that the data dictionary will be transactional and will be more secure during replication and management. One important thing to keep in mind is that MySQL 8.0 does not have MyISAM tables by default. In previous versions, we had MyISAM tables in system tables, though the default engine is InnoDB. Having a better data dictionary helps the MySQL query optimizer a lot by fetching the correct metadata and execution plans.

MySQL 8's support roles and history

In MySQL 8, there is one new feature that is well worth a special mention. Right on the MySQL server, you can now create roles, specify their privileges, and assign them to users. So, from now on, it will be an easy task for you because you will not need to remember which permissions a team X programmer needs, and whether a team QA must have Z privileges, and so on.

Let's take a concrete example:

To create a role, just run following command:

```
CREATE ROLE 'devops_developer', 'app_read', 'app_write';
```

Now give privileges to the role:

```
GRANT SELECT ON app_db.* TO 'app_read';
```

And, finally, share this role with a user:

```
GRANT 'app_read' TO 'read_username1'@'localhost',
'read_username2'@'localhost';
```

The other options available are as follows:

- **Mandatory roles**: This option is used to configure one or more roles that will persist from the MySQL configuration file, as follows:

```
[mysqld]
mandatory_roles='role1,role2@localhost,role5@%.yourcompany.com'
```

You can also use the following:

```
SET PERSIST mandatory_roles =
'role1,role2@localhost,role5@%.yourcompany.com';
```

- **How to check a role**: To check the privileges that have been allowed to a role, just run the following command:

```
mysql> SHOW GRANTS FOR 'userdev1'@'localhost';
```

The following is the output:

```
+---------------------------------------------------+
| Grants for userdev1@localhost                     |
+---------------------------------------------------+
| GRANT USAGE ON *.* TO `userdev1`@`localhost`      |
| GRANT `app_developer`@`%` TO `userdev1`@`localhost` |
+---------------------------------------------------+
```

However, this shows each role granted without any details of the privileges that the role represents. To also display role privileges, simply add a clause called USING, naming the granted roles for which the display of privileges would be like:

```
mysql> SHOW GRANTS FOR 'userdev1'@'localhost' USING 'app_developer';
```

The following is the output:

```
+-----------------------------------------------------------+
| Grants for userdev1@localhost                             |
+-----------------------------------------------------------+
| GRANT USAGE ON *.* TO `userdev1`@`localhost`              |
| GRANT ALL PRIVILEGES ON `app_db`.* TO `userdev1`@`localhost` |
| GRANT `app_developer`@`%` TO `userdev1`@`localhost`       |
+-----------------------------------------------------------+
```

There are many other options on the MySQL website.

For those who are Oracle DBAs, you will certainly find a resemblance to the commands you use in your environments, so this ROLE feature will not be new. However, in the MySQL world it is really a feature that will save a lot of time for MySQL DBAs.

MySQL 8 supports the creation and management of resource groups and permissions

A new feature that Oracle has added to MySQL 8.0 is the creation and management of resource groups that can assign **threads** to particular groups so that these threads run according to the resources available to the group.

Group attributes allow you to control resources to vary resource consumption by group threads as needed. DBAs can adapt them to different workloads.

Currently, the use of the CPU is a manageable resource—yes, you read it right, *manageable;* this use is represented by the concept of *virtual CPU* or *CPU cores*. At start-up, an assessment is carried out by the MySQL server as to the number of available virtual processors. DBAs, depending on their privilege, can then associate them with resource groups and assign threads.

This means that you can assign a group 2 virtual CPU to application A, for example, a group 1 virtual CPU to application B, and so on.

I can't wait to see my clients configure their group resources according to business needs; you can't imagine the headaches this will relieve.

As mentioned, virtual CPU resources can be assigned to different groups and given different priorities. Before we discover the resource groups and how they can benefit, let's take a look at the limitations first:

- Resource groups are not available if you install the *thread pool plugin* (MySQL Enterprise only).
- Resource groups are not available on macOS, which does not provide an API for linking processors to a thread.
- On FreeBSD and of course Solaris, the thread priorities of the resource group are ignored.
- On Linux, resource group thread priorities are ignored, unless CAP_SYS_NICE is configured.
- In Windows, threads run on one of five thread priority levels. The thread priority range of the resource group (from -20 to 19) corresponds to these levels.
- Resource group management applies specifically and exclusively to the server in question. Any changes made to the group's data dictionary table or SQL statements made in the resource group will be neither logged nor repeated.

Now that we know the limits of group resources, let's look at the practical point of view of what we will have.

Let's look at the regular problems that a DBA encounters everyday. He often faces the problem of slow reports, including slow requests, and finally the execution of **batch jobs**, which must be moved to **slaves** for normal use.

In this case, resource groups are a good solution and help solve the problems mentioned in the previous paragraph.

The following are two default groups that we cannot edit:

```
mysql> SELECT * FROM INFORMATION_SCHEMA.RESOURCE_GROUPS\G
```

The following is the output:

```
*************************** 1. row ***********************
RESOURCE_GROUP_NAME: USR_default
RESOURCE_GROUP_TYPE:
USER RESOURCE_GROUP_ENABLED: 1
VCPU_IDS: 0-8
THREAD_PRIORITY: 0
*********************** 2. row ***********************
RESOURCE_GROUP_NAME: SYS_default
RESOURCE_GROUP_TYPE: SYSTEM
RESOURCE_GROUP_ENABLED: 1
VCPU_IDS: 0-8
THREAD_PRIORITY: 0
```

There are two possible group types, SYSTEM and USER, which directly impact the priority values we will be able to assign to a group. This variation in allowed priorities and the attributed group type act as an identifier to protect system threads from CPU resource conflicts against user threads.

The available priority ranges related to each group type are set out in the following list:

- For SYSTEM resource groups, the priority range will be -20 to 0.
- For USER resource groups, the priority that you can choose is in the range of 0 to 19. A *thread* is the execution priority of the threads assigned to a resource group. Priority values range from −20 (the highest priority) to 19 (the lowest priority). The default value is 0, for SYSTEM and USER groups. SYSTEM groups have a higher priority than USER groups, which ensures that user threads never have a higher priority than SYSTEM threads.

So, what we can do is look to the `performance_schema` table to identify the `Thread_iq` for our report query and assign a specific resource group as follows:

```
CREATE RESOURCE GROUP ABCReporting
 TYPE = USER
 VCPU = 4-5
 THREAD_PRIORITY = 10;
CREATE RESOURCE GROUP Batch_job
 TYPE = USER
 VCPU = 6-8
 THREAD_PRIORITY = 8;
mysql> SELECT * FROM INFORMATION_SCHEMA.RESOURCE_GROUPS
 WHERE RESOURCE_GROUP_NAME = 'Batch_job'\G
```

We get the following output:

```
*************************** 1. row ***************************
    RESOURCE_GROUP_NAME: Batch_job
    RESOURCE_GROUP_TYPE: USER
 RESOURCE_GROUP_ENABLED: 1
               VCPU_IDS: 6-8
        THREAD_PRIORITY: 8
```

For resource group `ABCReporting`:

```
mysql> SELECT * FROM INFORMATION_SCHEMA.RESOURCE_GROUPS
 WHERE RESOURCE_GROUP_NAME = 'ABCReporting'\G
```

We get the following output:

```
*************************** 1. row ***************************
    RESOURCE_GROUP_NAME: ABCReporting

    RESOURCE_GROUP_TYPE: USER

 RESOURCE_GROUP_ENABLED: 1

               VCPU_IDS: 4-5

        THREAD_PRIORITY: 10
```

Now, let's look at some scenarios together.

We already have our huge ABC report query running on the server, and it consumes a lot of resources and slows everything down. In this case, we can find the `thread_id` of this ABC report query from the `performance_schema` table and assign a specific resource group to this `thread_id`:

```
SET RESOURCE GROUP ABCReporting FOR 4558;
```

Threads assigned to a report group run with their own resources, which you can modify as needed.

Let's say we're running a batch job script with `Batch_job` group resources at the same time. This means we need to decrease the priority and allocate fewer CPU resources to our reporting resource group. To do so, we use this:

```
ALTER RESOURCE GROUP ABCReporting

VCPU = 6

THREAD_PRIORITY = 19;
```

The MySQL 8.0 RESOURCE_GROUP feature is well-designed and easy-to-use, and, in certain cases, can prove to be quite helpful.

InnoDB enhancements

In MySQL 8.0, Oracle has improved or added features; let's look at these.

This step in MySQL is something many DBAs or developers are not aware of, because it is not something that we check everyday but it is important; we're talking about the maximum value of the **auto-increment counter**, which is registered in the **redo log** and changes each time during each checkpoint.

In addition to being saved in a series of private tables and visible only by MySQL, the auto-increment counter has been improved so it is more persistent during a restart of MySQL. This means that during a reboot, the new value will persist and not change as in previous releases.

Another improvement is the dynamic configuration of `Innodb_deadlock_detect`, which can be used to disable or enable this variable, which normally if it is active can affect the performance of MySQL in the case of highly competitive systems.

All temporary InnoDB tables are now created in the shared temporary tablespace that is in `ibtmp1`.

The following is a short summary of the changes that have been made and introduced in MySQL 8.0:

- The number of `InnoDB_undo_tablespaces` can now be changed during a startup or reboot
- The variable that gives an `Innodb_available_undo_logs` status has been removed, and may now be queried by the `SHOW VARIABLES LIKE 'command innodb_rollback_segments'`

The new `innodb_dedicated_server` configuration option, which is disabled by default, allows InnoDB to automatically configure the following options based on the amount of memory detected on the MySQL server, which will be very convenient for DBAs:

- `Innodb_buffer_pool_size`
- `Innodb_log_file_size`
- `innodb_flush_method`

The InnoDB storage engine now supports **atomic DDL**, which is a good thing and also guarantees that DDL operations will be fully committed or canceled, even if the server stops during the operation.

JSON enhancements functionalities

Oracle has been forced over time to adopt the new NoSQL trend because of the competition and also the fact that the concept of storage type document as JSON came to be much more practical at the management level; for some companies that have architectures such as **big data**, this became more of a constraint at the application level.

For these reasons, Oracle introduced for the first time in MySQL 5.7.8, the JSON data type, which is a type of specialized binary column, similar to a blob, but with additional features to optimize storage and recover the values of a JSON type column.

In the new version of MySQL 8.0, Oracle has added great features such as automatic validation, JSON document normalization, and automatic loading of values. There is also a restriction that must be taken into consideration, such as, for example, JSON columns that cannot be indexed.

By the way, the good news is that a JSON type column works very well.

In MySQL 8.0, path expressions for the JSON type now support **ranges**, which means that you can now fetch the first or the last element of a table; the following is an example:

```
mysql> CREATE TABLE t1 (doc JSON);
Query OK, 0 rows affected (0.01 sec)

mysql> INSERT INTO t1 VALUES ('[1, 2, 3, 4, 5]');
Query OK, 1 row affected (0.00 sec)

mysql> SELECT doc->"$[1 to 3]" FROM t1;
+------------------+
| doc->"$[1 to 3]" |
+------------------+
| [2, 3, 4]        |
+------------------+
1 row in set (0.00 sec)

mysql> SELECT doc->"$[last-2]" FROM t1;
+------------------+
| doc->"$[last-2]" |
+------------------+
| 3                |
+------------------+
1 row in set (0.00 sec)
```

The MySQL team also improved the performance of JSON, with optimizer support for partial updating and improved JSON handling in a number of cases, such as sorting data.

MySQL's Document Store permits you to treat MySQL as a document database style, with a set of CRS NoSQL APIs to directly access data. This feature was introduced in MySQL 5.7, the MySQL Document Store now gives you with consistent readings and writings. This gives it a very good advantage over other NoSQL databases, as developers or DBAs do not need to abandon transactional semantics. The data created in the MySQL Document Store is also accessible via the standard MySQL SQL.

On top of this, MySQL Document Store has improved its indexing capabilities. To improve spatial research, Oracle has added to MySQL 8.0 support for spatial indexing of GeoJSON type data in MySQL JSON documents, giving you an efficient spatial search of documents in the MySQL Document Store.

Keep in mind that JSON columns cannot be indexed directly. To create an index that indirectly references such a column, I suggest that you define a generated column that retrieves the information to be indexed and then create an index on the generated column, as shown in the following example:

```
mysql> CREATE TABLE jsonemp (
    -> c JSON,
    -> g INT GENERATED ALWAYS AS (c->"$.id")),
    -> INDEX i (g)
    -> );
Query OK, 0 rows affected (0.23 sec)

mysql> INSERT INTO jsonemp (c) VALUES
    > ('{"id": "1", "name": "Don"}'), ('{"id": "2", "name": "Lola"}'),
    > ('{"id": "3", "name": "Bob"}'), ('{"id": "4", "name": "Michele"}');
Query OK, 4 rows affected (0.05 sec)
Records: 4 Duplicates: 0 Warnings: 0

mysql> SELECT c->>"$.name" AS name
    > FROM jsonemp WHERE g > 2;




+--------+
| name   |
+--------+
| Don    |
| Lola   |
+--------+
2 rows in set (0.00 sec)

mysql> EXPLAIN SELECT c->>"$.name" AS name
    > FROM jsonemp WHERE g > 2\G
*************************** 1. row ***************************
           id: 1
  select_type: SIMPLE
        table: jsonemp
   partitions: NULL
         type: range
possible_keys: i
          key: i
      key_len: 5
          ref: NULL
         rows: 2
     filtered: 100.00
        Extra: Using where
```

In conclusion, we can see that JSON has been improved in terms of both operating and performance. For more details on all the changes that have been made, we suggest you visit the MySQL website (`https://www.mysql.com/`).

Invisible indexes from MySQL optimizer

You read that correctly—indexes can now be made invisible in MySQL 8.0!

From a performance or optimization point of view, this new MySQL 8.0 option is appreciated because you can essentially disable an index before deleting it. When you create an invisible index, it is always maintained normally, but the optimizer will not see it.

In other words, if you're not sure whether you need an index, you can mark it as invisible and the MySQL optimizer will not use it. After monitoring your server and monitoring performance, you can decide to reactivate it if you think that will result in improved performance.

As you probably already know, when the query optimizer can find an action plan to exploit them to their fullest, indexes can be of great assistance. They reduce execution time and improve the performance of your queries. However, we must keep in mind that they have a cost—that cannot be ignored. And although DBAs are generally conscious of the negative impact indexes can have on execution when manipulating data (inserting, updating), it is a simplification in itself. Lastly, since read performance also undergoes optimizer analysis for plan selection, it too can be somewhat obstructed by indexes.

Let's look at an example together, as follows:

```
mysql> SELECT * FROM sys.schema_unused_indexes;
+----------------+--------------+------------+
| object_schema  | object_name  | index_name |
+----------------+--------------+------------+
| Student1       | Classroom    | s          |
| Student2       | Classroom    | s_c        |
+----------------+--------------+------------+
2 rows in set (0.01 sec)
```

In this scenario, perhaps the server just started up. This does not guarantee that your end-of-month reports do not depend on these indexes. It can also make it hard to evaluate situations where indexes are repeated, and we can assume that if one of the indexes were to be dropped, another candidate would be selected instead. Perhaps you merely suspect that a given index is not necessary?

Let's go back to invisible indexes. When an index is not visible, the optimizer cannot use it because it does not see it. But it's still there and working, fulfilling its functions by checking for unique and referential restrictions. And if you decide that it was a bad idea, you will have the option to go back to the index and quickly make it visible again.

The optimizer switch has a switch named `use_invisible_index`, and this can be used to evaluate the execution plan of a query with an invisible index. Otherwise, optimizer hints are generally used for one of two major reasons:

- **Soft delete**: When, in production, an erase operation is being performed, it is always preferable to be able to see what changes will look like prior to making them permanent. To help you understand this, imagine your index as a recycling bin. If you come to realize the index in question is actually being used, a quick change of metadata is all you need to make it visible again—and the process is much less time-consuming than trying to recreate it or restoring it from a backup. For example:

```
ALTER TABLE classroom ALTER INDEX c INVISIBLE;
```

- **Staged rollout**: This means that every time you add indexes, it's important to consider that they can modify your existing query plans, sometimes in ways that will hurt MySQL's performance. With invisible indexes, you can organize the deployment of an index any time you choose: ideally, when traffic is lower and you can devote your attention to monitoring the system. For example:

```
ALTER TABLE Classroom ADD INDEX c (student1) INVISIBLE;
# after some time
ALTER TABLE Classroom ALTER INDEX c VISIBLE;
```

Now we can query the metadata as follows:

```
SHOW INDEXES FROM my_table;

| ----+------------+-------------+----------+------------+----------------------
| Table   | Non_unique | Key_name          | Seq_in_index | Column_name | Collation
| x_table | 1          | just_to_be_safe_idx | 1          | a           | A
| ----+------------+-------------+----------+------------+----------------------
```

The following is another example of a possible search for invisible indexes:

```
SELECT * FROM information_schema.statistics WHERE is_visible='NO';

*************************** 1. row ***************************
TABLE_CATALOG: def
TABLE_SCHEMA: student1
TABLE_NAME: Classroom
NON_UNIQUE: 1
INDEX_SCHEMA: student1
INDEX_NAME: c
SEQ_IN_INDEX: 1
COLUMN_NAME: Classroom
COLLATION: A
CARDINALITY: 7
SUB_PART: NULL
PACKED: NULL
NULLABLE:
INDEX_TYPE: BTREE
COMMENT: disabled
INDEX_COMMENT:
IS_VISIBLE: NO
```

In short, using `mysqldump`/`mysqlpump` to load a table in an older server will result in it becoming invisible. The same thing will happen if you synchronize replication from a newer server to an older server; just ensure the primary key can't be made into an invisible index.

Features deprecated in MySQL 8.0

Like all new MySQL versions, the following features are considered obsolete in MySQL 8.0, and may be removed in a future new release. When alternatives are displayed, applications must be updated to use them.

Since MySQL 8.0.4, the `validate_password` plugin has been re-enabled for use in the server component framework, and although it is still available, there are plans for it to be removed from future versions of MySQL.

The `ALTER TABLESPACE` and `DROP TABLESPACE ENGINE` clause will be removed from future releases.

The function `JSON_MERGE ()` is removed from MySQL 8.0.3. You should use `JSON_MERGE_PRESERVE ()` instead.

A quick look at the features removed from MySQL 8.0

It is important to note that the following items are obsolete and have been removed in MySQL 8.0. When messages are displayed for alternatives, applications must be updated to use them and the following is only a short list of all removed items. I invite you to visit MySQL website for more details:

- The `information_schema_stats` configuration has been replaced by `information_schema_stats_expiry`.
- InnoDB system views have been replaced:

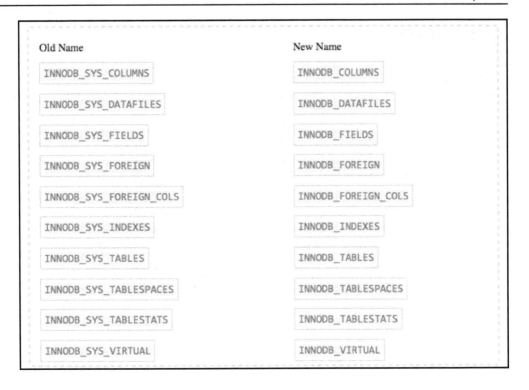

- The query cache has been removed, including FLUSH QUERY CACHE and RESET QUERY CACHE.
- Two MySQL storage engines currently provide native partition support: InnoDB and NDB. Of these, only InnoDB is supported by MySQL 8.0. Any attempt to create partitioned tables in MySQL 8.0 using another storage engine will fail.
- In MySQL 8.0, the data_locks table and sys schema views contain separate schema name and table name columns.

The topics mentioned in the preceding paragraph have an impact on the performance of MySQL.

Summary

In this chapter, we have covered all the new exciting features of MySQL 8.0 and their functionalities, and reviewed deprecated and removed features. We have seen the main reasons why Oracle has gone so far with its development of the global data dictionary in MySQL 8.0.

We covered MySQL support roles and history; we covered one new feature on the MySQL server, in which you can now create roles, specify their privileges, and assign them to users. We learned that a new feature that Oracle has added to MySQL 8.0 is the creation and management of resource groups; we can assign threads to particular groups so that these threads run according to the resources available to the group. We also looked at enhancements in InnoDB and JSON, and we learned about invisible indexes from MySQL's optimizer. Lastly, we looked at features that have been deprecated and removed from MySQL 8.0.

In the next chapter, we will show you how to index your data for high performance, with advanced tips and techniques.

3
Indexing Your Data for High Performance

This chapter explains how to optimize MySQL performance by using indexes and query execution plans, and provides examples. Optimization involves a good understanding of the MySQL optimizer and index strategy and, finally, a solid knowledge of how indexes and queries work together.

In this chapter, we will cover the following topics:

- How does the MySQL optimizer think in MySQL 8.0?
- What kind of data type should I consider indexing first and why?
- Why should I have a good index strategy?
- What impact does an index have on MySQL performance?
- How to display and analyze a table structure
- How to efficiently read MySQL query execution plans
- How to know when to create an index
- Using multiple columns in an index
- Organizing columns in an index for best performance
- Case study 1 – how to use the explain plan tool in MySQL 8.0
- Case study 2 – how to display and analyze a table structure versus the explain plan tool
- Case study 3 – how to organize your columns in an index

How does MySQL optimizer think in MySQL 8.0?

Let's look at the main improvements in the MySQL 8.0 optimizer:

- MySQL 8.0 now more effectively supports advanced SQL features such as common table expressions, windowing functions, and the `grouping()` function
- One feature that DBAs will appreciate is the invisible index
- More tips in Query Rewrite Plugin
- On the performance side, the cost model has really been improved for superior performance
- Histogram statistics in MySQL 8.0 improve the statistics based on data distribution

I've always mentioned that to get optimal performance, you need to understand how MySQL thinks or reacts to your queries; this step in understanding is much more important than you think. For example, have you ever had situations where a complex query did not use the index that it had to use?

Let's have a look at how the high-level optimizer responds, that is, how it is organized and structured, to help you easily master the world of the optimizer.

The query optimizer takes queries as input and produces an execution plan as output. The following is an organizational chart that will help you understand this:

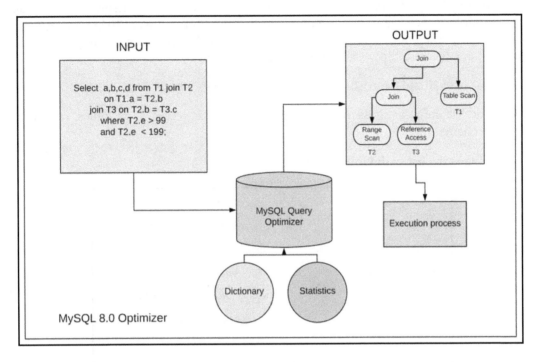

As you may have noticed, the queries or the SQL language work like a GPS. That is to say that it works like when you enter an address in your GPS; it will make sure to propose different routes to get to your destination, which will also be done by the optimizer.

So, the SQL language is called **declarative**. This means that it conveys a final state rather than a procedure for how to get there. Since the GPS or the optimizer will offer you the best way, sometimes the route will not necessarily be the one that you had planned, depending on the parameters (indexes, memory cache, and so on).

In short, the way that MySQL evaluates or makes its decisions about how it executes your queries is based on a methodology called cost-based optimization, so if we simplify this mechanism, it would look like this:

1. Assign a cost to each operation
2. Evaluate how many possible operations each plan needs
3. Make a total of these operations
4. Finally, choose the plan that will cost the least possible amount

In fact, the MySQL optimizer will not evaluate every possibility imaginable, as it is limited in its methodology. For example, if you have four tables that you want to join in a query and imagine that each table has at least four indexes, it will give you a result that MySQL cannot evaluate because the possibilities are enormous.

But how do we evaluate the costs for each operation? Here's how.

You will find the default values in the `server_cost` and `engine_cost` tables, which are in the `mysql` schema.

The following is the list of default values:

Cost	Operation
40	disk_temptable_create_cost
1	disk_temptable_row_cost
2	memory_temptable_create_cost
0.2	memory_temptable_row_cost
0.1	key_compare_cost
0.2	row_evaluate_cost
1	io_block_read_cost
1	memory_block_read_cost

So, as you can see, MySQL since version 5.7 assesses the evaluation possibilities in relation to a cost per operation, which will determine the most appropriate action to take for effective performance, and we should particularly highlight that in MySQL version 8.0, Oracle has introduced a new feature where the methodology adapts to the percentage of indexing in the Memory/InnoDB Buffer Pool, which was not done before.

What kind of data type should I consider indexing first and why?

From a performance point of view, creating indexes is essential for system performance and future maintenance of your MySQL server database. Choosing the right indexes can give a significant boost to your application's performance.

In principle, the less space the column takes up, the faster your index will be. So, for example, what would be the column that would be the best candidate for a quick index, an INT or VARCHAR?

The answer would obviously be INT because the space used will be less than the VARCHAR. So, if performance is critical for you—and is probably why you're reading this book—I'll tell you that if you have the chance to have the smallest number possible, the better your index's performance will be. I'll give you an example: it is much better to create an index on a zip code than postal code and country. It is definitely not recommended to create indexes on small tables. Also, the data type helps you predict how many records you will have in your table.

Here is another example: if you foresee using the INT type, it means that your maximum capacity to have records will be 4 billion pieces of unsigned data. In your case, perhaps you don't plan to have more than 20,000 customers in your database; it would make sense to use the SMALLINT, as you will be able to have a maximum of 32,767 customers with an unsigned SMALLINT:

Type	Storage	Minimum Value	Maximum Value
	(Bytes)	(Signed/Unsigned)	(Signed/Unsigned)
TINYINT	1	-128	127
		0	255
SMALLINT	2	-32768	32767
		0	65535
MEDIUMINT	3	-8388608	8388607
		0	16777215
INT	4	-2147483648	2147483647
		0	4294967295
BIGINT	8	-9223372036854775808	9223372036854775807
		0	18446744073709551615

However, keep in mind that your optimization strategy with indexes must take into consideration that the more indexes you use, the more you will have to take into account that your updates, insertion, and deletion of records will be affected in their performance. It would be wise to have a balance between indexes and other operations on your data.

Why should I have a good index strategy?

Indexing your data is so broad that it's hard to know what to do and what not to do when developing your indexing strategies. You will agree with me that if you create indexes it is to improve the response time of your requests or applications, but indexing data is a balancing act.

Each index is a table that's managed by the system, so each addition or modification to the data in a table of your application potentially implies, as already mentioned in this book, the updating of these indexes, which can slow the performance of the updates to the data files.

The important points that you need to consider in your indexing strategy are as follows:

- Create a primary key (generally, the column will end with `id`)
- Predict the columns that will often be queried in your application with the `WHERE`, `GROUP BY`, `HAVING`, and `ORDER BY` clauses
- You should have an index on the columns that will be used with functions, such as `SUM ()`, `COUNT ()`, `MIN ()`, `MAX ()`, and `AVG ()`; you will benefit from this performance-wise
- Do not overload your database with too many indexes, as it will impact on the performance of MySQL
- Predict secondary keys with unique indexes to speed up join queries (usually, columns that end with `_id`)
- As a rule, `usernames` or `emails` columns are good candidates for indexing
- Some columns like `URL`; most applications usually have a `UUID`

Another important aspect of the index strategy would be to know in which situation we should not create indexes.

In some cases, indexes can affect performance and sometimes these same indexes should not exist. Sometimes, it's better to ignore query performance for indexes and go with a full table scan. Let's discuss the cases in which it is best to avoid indexes.

An index may not be useful for a table with few columns if a large percentage of its records are still extracted from it, as the creation of an index will not stop a full scan. Also, we must remember that erasing the primary key or foreign keys can have unfortunate consequences.

Often enough, static data tables on the smaller side are sufficiently so as to be read as a full scan rather than an index reading.

As a general rule, indexes should only be created on a small proportion of a table's columns. Large indexes of composite types can be excessively large in comparison to their table. It is important to consider the index-table size ratio, as the larger it is, the less useful your index will be in reducing the physical space to read.

What impact does an index have on MySQL performance?

Although adding indexes can help optimize the performance of your queries, adding indexes has a significant cost on MySQL performance.

In fact, when an index is added to a table, the performance of the writing is affected. Let me show you this from the `music_album` table. By examining the definition of the current table, you will notice a large number of indexes:

```
CREATE TABLE music_album (
  music_album_id int(10) unsigned NOT NULL,
  music_artist_id int(10) unsigned NOT NULL,
  music_album_type_id int(10) unsigned NOT NULL,
  name varchar(255) NOT NULL,
  first_released year(4) NOT NULL,
  music_country_id smallint(5) unsigned DEFAULT NULL,
  PRIMARY KEY (music_album_id),
  KEY artist_id (music_artist_id),
  KEY country_id (music_country_id),
  KEY music_album_type_id (music_album_type_id),
  KEY idx1 (music_country_id,music_album_type_id),
  KEY idx2 (music_album_type_id, music_country_id)
) ENGINE=InnoDB DEFAULT CHARSET=latin1
```

Table: music_album

By performing a simple benchmarking test, we can test the insertion rate of the current music album table with the original definition that included fewer indexes:

```
DROP TABLE IF EXISTS test1;
CREATE TABLE test1 LIKE music_album;
INSERT INTO test1 SELECT * FROM music_album;
DROP TABLE test1;

CREATE TABLE test1 LIKE music_album;
ALTER TABLE test1 DROP INDEX first_released, DROP
INDEX music_album_type_id,
DROP INDEX name, DROP INDEX music_country_id,
DROP INDEX idx1, DROP INDEX idx2;
INSERT INTO test1 SELECT * FROM music_album;
DROP TABLE test1;
```

The following are the test results:

```
# Insert with indexes
Query OK, 563881 rows affected (23.34 sec)

# Insert without indexes
Query OK, 563881 rows affected (7.54 sec)
```

Did you notice that inserting data into the table with additional indexes was four times slower?

This test is quite basic and there are, of course, several other elements that can negatively affect insertion speed, but it provides a clear example of how adding indexes to a table can impair writing performance.

One of the index optimization tasks is to delete duplicate indexes. Although locating an identical index is not a complicated task, it is also common to see indexes that are subsets of other indexes, or that correspond to the primary key. Any index found in the left-most part of another index is a duplicate index that will not be used. The following is an example:

```
CREATE TABLE music_album (

...

PRIMARY KEY (music_album_id),
KEY artist_id (music_artist_id),
KEY country_id (music_country_id),
KEY music_album_type_id (music_album_type_id),
KEY idx1 (music_country_id,music_album_type_id),
KEY idx2 (music_album_type_id, music_country_id)

...
```

The `music_country_id` index is actually a duplicate due to the `idx2` index.

How to display and analyze a table structure

As we know, commands for SQL queries are both simple and easy to learn. Yet the efficiency of different queries and database functions can vary, and as the volume of information you are storing increases, this becomes more and more important. The same is true if your database supports a website, or if your site is experiencing heavier traffic.

In the context of optimizing your queries, it is very important to have an understanding at this stage regarding the display of the structure of a table in MySQL. Thanks to this display, you will be able to interpret from the explain plan, refer to it, and find a solution to your query performance problem.

When we display the structure of a table, this structure always tells me a little story about the following important points:

- How is the table used or will be used?
- The table will also tell me what types of data are stored.
- What are the columns that are indexed?
- Do we find triggers?
- Do we have a primary and/or secondary key?
- Do we have comments that will help us understand the types of columns?

To see the history of a table, we must use the following command:

```
show create table [table name]\G
```

Let's take a simple example:

```
mysql> show create table yourexample_table\G
***************1 row***********************
        Table: yourexample_table
Create Table: CREATE TABLE `yourexample_table` (
   `id` int(11) NOT NULL AUTO_INCREMENT,
   `name` varchar(50) DEFAULT NULL,
   `address` varchar(140) DEFAULT NULL,
   `username` varchar(20) DEFAULT NULL,
   PRIMARY KEY (`id`),
   KEY `username` (`username`)
) ENGINE=InnoDB DEFAULT CHARSET=latin1
1 row in set (0.00 sec)
```

We use the `show create table` command because no other command will give the same details as `DESC`, for example, in the case of an optimization.

Did you know that explain can return the same information on the table as the `DESC` command?

The following are the details:

```
mysql> explain yourexample_table;
+-----------+--------------+------+-----+---------+----------------+
| Field     | Type         | Null | Key | Default | Extra          |
+-----------+--------------+------+-----+---------+----------------+
| id        | int(10)      | NO   | PRI | NULL    | auto_increment |
| name      | varchar(50)  | YES  |     | NULL    |                |
| address   | varchar(140) | YES  |     | NULL    |                |
| username  | varchar(20)  | YES  | MUL | NULL    |                |
+-----------+--------------+------+-----+---------+----------------+
4 rows in set (0.00 sec)

mysql> desc yourexample_table;
+-----------+--------------+------+-----+---------+----------------+
| Field     | Type         | Null | Key | Default | Extra          |
+-----------+--------------+------+-----+---------+----------------+
| id        | int(10)      | NO   | PRI | NULL    | auto_increment |
| name      | varchar(50)  | YES  |     | NULL    |                |
| address   | varchar(140) | YES  |     | NULL    |                |
| username  | varchar(20)  | YES  | MUL | NULL    |                |
+-----------+--------------+------+-----+---------+----------------+
4 rows in set (0.00 sec)
```

In our example, we have two indexes for our table, the first of which is the primary key (id column). The second is the index we added for the username column. So, we can see that the queries using this column will be more efficient than if the index did not exist.

In other words, when analyzing a table structure, we must look at whether we have factors that can affect MySQL performance, such as the following:

- Do we have **triggers**?
- Do we have **foreign keys**?

Let's look at another example together, of a more complex table this time:

```
mysql> SHOW CREATE TABLE complex_example_table\G
*************************** 1. row ***************************
        Table: complex_example_table
Create Table: CREATE TABLE `complex_example_table` (
  `ID1` int(10) NOT NULL auto_increment,
  `ID2` int(10) NOT NULL default '0',
  `STORYB` varchar(200) NOT NULL default '',
  `STORYC` varchar(180) default NULL,
  PRIMARY KEY  (`ID1`,`ID2`,`STORYB`),
  KEY `STORYB` (`STORYB`,`STORYC`),
  KEY `STORYC` (`STORYC`),
  CONSTRAINT `IDX_ID1_ID2` FOREIGN KEY (`ID1`, `ID2`)
REFERENCES `complex_example_table` (`ID1`, `ID2`)
ON DELETE CASCADE ON UPDATE CASCADE,
CONSTRAINT `IDX_` FOREIGN KEY (`STORYB`, `STORYC`)
REFERENCES `second_example_table` (`STORYB`, `STORYC`)
ON DELETE CASCADE ON UPDATE CASCADE
) ENGINE=INNODB CHARSET=utf8
```

As you can see in our preceding example, we have triggers like these:

```
1. REFERENCES `complex_example_table` (`ID1`, `ID2`) ON DELETE
   CASCADE ON UPDATE CASCADE
2. REFERENCES `second_example_table` (`STORYB`, `STORYC`) ON DELETE
   CASCADE ON UPDATE CASCADE
```

And we have a FOREIGN KEY constraint:

```
• CONSTRAINT `IDX_` FOREIGN KEY (`STORYB`, `STORYC`) REFERENCES
  `second_example_table` (`STORYB`, `STORYC`)
```

Depending on the number of records we will have in our primary table, `complex_example_table`, triggers #1 and #2 that we identified previously may be a factor that will influence the performance of our queries, and even MySQL in general.

We agree that the need to have a DELETE CASCADE trigger is part of a traditional data model to ensure the data integrity of your child tables, while not leaving orphan records in the child table. However, in the field of query performance optimization for large databases, the DELETE CASCADE trigger will have a negative impact on performance, in that it does the following:

- It creates InnoDB deadlocks
- It slows down your requests

Let's look at an example to show you the impact:

```
CREATE TABLE parent (
id INT NOT NULL AUTO_INCREMENT,
bogus_column char(32),
PRIMARY KEY (id)
) ENGINE=InnoDB;

CREATE TABLE child (
id INT NOT NULL AUTO_INCREMENT,
parent_id INT NOT NULL,
bogus_column char(32),
PRIMARY KEY (id),
KEY (parent_id),
CONSTRAINT child_ibfk_1 FOREIGN KEY (parent_id) REFERENCES parent (id)
) ENGINE=InnoDB;

INSERT INTO parent (bogus_column)
VALUES ('aaa'), ('bbb'), ('ccc'), ('ddd'), ('eee');

INSERT INTO child (parent_id,bogus_column) VALUES
(1, 'aaa'), (2,'bbb'), (3, 'ccc'),
(4, 'ddd'), (5, 'eee');
```

```
START TRANSACTION; # session1
START TRANSACTION; # session2

# session1
UPDATE child SET parent_id = 5â€¨ WHERE parent_id = 4;

#session2
UPDATE parent SET bogus_column = 'new!' WHERE id = 4;
```

In our previous instructions, you may have noticed that session2 will block the wait for a lock. But where is this lock? We can find the answer in the information_schema.innodb_locks table:

```
mysql> SELECT * FROM information_schema.innodb_locks\G
*************************** 1. row ***************************
    lock_id: 87035:1300:3:6
lock_trx_id: 87035
  lock_mode: X
  lock_type: RECORD
 lock_table: `test`.`parent`
 lock_index: `PRIMARY`
 lock_space: 1300
  lock_page: 3
   lock_rec: 6
  lock_data: 5
*************************** 2. row ***************************
    lock_id: 87034:1300:3:6
lock_trx_id: 87034
  lock_mode: S
  lock_type: RECORD
 lock_table: `test`.`parent`
 lock_index: `PRIMARY`
 lock_space: 1300
  lock_page: 3
   lock_rec: 6
  lock_data: 5
2 rows in set (0.00 sec)
```

Let's take the same example, but without foreign key constraints blocking our last instructions. As you can see, the expected output changes, as follows:

```
mysql> SELECT * FROM information_schema.innodb_locks;
Empty set (0.00 sec)
```

In this section, you have learned how to display the structure of a table to see its history and analyze it. We also saw the impact of triggers on performance. In the next section, we will see when an index becomes necessary for the performance of your database.

How to efficiently read MySQL query execution plans

When you run a query, MySQL query optimizer tries to design an optimal execution plan for the query. You can see the plan information by mentioning EXPLAIN before your request.

EXPLAIN is one of the most powerful tools at your disposal to understand and optimize your MySQL queries that are slow or perhaps you have doubts regarding their performance, but unfortunately, many DBAs or developers rarely use them.

In this section, I will show you how to interpret the results of EXPLAIN and how to use it to optimize your queries.

How to effectively read the EXPLAIN results

The role of the EXPLAIN tool is to display the running cost before executing your DML queries; it's like asking your vendor for a price estimate for goods before you buy. In other words, MySQL uses EXPLAIN to explain how it will execute your DML, including the table structure. Please note that since MySQL 5.7, the DML (Select, Update, Delete, Insert, and Replace) commands are allowed in EXPLAIN—that's why we will not just mention SELECT in our explanations.

The syntax and possible parameters are as follows:

```
    {EXPLAIN | DESCRIBE | DESC}
     tbl_name [col_name | wild]
{EXPLAIN | DESCRIBE | DESC}
    [explain_type]
    {explainable_stmt | FOR CONNECTION connection_id}
explain_type: {
  | FORMAT = format_name
}
format_name: {
    TRADITIONAL
  | JSON
```

```
    }
explainable_stmt: {
    SELECT statement
  | DELETE statement
  | INSERT statement
  | REPLACE statement
  | UPDATE statement
}
```

By the way, remember that in order to use EXPLAIN, your user must have the SELECT privilege, and for the views, the SHOW VIEW privilege.

Let's analyze the output of a simple query to familiarize ourselves with the columns returned by EXPLAIN, and we will get to more complex outputs gradually.

Here is a simple example:

```
mysql> explain select * from tbl_report\G
*************************** 1. row ***************************
           id: 1
  select_type: SIMPLE
        table: tbl_report
   partitions: NULL
         type: ALL
possible_keys: NULL
          key: NULL
      key_len: NULL
          ref: NULL
         rows: 1
     filtered: 100.00
        Extra: NULL
1 row in set, 1 warning (0.00 sec)
```

With the help of EXPLAIN, you will be able to see from which table you are missing indexes and make the necessary adjustments to optimize your queries. Keep in mind that you may need to run EXPLAIN to get your query to an optimal level.

There are a lot of customers who often ask me the following question:

Why does my query not use my indexes?

There are several reasons why MySQL does not use the indexes it should in its optimizer, but the main one is often just because the statistics are not up to date. To refresh the statistics that MySQL uses to make decisions on the use of indexes, just run the following command:

```
analyze table [table_name];
ANALYZE TABLE clients;
```

The following is the result:

```
+------------------------+----------+----------+----------+
| Table                  | Op       | Msg_type | Msg_text |
+------------------------+----------+----------+----------+
| app.clients            | analyze  | status   | OK       |
+------------------------+----------+----------+----------+
```

 If you have tables with millions of records, keep in mind that there will be a table lock for a short time, so I suggest you proceed with this command during quieter periods.

The EXPLAIN PLAN columns for MySQL 8.0 are explained as follows:

Column	JSON Name	Explanation
id	select_id	The SELECT identifier (DML)
select_type	None	The SELECT type (See below for details)
table	table_name	The table name for the output row
partitions	partitions	The matching partition names
type	access_type	The join type (Inner_join...)
possible_keys	possible_keys	The possible indexes that MySQL can use
key	key	The potential index that it can be chosen
key_len	key_length	The length of the potential key
ref	ref	The columns compared to the index chosen
rows	rows	Estimate of rows that will be taken in consideration
filtered	filtered	% of rows filtered by table condition
Extra	None	Additional helpful information

Let's explain each of the items you can see in the previous table.

id (JSON name: select_id)

This item is a sequential reference used by MySQL inside a query. If you notice an EXPLAIN analysis that has multiple lines, you will see that the output will have sequential numbering to help you find it yourself.

select_type (JSON name: none)

This type is the one with the most information and contains the most references to help you see what type of DML, like SELECT, for example, will be interpreted by MySQL.

Let's look at the choices that MySQL offers for this option:

select_type Value	JSON Name	Explanation
SIMPLE	None	Simple SELECT (doesn't include UNION or subqueries)
PRIMARY	None	First most important SELECT
UNION	None	Second SELECT in a UNION
DEPENDENT UNION	dependent (true)	Second SELECT in a UNION, dependent on the outer query
UNION RESULT	union_result	Result of the UNION
SUBQUERY	None	First SELECT in a subquery
DEPENDENT SUBQUERY	dependent (true)	First SELECT in a subquery, dependent on the outer query
DERIVED	None	Derived table style SELECT (subquery in FROM clause)
MATERIALIZED	materialized_from_subquery	Materialized subquery (New option)
UNCACHEABLE SUBQUERY	cacheable (false)	A subquery where the result cannot be cached and have to be re-evaluated for each row from the outer query
UNCACHEABLE UNION	cacheable (false)	The second select in a UNION that is part of an uncacheable subquery

Let's go over the options for the table.

table (JSON name: table_name)

This item refers to a name in a table that is used by the record that is part of the EXPLAIN plan.

partitions (JSON name: partitions)

The item demonstrates which record will be used by the query in the context that there is a partition of a table.

type (JSON name: access_type)

The purpose of TYPE is to bring out the type of join used in the query. There are some different types that are not necessarily placed in the order of display, but rather by type of join, and here are these different types:

system	Applies to system tables and contains a record.
const	This type is very fast because it will read the record only once since it refers to a given value. Here is an example: SELECT * FROM clients WHERE ID=1;
eq_ref	This type, outside the const, is the best choice because it will be used in all index possibilities and a record is read among the combinations of the previous tables. Here is an example: SELECT * FROM clients,invoices WHERE clients.ID=invoices.clientID;
ref	All the records that can be found a table in its index. It is best, for optimal performance, that the ref is used with an indexed column. Here is an example: SELECT * FROM clients WHERE ID=1;
fulltext	This type is specifically for fulltext searches from an index.
ref_or_null	This type is very similar to ref, but with the exception that MySQL will do extra work to find records that will be NULL. Here is an example: SELECT * FROM clients WHERE ID=1 OR last_billing IS NULL;

`index_merge`	This type indicates that MySQL uses the Index Merge Optimization. You will notice in this case that the `key_len` type contains a larger list of values because this one is used by the indexes.
`unique_subquery`	This type replaces `eq_ref` with some values of the `IN ()` function in subqueries. Here is an example: `10 IN (SELECT ID FROM clients WHERE ID < 100000)`
`index_subquery`	This type is similar to `unique_subquery`, but will replace the `IN ()` and will only be used generally for non-unique values.

`range`	This type will be used in an extended comparison between two values and `EXPLAIN` will show you which index is used.
	Here is an example:
	`SELECT * FROM clients`
	`WHERE ID BETWEEN 1000 and 2000;`

`index`	This type is the same, except that the full scan is completely in the index and not at the table level. If all the criteria correspond to the index, then in the extra column you will have more explanations.
`all`	This type is of course not desirable for optimization because it indicates that MySQL will do a full scan of the table and will not use any indexes.

EXPLAIN extra information

One of the important columns of `EXPLAIN` is, of course, the `EXTRA` column. This column contains additional information on how MySQL will support your query.

 A quick note: if you want your queries to be faster, take a look in the `EXTRA` column and try to see messages such as `Using Filesort` and `Using Temporary Table`; we will revisit these two messages later.

Let's take a look at the list of the most important messages you'll find in the `EXPLAIN` view:

- **Full scan on NULL key**: This message is displayed when MySQL cannot access an index for a subquery.
- **Impossible HAVING**: The `HAVING` clause cannot select any records.
- **Impossible WHERE**: Similar to `HAVING` because it cannot find records.

- **Not exists**: As a general rule, MySQL has been able to optimize the LEFT JOIN but is not able to evaluate the previous tables, and is only able to find a single record. Here is an example:

```
SELECT * FROM clients LEFT JOIN clients_history ON
clients.id=clients_history.id WHERE t2.id IS NULL;
```

Suppose clients_history.id is defined as NOT NULL. In this case, MySQL scans clients and looks for rows in clients_history using values from clients.id. If MySQL finds a matching line in clients_history, it knows that clients_history.id can never be NULL and does not scan the rest of the rows of clients_history with the same ID value.

- **Using filesort**: MySQL must do additional work to find the records in the requested ranking. The ranking is done by browsing all the records relative to the join. MySQL will need to store the search key and pointer records that are found. Then, the records found will be sorted according to the order requested.
- **Using index**: This message is for guidance only and to tell you that MySQL used an index to execute your query.
- **Using index condition**: MySQL tells you that it has worked with tables and index tuples to read records through an index.
- **Using join buffer**: MySQL here indicates that the joins that were previously executed were stored in a memory called join_buffer. It is not advisable to have a message like this, because if you do not have enough memory, MySQL will use the disk to compensate the execution.
- **Using temporary**: MySQL will display this message when you use a Group By or Sort By. The job MySQL must do is to store your data in a temporary table to work with the records. The other situation to know why MySQL should use temporary tables, is the lack of memory, so it will need to revise the RAM requirements.

We will see a more complex EXPLAIN model in case study # 2.

In this section, you learned how to effectively read the EXPLAIN tool and how to interpret the execution plan view. In our next section, we will explore when the creation of an index is necessary.

How to know when to create an index

An index at the database level is the same principle as having an index at the end of a book. This is a completely separate section of the content from the rest of the book. So, do you see where I'm going with this? For example, if you are looking for a specific value, you can go to the index and search for it (the indexes are ordered, so finding things in this section is much faster than passing each page of the book).

A database index is an ordered list of relevant information that's used to expedite the search for records that match the criteria.

Specifically, you create an index when you have information that you need to look for frequently and need a quick answer for.

In other words, indexes prevent the DBMS from scanning the entire table looking for matching values, and they also help when you need to sort on a column.

Keep in mind that if you want to combine several columns in an index, the consequence will be that your queries will have the same number of columns in the WHERE clauses and in the same order.

The five general rules to know when it is appropriate to create an index would be to respond positively to the following questions:

- Can you index each primary key?
- Can you index each foreign or secondary key?
- Can you index each column used in a JOIN clause?
- Can you index each column used in a WHERE?
- Can you index each column used in a GROUP BY clause?
- Can you index each column used in an ORDER BY clause?
- Are you going to generate reports?

In other words, indexes become necessary when you plan to use joins, that is, WHERE, GROUP BY, and ORDER BY.

Also, if your table is very small, for example only a few employees, it is more difficult to use an index than to let MySQL do a full scan of the table. Indexes are only useful with tables that have a lot of records.

There are many cases in which a single multi-column type index would give you better performance than multiple indexes for a single column. At the same time, keep in mind that your indexing strategy should include the impact on other SQL commands, such as insert, update, and delete.

Evidently, even when it comes to a very simple table, there is a lot to consider when working with indexes.

The following is a small example of a simple table structure to help you understand:

```
CREATE TABLE employees (
ID INT,
employee_name VARCHAR(50),
employee_salary decimal(10,2),
hired_date (date)
)
```

The ID column is just an integer (INT) that can hold a very large number. In a real-life situation, there is a good chance I would have left this data type unsigned, since employee IDs cannot be negative. Plus, because of the size and the type of number, we would never have enough employees anyway.

You will probably consider automatically incrementing the column, and incrementing the primary key automatically, based on how the data will be entered.

Another tip is that the name of the employee is a VARCHAR (50) that should cover the names of most people. I don't think this column is updated very often, so if you think you have a lot of employees, it would be a column to be indexed.

In the next section, we will reflect on when an index with multiple columns is needed.

Multiple column index versus multiple indexes

When discussing indexes, there is another question people often bring up: should we be using multiple columns in an index or multiple indexes on unique columns?

One mistake we often make is not taking the time to understand how indexing works and what we think is correct, indexing all columns used in queries separately.

In this case, you end up with a table that has multiple indexes. But these indexes end up having only one column. This kind of problem can be seen very quickly.

If you have queries with multiple columns in a WHERE clause, you will probably need multiple indexes that will contain multiple columns for optimal performance. But wait, we must keep in mind that indexing all possible combinations, thinking that you will get better performance, may very well have an opposite effect.

Let's use an example of indexes with unique columns:

```
mysql> show create table people \G
*************************** 1. row ***************************
        Table: people
Create Table: CREATE TABLE `people` (
  `firstname` varchar(50) NOT NULL DEFAULT '',
  `lastname` varchar(50) NOT NULL DEFAULT '',
  `mobile` varchar(20) NOT NULL DEFAULT '',
  `birthday` date NOT NULL,
  `home_id` smallint(6) DEFAULT NULL,
  `ID` int(11) NOT NULL AUTO_INCREMENT,
  PRIMARY KEY (`ID`),
  KEY `birthday` (`birthday`,`lastname`)
) ENGINE=InnoDB AUTO_INCREMENT=9 DEFAULT CHARSET=latin1
1 row in set (0.00 sec)
```

Here is our table structure:

```
mysql> show create table people\G
*************************** 1. row ***************************
```

```
Table: people
Create Table: CREATE TABLE `people` (
  `firstname` varchar(50) NOT NULL DEFAULT '',
  `lastname` varchar(50) NOT NULL DEFAULT '',
  `mobile` varchar(20) NOT NULL DEFAULT '',
  `birthday` date NOT NULL,
  `home_id` smallint(6) DEFAULT NULL,
  `ID` int(11) NOT NULL AUTO_INCREMENT,
  PRIMARY KEY (`ID`)
) ENGINE=InnoDB AUTO_INCREMENT=9 DEFAULT CHARSET=latin1
1 row in set (0.00 sec)
```

As you may have noted, this table only has one primary key. Let's look at a query that could use two different indexes on the people table, depending on the filtering of the WHERE clause. Now, let's create these indexes:

```
mysql> ALTER TABLE people
ADD INDEX (birthday),
ADD INDEX (lastname);
Query OK, 0 rows affected (0.04 sec)
Records: 0  Duplicates: 0  Warnings: 0
```

If we think efficiently, it will be more efficient to combine DML statements for a given table whenever possible. For example, if you choose to run ALTER commands as two individual commands, the following will happen:

```
mysql> ALTER TABLE people  DROP index birthday, drop index lastname;
Query OK, 0 rows affected (0.03 sec)
Records: 0  Duplicates: 0  Warnings: 0

mysql> ALTER TABLE people ADD INDEX (birthday);
Query OK, 0 rows affected (0.05 sec)
Records: 0  Duplicates: 0  Warnings: 0

mysql> ALTER TABLE people  ADD INDEX (lastname);
Query OK, 0 rows affected (0.04 sec)
Records: 0  Duplicates: 0  Warnings: 0
```

Imagine if you had a table with over a million records in production and an ALTER command took 90 minutes or 8 hours; it's a huge saving.

Keep in mind that creating an index is a time-consuming operation, depending on the size of your table, and can block all your operations on that same table. In optimization, we must also think about efficiency and impact on all operations. You can combine the creation of multiple indexes on any table with a single instruction, ALTER.

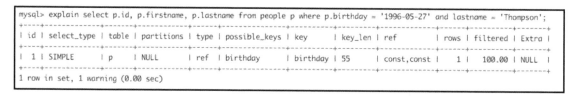

```
mysql> explain select p.id, p.firstname, p.lastname from people p where p.birthday = '1996-05-27' and lastname = 'Thompson';
+----+-------------+-------+------------+------+---------------+----------+---------+-------------+------+----------+-------+
| id | select_type | table | partitions | type | possible_keys | key      | key_len | ref         | rows | filtered | Extra |
+----+-------------+-------+------------+------+---------------+----------+---------+-------------+------+----------+-------+
|  1 | SIMPLE      | p     | NULL       | ref  | birthday      | birthday | 55      | const,const |   1  |   100.00 | NULL  |
+----+-------------+-------+------------+------+---------------+----------+---------+-------------+------+----------+-------+
1 row in set, 1 warning (0.00 sec)
```

As you may have noticed, MySQL does not seem to know which index to use because it tells us that there are two possible indexes or keys. As we said earlier, the optimizer is like a GPS in that it shows two different (possible_keys) ways and chooses (key column) the best path.

If you have noticed—and many people ask this question, as I already mentioned in one of the previous sections—why doesn't MySQL use the right index?

Just as in our example, the WHERE clause contains two indexed columns and MySQL does not seem to know exactly which of these indexes is used, because they have the same cardinality or weight; that's why MySQL shows more than one potential key.

Now that you understand the potential impact on query performance and the potential confusion, let's take a look at the other option that MySQL offers us to address this issue.

The other option offered is what we call indexing on multiple columns, or **compound** indexes.

Let's delete the indexes we created earlier:

```
mysql> ALTER TABLE people  DROP index birthday, drop index lastname;
Query OK, 0 rows affected (0.04 sec)
Records: 0  Duplicates: 0  Warnings: 0
```

And here is our table structure:

```
mysql> show create table people \G
*************************** 1. row ***************************
       Table: people
Create Table: CREATE TABLE `people` (
  `firstname` varchar(50) NOT NULL DEFAULT '',
  `lastname` varchar(50) NOT NULL DEFAULT '',
  `mobile` varchar(20) NOT NULL DEFAULT '',
  `birthday` date NOT NULL,
  `home_id` smallint(6) DEFAULT NULL,
  `ID` int(11) NOT NULL AUTO_INCREMENT,
  PRIMARY KEY (`ID`),
  KEY `birthday` (`birthday`,`lastname`)
) ENGINE=InnoDB AUTO_INCREMENT=9 DEFAULT CHARSET=latin1
1 row in set (0.00 sec)
```

Now, let's create an index of the COMPOUND type:

```
mysql> ALTER TABLE people add  index (birthday, lastname);
Query OK, 0 rows affected (0.05 sec)
Records: 0  Duplicates: 0  Warnings: 0
```

Here is the new people table structure:

```
mysql> show create table people \G
*************************** 1. row ***************************
       Table: people
Create Table: CREATE TABLE `people` (
  `firstname` varchar(50) NOT NULL DEFAULT '',
  `lastname` varchar(50) NOT NULL DEFAULT '',
  `mobile` varchar(20) NOT NULL DEFAULT '',
  `birthday` date NOT NULL,
  `home_id` smallint(6) DEFAULT NULL,
  `ID` int(11) NOT NULL AUTO_INCREMENT,
  PRIMARY KEY (`ID`),
  KEY `birthday` (`birthday`,`lastname`)
) ENGINE=InnoDB AUTO_INCREMENT=9 DEFAULT CHARSET=latin1
1 row in set (0.00 sec)
```

As you can see, we have an index now that combines two columns, so let's look at EXPLAIN with the same query:

```
mysql> explain select p.id, p.firstname, p.lastname from people p where p.birthday = '1996-05-27' and lastname = 'Thompson';
+----+-------------+-------+------------+------+---------------+----------+---------+-------------+------+----------+-------+
| id | select_type | table | partitions | type | possible_keys | key      | key_len | ref         | rows | filtered | Extra |
+----+-------------+-------+------------+------+---------------+----------+---------+-------------+------+----------+-------+
|  1 | SIMPLE      | p     | NULL       | ref  | birthday      | birthday | 55      | const,const |    1 |   100.00 | NULL  |
+----+-------------+-------+------------+------+---------------+----------+---------+-------------+------+----------+-------+
1 row in set, 1 warning (0.00 sec)
```

By combining two columns in an index, we fixed the confusion that MySQL had beforehand, and in addition we got 100% filtering.

The important thing here is to remember that we have to realize that indexes have to be adjusted to the needs of our queries; it's a question of best practices and strategizing. Again, it is not the amount of indexes that counts, but rather the correct answer to the needs of our queries. We must also evaluate the needs of our queries because if we have all kinds of different queries, we will have a quantity as a result, and we'll be in a vicious circle that affects the performance of MySQL.

In this section, you learned the difference between indexes with unique columns and indexes with multiple columns.

In the next section, you will discover how to organize your columns in an index against your queries.

How to organize your columns in an index for good performance

In this section, we will specifically cover the order of the columns in a multi-column index or COMPOUND type. The order in which you will put your columns will allow you to have queries that perform. Now, in what order should we put them? It depends on how you are going to query your table with your queries. An index can be used to perform an exact search or filtering with the WHERE clause.

A specific search is when the values of all columns in the index are specified and the query uses exactly the same order.

We can say that this type of index is defined as follows:

```
index( col_A, col_B, col_C )
```

The advantage of a COMPOUND index is beneficial for a query if it uses these columns in joins, filtering, and sometimes in a particular selection. There will be other benefits for queries that use the left-most subset of columns of this type of COMPOUND index. Thus, the preceding index will also answer queries that require the following:

- index(col_A, col_B, col_C)
- index(col_A, col_B)
- index(col_A)

In other words, a COMPOUND type index is based on the concept (MostSelective, SecondMost, Less) and will only be effective when the MostSelective column is specified. This type of index can become your best friend in optimizing your queries if the order is respected, and will eliminate creating other indexes for no reason.

Another point to consider regarding this type of index is that it will not be effective in the case of * index(col_A, col_C).

Did you notice that column B is missing in this case, because MySQL will not consider the index? You will have a full scan in your EXPLAIN, as shown in the following screenshot. We reversed the columns to show you that if you do not respect the column order, MySQL will not consider the index:

```
mysql> explain select p.id, p.firstname, p.lastname from people p where lastname = 'Thompson' and p.birthday = '1996-05-27';
+----+-------------+-------+------------+------+---------------+------+---------+------+------+----------+-------------+
| id | select_type | table | partitions | type | possible_keys | key  | key_len | ref  | rows | filtered | Extra       |
+----+-------------+-------+------------+------+---------------+------+---------+------+------+----------+-------------+
|  1 | SIMPLE      | p     | NULL       | ALL  | NULL          | NULL | NULL    | NULL |    8 |    12.50 | Using where |
+----+-------------+-------+------------+------+---------------+------+---------+------+------+----------+-------------+
1 row in set, 1 warning (0.00 sec)
```

In the opposite case—remember from our previous section our table that had a COMPOUND index:

```
mysql> show create table people \G
*************************** 1. row ***************************
       Table: people
Create Table: CREATE TABLE `people` (
  `firstname` varchar(50) NOT NULL DEFAULT '',
  `lastname` varchar(50) NOT NULL DEFAULT '',
  `mobile` varchar(20) NOT NULL DEFAULT '',
  `birthday` date NOT NULL,
  `home_id` smallint(6) DEFAULT NULL,
  `ID` int(11) NOT NULL AUTO_INCREMENT,
  PRIMARY KEY (`ID`),
  KEY `birthday` (`birthday`,`lastname`)
) ENGINE=InnoDB AUTO_INCREMENT=9 DEFAULT CHARSET=latin1
1 row in set (0.00 sec)
```

We had the following EXPLAIN:

```
mysql> explain select p.id, p.firstname, p.lastname from people p where p.birthday = '1996-05-27' and lastname = 'Thompson';
+----+-------------+-------+------------+------+---------------+----------+---------+-------------+------+----------+-------+
| id | select_type | table | partitions | type | possible_keys | key      | key_len | ref         | rows | filtered | Extra |
+----+-------------+-------+------------+------+---------------+----------+---------+-------------+------+----------+-------+
|  1 | SIMPLE      | p     | NULL       | ref  | birthday      | birthday | 55      | const,const |  1   | 100.00   | NULL  |
+----+-------------+-------+------------+------+---------------+----------+---------+-------------+------+----------+-------+
1 row in set, 1 warning (0.00 sec)
```

So as you can see, the order of columns from left to right will be very important for your query to be optimal.

In this section, you learned that the order of the columns is very important in a COMPOUND index type and that this index is very efficient. You also learned that if you do not respect the number of columns, MySQL just ignores this index.

In our next section, we will look at how to use an EXPLAIN plan with MySQL 8.0.

Case study 1 – how to use the EXPLAIN plan tool in MySQL 8.0

As we have already explained in our previous sections, EXPLAIN describes how MySQL plans to execute any query. That is, it is a pre-execution tool, without affecting the performance of your database, not to compare with the profiling of a query that is another tool of MySQL.

The following table shows the EXPLAIN syntax in the most important versions of MySQL:

MySQL 8.x	MySQL 5.7	MySQL 5.6

{EXPLAIN | DESCRIBE | DESC}
   tbl_name [col_name | wild]
	{EXPLAIN | DESCRIBE | DESC}
	   tbl_name [col_name | wild]
		{EXPLAIN | DESCRIBE | DESC}
		   tbl_name [col_name | wild]

{EXPLAIN | DESCRIBE | DESC}
   [explain_type]
   {explainable_stmt | FOR CONNECTION connection_id}
	{EXPLAIN | DESCRIBE | DESC}
	   [explain_type]
	   {explainable_stmt | FOR CONNECTION connection_id}
		{EXPLAIN | DESCRIBE | DESC}
		   [explain_type]
		   explainable_stmt

explain_type: {
  | FORMAT = format_name
}
	explain_type: {
	  EXTENDED
	  | PARTITIONS
	  | FORMAT = format_name
	}
		explain_type: {
		  EXTENDED
		  | PARTITIONS
		  | FORMAT = format_name
		}

format_name: {
  TRADITIONAL
  | JSON
}
	format_name: {
	  TRADITIONAL
	  | JSON
	}
		format_name: {
		  TRADITIONAL
		  | JSON
		}

explainable_stmt: {
  SELECT statement
  | DELETE statement
  | INSERT statement
  | REPLACE statement
  | UPDATE statement
}
	explainable_stmt: {
	  SELECT statement
	  | DELETE statement
	  | INSERT statement
	  | REPLACE statement
	  | UPDATE statement
	}
		explainable_stmt: {
		  SELECT statement
		  | DELETE statement
		  | INSERT statement
		  | REPLACE statement
		  | UPDATE statement
		}

EXPLAIN options

I will not describe the EXPLAIN options in detail again, because we have already done so in the *How to efficiently read MySQL query execution plans* section. However, I will explore the most important options that DBAs and developers are not used to working with, and give you a better understanding of EXPLAIN so that you can manage it properly.

The DESCRIBE and EXPLAIN commands are synonyms or similar. In practice, DESCRIBE is often used to get a quick overview of the table structure, while EXPLAIN is used to get a pre-execution of queries expressed as a plan.

In the preceding table, we have an option that is new since MySQL 5.7, and this option is FOR CONNECTION connection_id. As you may have probably noticed, this option allows us to execute an EXPLAIN on a connection directly and observe its live performance. We will see this option with an example.

Let's continue our explanations before our examples. You will also notice that the EXPLAIN_TYPE option no longer contains EXTENDED and PARTITIONS. These options are now default and cannot be used as parameters anymore in MySQL 8.0.

In the release of MySQL 8.0, the output JSON format is encouraged much more because it gives you additional information that EXPLAIN with TRADITIONAL will not give you.

So, as you can see, the MySQL 8.0 EXPLAIN version is similar to version 5.7, but with more orientation to the JSON format and now defaults with the advantage of giving you good information relevant to the output.

Let's look at an execution plan (EXPLAIN) with MySQL 8.0, using a JSON output format with explanations:

```
mysql> explain FORMAT=JSON  select p.id, p.firstname, p.lastname from people p where lastname = 'Thompson' and p.birthday =
'1996-05-27'\G
*************************** 1. row ***************************
EXPLAIN: {
  "query_block": {
    "select_id": 1,
    "cost_info": {
      "query_cost": "2.60"          <---- 1
    },
    "table": {
      "table_name": "p",
      "access_type": "ALL",
      "rows_examined_per_scan": 8,   <---- 2
      "rows_produced_per_join": 1,
      "filtered": "12.50",                   3
      "cost_info": {
        "read_cost": "2.40",         <----
        "eval_cost": "0.20",
        "prefix_cost": "2.60",              4
        "data_read_per_join": "136"  <----
      },                                  5
      "used_columns": [
        "firstname",
        "lastname",
        "birthday",
        "ID"
      ],
      "attached_condition": "((`addresses`.`p`.`birthday` = '1996-05-27') and (`addresses`.`p`.`lastname` = 'Thompson'))"
    }
  }
}
```

The following is the structure of the `people` table:

```
mysql> show create table people G
***** 1. row ************
        Table: people
Create Table: CREATE TABLE `people` (
   `firstname` varchar(50) NOT NULL DEFAULT '',
   `lastname` varchar(50) NOT NULL DEFAULT '',
   `mobile` varchar(20) NOT NULL DEFAULT '',
   `birthday` date NOT NULL,
   `home_id` smallint(6) DEFAULT NULL,
   `ID` int(11) NOT NULL AUTO_INCREMENT,
   PRIMARY KEY (`ID`)
) ENGINE=InnoDB AUTO_INCREMENT=9 DEFAULT CHARSET=latin1
1 row in set (0.00 sec)
```

//

- `Cost_info:Query_cost`: This is the effort that the optimizer must make to execute your query in terms of units. This option is in tandem with the `ACCESS_TYPE`.

  For example, if you had a table with a record count of over a million and no indexes, instead of 2.60 units, you would have a number like 50 units or more. Here, we have a figure of 2.60 units because the `FULL SCAN (ALL)` is done with a number of 6 records. So, the bigger the number in the `COST_INFO` option, the worse your query will perform and the longer the response time will be optimal.

- `rows_examined_per_scan`: This option tells you how many records have been scanned into the table. In our preceding example, you have the number 8.

- `rows_produced_per_join`: The number of records that have been processed in a join is suggested to be small, to keep the execution of your query.

- `read_cost`: This option tells you the cost in units or effort that the optimizer must pay to read the data; in our example, the effort in unit tells us that the reading is very fast because we have a low value of 2.40.

- `data_read_per_join`: Here, we have an indicator of the number of records that have been seen or read in a join; again, it is better to have a small number at this level for optimal performance, otherwise you will need to review the join types and correct them to get a favorable optimization.

In this case study, you learned the `EXPLAIN` plan of MySQL 8.0 and also the benefits of `JSON` format output.

In the next case study, you will learn how to analyze and display a table structure across `EXPLAIN`.

Case study 2 – how to display and analyze a table structure versus the EXPLAIN plan tool

We will explore the following in this section:

- Running a plan with `EXPLAIN`
- How to display the structure of a table for our execution plan (`EXPLAIN`)
- Finally, how to compare the structure of a table with respect to an execution plan (`EXPLAIN`)

Let's take the example from case study 1 but this time show you a full scan by using the EXPLAIN command to display the structure of the people table as its DESC synonym would:

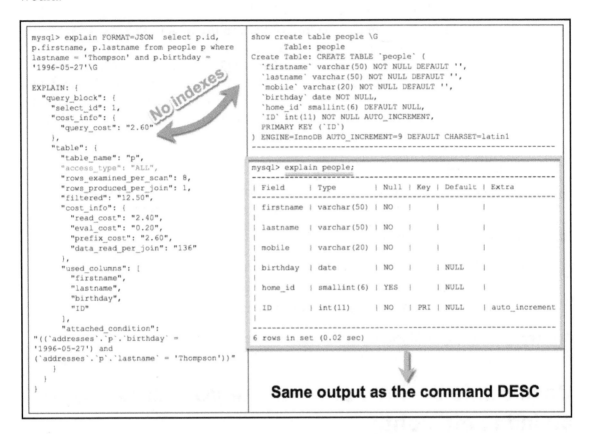

```
mysql> explain FORMAT=JSON  select p.id,
p.firstname, p.lastname from people p where
lastname = 'Thompson' and p.birthday =
'1996-05-27'\G

EXPLAIN: {
  "query_block": {
  "select_id": 1,
  "cost_info": {
    "query_cost": "2.60"
  },
  "table": {
  "table_name": "p",
  "access_type": "ALL",
  "rows_examined_per_scan": 8,
  "rows_produced_per_join": 1,
  "filtered": "12.50",
  "cost_info": {
    "read_cost": "2.40",
    "eval_cost": "0.20",
    "prefix_cost": "2.60",
    "data_read_per_join": "136"
  },
  "used_columns": [
    "firstname",
    "lastname",
    "birthday",
    "ID"
  ],
  "attached_condition":
"((`addresses`.`p`.`birthday` =
'1996-05-27') and
(`addresses`.`p`.`lastname` = 'Thompson'))"
    }
  }
}
```

No indexes

```
show create table people \G
       Table: people
Create Table: CREATE TABLE `people` (
  `firstname` varchar(50) NOT NULL DEFAULT '',
  `lastname` varchar(50) NOT NULL DEFAULT '',
  `mobile` varchar(20) NOT NULL DEFAULT '',
  `birthday` date NOT NULL,
  `home_id` smallint(6) DEFAULT NULL,
  `ID` int(11) NOT NULL AUTO_INCREMENT,
  PRIMARY KEY (`ID`)
) ENGINE=InnoDB AUTO_INCREMENT=9 DEFAULT CHARSET=latin1
```

```
mysql> explain people;
```

Field	Type	Null	Key	Default	Extra
firstname	varchar(50)	NO			
lastname	varchar(50)	NO			
mobile	varchar(20)	NO			
birthday	date	NO		NULL	
home_id	smallint(6)	YES		NULL	
ID	int(11)	NO	PRI	NULL	auto_increment

6 rows in set (0.02 sec)

Same output as the command DESC

When we want to optimize a query, we have to examine it with the following steps:

1. Run the execution plan (EXPLAIN) on the query preceding your query, with the word EXPLAIN
2. Observe which part of your EXPLAIN can have the word ALL in the ACCESS_TYPE line, or any other signs that your query needs attention

3. Analyze the table structure of the query that seems to have a performance problem with the `SHOW CREATE TABLE [tablename]\G` command, asking the following questions:
   1. Is there at least one primary key?
   2. Is there an index on columns that you use in your `WHERE`, `GROUP BY`, `ORDER BY`, and `HAVING` clauses?
      1. If the answer to reference (2) is no, the next question would be, do I need a `COMPOUND` index that will cover the columns used in `WHERE`, `GROUP BY`, and `ORDER BY`, or do I just need an index that will be used in the `WHERE` clause with a single referenced column?

4. Modify your query if necessary to use in your indexes
5. Generally, steps 1 to 3 are sufficient, but depending on the complexity of your query, you may need to repeat them until your query is optimized

In this section, you learned the following:

- How to run an execution plan with `EXPLAIN`
- How to display the structure of a table for our execution plan (`EXPLAIN`)
- How to compare a table structure against an execution plan (`EXPLAIN`)

In the next section, you will learn how to organize your columns in your indexing strategy.

Case study 3 – how to organize your columns in an index efficiently

In this section, we'll learn how to organize columns in indexes so that your queries are maximized.

Here's a visual representation to help you understand how to organize your columns with the `WHERE`, `GROUP BY`, and `ORDER BY` clauses:

In the following table, we will represent the index requirements in relation to the number of columns:

Only 1 column	2 columns	3 columns et plus
We include these instructions: 1. Operators: <>= 2. LIKE & NOT LIKE 3. IN() & NOT IN()	We include these instructions: 1. BETWEEN & NOT 2. AND & OR 3. Operators: <>= 4. NOT 5. LIKE & NOT LIKE	We include these instructions: 1. All instructions from column #1 and #2 2. Parenthesis We exclude all sub-queries.
Index strategies	Index strategies	Index strategies
• Primary key • Unique index • Partial index	• Partial index • Compound	• Compound

Remember that the COMPOUND index must be used or interpreted from left to right, and all columns must be supported.

In the indexing strategy, always keep in mind that single-column indexes in complex queries are not the most efficient, but COMPOUND indexes are the ones you should consider to cover the WHERE, GROUP BY, and ORDER BY clauses.

Speaking of the WHERE, GROUP BY, and ORDER BY clauses, I suggest a COMPOUND index in similar cases to the following example.

Here is our table structure:

```
mysql> show create table people \G
***** 1. row ************
        Table: people
Create Table: CREATE TABLE `people` (
  `firstname` varchar(50) NOT NULL DEFAULT '',
  `lastname` varchar(50) NOT NULL DEFAULT '',
  `mobile` varchar(20) NOT NULL DEFAULT '',
  `birthday` date NOT NULL,
  `home_id` smallint(6) DEFAULT NULL,
  `ID` int(11) NOT NULL AUTO_INCREMENT,
  PRIMARY KEY (`ID`)
) ENGINE=InnoDB AUTO_INCREMENT=9 DEFAULT CHARSET=latin1
1 row in set (0.00 sec)
```

Here is our execution plan (EXPLAIN):

```
explain FORMAT=JSON SELECT firstname, lastname, COUNT(*) as number
FROM people
WHERE birthday BETWEEN '1964-01-01' AND '2018-09-01'
GROUP BY lastname
ORDER BY birthday;
```

Here is the result:

```
EXPLAIN: {
  "query_block": {
    "select_id": 1,
    "cost_info": {
      "query_cost": "2.60"
    },
    "ordering_operation": {
      "using_filesort": true,
      "grouping_operation": {
        "using_temporary_table": true,
        "using_filesort": false,
        "table": {
          "table_name": "people",
          "access_type": "ALL",
          "rows_examined_per_scan": 8,
          "rows_produced_per_join": 1,
          "filtered": "12.50",
          "cost_info": {
            "read_cost": "2.40",
            "eval_cost": "0.20",
            "prefix_cost": "2.60",
            "data_read_per_join": "136"
          },
          "used_columns": [
            "firstname",
            "lastname",
            "birthday",
            "ID"
          ],
          "attached_condition": "(`addresses`.`people`.`birthday` between '1964-01-01' and '2018-09-01')"
        }
      }
    }
  }
}
```

As indicated by the execution plan (EXPLAIN), we have a full scan because no indexes exist.

Have you noticed that EXPLAIN gives us the columns in an interpreted order, and also that this information facilitates our optimization task because we will create the COMPOUND index with the columns in the same order?

```
"used_columns": [
    "firstname",
    "lastname",
    "birthday",
    "ID"
```

Creating a missing index

Now, let's create a COMPOUND index, as we have indicated in our suggestions table for the previous indexes:

```
mysql> ALTER TABLE people ADD INDEX (firstname,lastname,birthday,ID);
Query OK, 0 rows affected (0.08 sec)
Records: 0  Duplicates: 0  Warnings: 0
```

Let's see the result after creating the index. Here is our new table structure after creating an index:

```
mysql> show create table people \G
*************************** 1. row ***************************
       Table: people
Create Table: CREATE TABLE `people` (
  `firstname` varchar(50) NOT NULL DEFAULT '',
  `lastname` varchar(50) NOT NULL DEFAULT '',
  `mobile` varchar(20) NOT NULL DEFAULT '',
  `birthday` date NOT NULL,
  `home_id` smallint(6) DEFAULT NULL,
  `ID` int(11) NOT NULL AUTO_INCREMENT,
  PRIMARY KEY (`ID`),
  KEY `firstname` (`firstname`,`lastname`,`birthday`,`ID`)
) ENGINE=InnoDB AUTO_INCREMENT=9 DEFAULT CHARSET=latin1
1 row in set (0.00 sec)
```

Here is the result of our TRADITIONAL execution plan:

```
| id | select_type | table  | partitions | type  | possible_keys | key       | key_len | ref  | rows | filtered | Extra

|  1 | SIMPLE      | people | NULL       | index | firstname     | firstname | 111     | NULL |   8  |  12.50   | Using where;
                                                                                                                 Using index;
                                                                                                                 Using temporary;
                                                                                                                 Using filesort
```

Here is the result of our execution plan in JSON format:

```
EXPLAIN: {
  "query_block": {
    "select_id": 1,
    "cost_info": {
      "query_cost": "2.60"
    },
    "ordering_operation": {
      "using_filesort": true,
      "grouping_operation": {
        "using_temporary_table": true,
        "using_filesort": false,
        "table": {
          "table_name": "people",
          "access_type": "index",
          "possible_keys": [
            "firstname"
          ],
          "key": "firstname",
          "used_key_parts": [
            "firstname",
            "lastname",
            "birthday",
            "ID"
          ],
          "key_length": "111",
          "rows_examined_per_scan": 8,
          "rows_produced_per_join": 1,
          "filtered": "12.50",
          "using_index": true,
          "cost_info": {
            "read_cost": "2.40",
            "eval_cost": "0.20",
            "prefix_cost": "2.60",
            "data_read_per_join": "136"
          },
          "used_columns": [
            "firstname",
            "lastname",
            "birthday",
            "ID"
          ],
          "attached_condition": "(`addresses`.`people`.`birthday` between '1964-01-01' and '2018-09-01')"
        }
      }
    }
  }
}
```

In our MySQL report output, MySQL took into consideration the COMPOUND index; here is a good example of optimization that can be applied for simple and complex queries.

In this section, you learned how to organize columns in indexes so that your queries are maximized. Similarly, we have explored how to take advantage of the output of the execution plan in JSON format.

In the next section, we will share tips and techniques for your benefit.

Tips and techniques

In this section, I will share the five most popular tips and we will review a real case of a company that is facing a performance problem with a query in MySQL.

The five general rules for your indexes

The five general rules to know when it is appropriate to create an index would be to respond positively to the following questions:

- Can you Index each primary key?
- Can you Index each foreign or secondary key?
- Can you Index each column used in a JOIN clause?
- Can you Index each column used in a WHERE?
- Can you Index each column used in a GROUP BY clause?
- Can you Index each column used in an ORDER BY clause?
- Are you going to generate reports?

In other words, indexes become necessary when you plan to use joins, that is, WHERE, GROUP BY, and ORDER BY.

If your table is very small, for example, only a few employees, it is more difficult to use an index than to let MySQL do a full scan of the table. Indexes are only useful with tables that have a lot of records.

Use the COMPOUND index more often in complex queries to reduce the number of indexes.

Tip 2 – the five general rules to optimize your queries

When we want to optimize a query, we have to examine it by performing the following steps:

1. Run the execution plan (EXPLAIN) on the query preceding your query with the word EXPLAIN
2. Observe which part of your EXPLAIN can have the word ALL in the ACCESS_TYPE line or any other signs that your query needs attention
3. Analyze the table structure whose query seems to have a performance problem with the SHOW CREATE TABLE [tablename] G command asking you the following questions:
    1. Is there at least one primary key?
    2. Is there an index on columns that you use in your WHERE, GROUP BY, ORDER BY, and HAVING clauses?
    3. If the answer to reference (b) is no, the next question would be: do I need a COMPOUND index that will cover the columns used in WHERE, GROUP BY, ORDER BY or do I just need an index that will be used in the WHERE clause with a single referenced column?
4. Modify your query if necessary for use with your indexes
5. Generally, Steps 1 to 3 are sufficient, but depending on the complexity of your query, you may need to repeat them until your query is optimized

Tip 3 – understand your material resources

To work, a database server needs a good balanced dose of four core resources:

- CPU or processors
- RAM or live memory
- Disks
- Networks

If one of them is weak or overloaded, the database server will be impacted in performance.

One of the optimization tasks is to understand the material resources, which can be divided into two categories—the best choice of hardware and the identification of problems.

When choosing hardware for MySQL, we must ensure that we have powerful components, even if we have virtualization. It is important that we have a balance between these components. I have noticed over time that companies choose servers with processors and hard disks that are fast, but that require a lot of memory work.

One of the most important components is memory, and then CPU. MySQL 8.0, for example, with its multi-threading, will use memory and CPU.

In terms of problem identification, one of the most important tasks is to check the performance and the use of the four resources mentioned here, keeping a close eye on whether they work well or not. In your search to find the source of the problem, your attention will be focused on RAM and CPU.

This knowledge can help solve problems quickly outside of query optimization.

Tip 4 – the configuration is not the only thing to take into consideration

Typically, database administrators or developers tend to spend too much time tweaking their MySQL server configurations. Since they optimize too many parameters at once, the result in general will impact performance. I saw a lot of optimized servers that were worse after these changes, lacking memory and working poorly when the workload became a little more intense.

Another mistake that most people make is to keep the default values provided by MySQL, which are conceived for general purposes only and are very outdated and probably not suited to your situation. It is best to have a good basic configuration and change other parameters only if necessary.

In most cases, you can achieve 95% of the maximum performance of the server by setting about ten parameters correctly. Of course, the more complex your situation is, the better it will be to call on an expert who will recommend the right configuration and manipulation. I have also seen companies who try to use server tuning tools that turn out to give instructions that make no sense for specific cases like yours. Some will offer you dangerous and imprecise tips, such as cache hit ratios and memory usage formulas. These tools will offer you inaccurate adjustments and inaccurate times.

Tip 5 – recommendations on the performance of the MySQL architecture

Over time, I noticed that most companies use a single MySQL server to process their reads and writes. When I mention reads, I include daily, monthly, and annual reports, plus other queries that will generate results.

In the evolution of a company, it is quite normal that your MySQL database will have more and more pressure because it will be limited in material resources, so the requests will not have been optimized. The people who work in the infrastructure and development department will be overwhelmed by the growth of the company.

When the company evolves quickly, there will be three things to consider to keep your MySQL performing:

- Optimize your requests to begin with if possible
- Decentralize your MySQL architecture with replication
- Increase hardware resources by optimizing the MySQL configuration

I invite you to review the previous sections so that you can optimize your queries as quickly as possible, without having too much of an impact on your website or application.

Regarding the decentralization of your MySQL architecture, the best strategy would be to create replicas (called slaves in the MySQL world) and execute your reports on replicas by specializing them in relation to the report objectives.

Finally, if you see that you have optimized your queries properly, that you have decentralized your reports to replications, and that your MySQL primary server is still slow in performance, you will need to consider increasing the hardware resources.

A technical case study

A company that specializes in smart cards had a MySQL performance problem, and here is its case study.

In short, the company has the following problems:

- 5,000% CPU usage
- 40-50% disk usage for MySQL temporary tables
- Queries pile up on top of each other
- There are some dead locks

The problems that this company faces are common to other companies that are in a phase of fast expansion, and unfortunately the people working for this company are overworked and do not know where to start to solve the problem.

The first thing we did was we changed some important parameters in the configuration, which were very basic to begin with.

We improved the performance by about 30%, so we now have this:

- 3,500% CPU usage
- Still 40-50% disk usage for MySQL temporary tables
- Queries pile up on top of each other
- There are some dead locks

As I mentioned in the previous sections, configuration will not work miracles in this case.

The second thing we did was that we increased the RAM from 16 GB to 32 GB.

We have improved the performance by 15%, so we now have this:

- 2,700% CPU usage
- Still 40-50% disk usage for MySQL temporary tables
- Queries pile up on top of each other
- There are some dead locks

We are improving the situation, but MySQL is still overloaded. It should be noted that MySQL coexists on the same server as the web server (Apache) on a Linux Red Hat server.

Have you noticed that we have done the steps in reverse to what we have shared so far, and that the performance is still not significant?

The next step, which should have been the first, is to take the top three slow queries and optimize them. We did the exercises and what do you think we noticed? There were missing indexes of which a very important one which concerns the most greedy query of material resources, the COMPOUND index.

As soon as we added two simple indexes to unique columns in some tables, and a COMPOUND in the main table, we lowered the workload on the MySQL server, as follows:

- 30% CPU usage
- 45% disk I/O usage
- Queries do not pile up any more
- Fast response time
- No more dead locks

The moral of this story is to take the time to review the slowest queries first, analyze them with the execution plan (EXPLAIN), and see if it is optimization that solves the performance issue. As a consequence of taking the time to review the slowest queries, we took some pressure off MySQL. We'll now have a better idea of whether we need to add more hardware resources and whether we need to adjust the MySQL configuration.

One last tip: avoid having MySQL in cohabitation with your application server, because they are very greedy with RAM and processors.

Summary

What is very important in the field of optimization is to understand how the MySQL optimizer thinks when using the tools that are available, such as EXPLAIN.

In addition to understanding and familiarizing yourself with the MySQL EXPLAIN tool, you must apply the steps we explained in organizing your columns in the order in which you use the WHERE, GROUP BY, and ORDER BY commands.

We also shared the new MySQL 8.0 features for EXPLAIN and other components.

In the next chapter, we will show you advanced performance techniques for the large queries that you can use in your projects.

4

Advanced Data Techniques for Large Queries

In the previous chapters, we learned how to use indexes, and execution plans, and looked at the best way to analyze a table structure. In this chapter, we will be learning how to analyze and optimize large MySQL queries, and look at some tips and techniques.

We all know that a full scan on a huge table will impact your database performance, and we will learn how to avoid it. We will also review the new MySQL 8.0 partition features and improvements.

This chapter will cover the following:

- The most important variables are full scan indicators
- Partitioning a table:
  - Overview of partitioning in MySQL 8.0
  - Partitioning types available
  - Horizontally partitioning your data
  - Managing partitions:
    - Option #1: RANGE partitioning
    - Option #2: LIST partitioning
    - Option #3: HASH partitioning
    - Option #4: KEY partitioning
- Using partitions:
  - Partition pruning
- Getting rid of unused and duplicate indexes:
  - Unused indexes
  - Duplicate indexes
  - Bonus: potentially missing indexes

- The most important query optimizations:
  - Optimizing a query with the WHERE clause
  - Optimizing a query with the GROUP BY clause
  - Optimizing a query with the ORDER BY clause
- Temporary tables
- Case study 1 – example of how to optimize a complex query
- Case study 2 – how to optimize sort indexes
- Tips and techniques
- Summary

The most important variables are full-scan indicators

The high season is coming for your business, and you wonder how you will manage the load on your MySQL database.

Stress tests can help you, but it's not a good idea to run them in a production environment. In this case, we can use two important variables that can come to your aid and are called Select_scan and Select_full_join. Of course, other MySQL counters could also give you an idea of the number of queries that will impact MySQL performance, which could lead to performance degradation as the load or pressure increases on your database.

The Select_scan variable in the MySQL SHOW GLOBAL STATUS report shows the number of full scans performed since the last MySQL restart (because every time you restart MySQL, all variables are reset to 0).

The Select_full_join variable is another important indicator that we will look at in the optimization domain to help us see whether MySQL is doing a lot of work with joins. Of course, a small number means that you can ignore join optimization and focus on other variables.

A full scan of a small table is fast, so that missing indexes can be ignored until the load increases or the amount of data increases as already mentioned in previous chapters.

 To avoid performance issues, I strongly suggest that any new features added to your application or website should be tested against the amount of data you have in production, so that the indexes can be created in production before deployment.

Let's look at an example together:

```
mysql> SHOW GLOBAL STATUS\G
```

The following is our extraction only the variables that we need:

```
*************************** 303. row ***************************
Variable_name: Select_full_join
        Value: 0
*************************** 304. row ***************************
Variable_name: Select_full_range_join
        Value: 0
*************************** 305. row ***************************
Variable_name: Select_range
        Value: 1
*************************** 306. row ***************************
Variable_name: Select_range_check
        Value: 0
*************************** 307. row ***************************
Variable_name: Select_scan
        Value: 56
```

In our previous example, the `Select_scan` tells us that it has had 56 full scans in tables next to the SELECT statement. So, this indicator will help you your optimization in MySQL is overloaded. As for the other variables, as you have noticed, we can ignore most of them because the indicators are either zero or very small.

Another trick is `Select_scan` but in a continuous way, by running the following:

```
mysqladmin -r -i 10 extended-status | grep "Select_scan"
```

This command will display the same results we got manually, but this time the display will be continuously live every 10 seconds.

The indicators that we have demonstrated in this section will be useful before starting to optimize your queries to give you an idea of where to start.

In the next section, we will see how to begin to partition a table in all its stages in the MySQL 8.0 release.

Partitioning a table

First, let's define what partitioning a table is. Partitioning a table in MySQL is how MySQL divides its actual data into separate tables, but it is always treated as a single table by the SQL layer.

An overview of partitioning in MySQL 8.0

When partitioning, it is critical to find a partition key. It is important to make sure that the searches we are going to do in a table go to the correct partition or group of partitions. This means that all commands, for example `SELECT`, `UPDATE`, `DELETE`, must include this column in the `WHERE` clause to ensure efficiency in the use of these partitions.

Generally, the best practice is to add the partition key to the primary key with auto incrementation enabled, that is, `PRIMARY KEY` (customer ID example, ID). If you do not have well-designed and small columns for this composite primary key, it could augment all your secondary indexes for no reason.

You can partition by range or hash. The former is excellent and popular because you have known groups of IDs in each table, and this helps when querying partition IDs.

Hash partitioning balances the load on the table and allows you to write simultaneously to the partitions.

In MySQL 8.0, you can allow partition on InnoDB tables.

Available partitioning type

MySQL partitioning is an option that improves performance, management, and maintenance, and also reduces the cost of storing large amounts of data.

Partitioning makes it possible to organize and subdivide tables, indexes, and smaller index tables. The impact of this partitioning will be that queries will access only a fraction of the data and will execute more quickly because there is less data to analyze.

In this section, we will cover the types of partitioning available in MySQL 8.0. There are two major forms of partitioning: horizontal and vertical, and an additional four types: range, list, hash, and key.

Horizontally partitioning your data

Horizontal partitioning is used to divide your table records into multiple partitions.

All columns defined in a table are in each defined partition. The whole partition can be organized individually or as a set. For example, a table that contains a transaction as a subscription to your website for the entire year will be partitioned horizontally into twelve separate partitions, and each partition will contain one month's data.

Managing partitions

In this section, we will cover options for managing partitions.

Some options that we will look into are the following:

- RANGE partitioning
- LIST partitioning
- HASH partitioning
- KEY partitioning

RANGE partitioning

Partitioning of this type has an impact on partition records based on the values of columns within a given scope.

The RANGE partition is organized from an interval between two values as long as these values do not overlap, and are set using the VALUES LESS THAN operator.

The basic syntax for creating a partition with RANGE is as follows:

```
PARTITION BY RANGE (Column ID) (
    PARTITION p0 VALUES LESS THAN (Num1),
    PARTITION p1 VALUES LESS THAN (Num2),
    PARTITION p2 VALUES LESS THAN (Num3),
    PARTITION p3 VALUES LESS THAN (Num4)
);
```

In our following examples, suppose you create a table to store employee records for a pizza chain of 30 restaurants, numbered from 1 to 30.

This table can be partitioned by intervals in several ways, depending on your needs—for instance, by using the resto_id column as follows:

```
CREATE TABLE employees (
    id INT NOT NULL,
    firstname VARCHAR(30),
    lastname VARCHAR(30),
    datehired DATE NOT NULL DEFAULT '1999-01-01',
    datefinished DATE NOT NULL DEFAULT '9999-12-31',
    job_id INT NOT NULL,
    resto_id INT NOT NULL
)
PARTITION BY RANGE (resto_id) (
    PARTITION p0 VALUES LESS THAN (6),
    PARTITION p1 VALUES LESS THAN (11),
    PARTITION p2 VALUES LESS THAN (16),
    PARTITION p3 VALUES LESS THAN (21),
    PARTITION p4 VALUES LESS THAN (31));
```

As you can see, in the preceding example, partitioning lines that correspond to workers of restaurants 1 to 5 and are stored in the p0 partition, while those for restaurants 6 to 10 are stored in partition p1, and so on, through to p4. Do observe that there is a logic to each partition, as well as a lowest-to-highest order.

It is easy to determine that a new record containing data, for example: (53, 'Sia', 'lalonde', '1999-06-24', NULL, 14), is inserted into the partition p2, but what happens when your restaurant adds its 31st store?

In our example, no rule has been defined for records with resto_ids beyond 30, and since MySQL does not know where to put it, an error occurs. Such an error can be prevented by using the VALUES LESS THAN option or a type that will handle all other records by mentioning them in the CREATE TABLE command, which provides all values greater than the highest value.

The MAXVALUE represents an INTEGER value always greater than the largest possible INTEGER value.

Now, any row whose value for the resto_id column is greater than or equal to 24 will be stored in the p5 partition.

You can still use the ALTER TABLE command to add new partitions for future restaurants, for example as follows:

```
CREATE TABLE employees (
    id INT NOT NULL,
    firstname VARCHAR(30),
    lastname VARCHAR(30),
    datehired DATE NOT NULL DEFAULT '1999-01-01',
    datefinished DATE NOT NULL DEFAULT '9999-12-31',
    job_id INT NOT NULL,
    resto_id INT NOT NULL
)
PARTITION BY RANGE (resto_id) (
    PARTITION p0 VALUES LESS THAN (6),
    PARTITION p1 VALUES LESS THAN (11),
    PARTITION p2 VALUES LESS THAN (16),
    PARTITION p3 VALUES LESS THAN (21),
    PARTITION p4 VALUES LESS THAN (31),
    PARTITION p5 VALUES LESS THAN MAXVALUE);
```

In MySQL 8.0, it is possible to partition a table with the RANGE type according to the value of a column such as TIMESTAMP, using the UNIX_TIMESTAMP () function, as follows:

```
CREATE TABLE inventory_monthly_report (
    inv_report_id INT NOT NULL,
    inv_report_status VARCHAR(20) NOT NULL,
    inv_report_status_updated TIMESTAMP NOT NULL DEFAULT
CURRENT_TIMESTAMP ON UPDATE CURRENT_TIMESTAMP
)
PARTITION BY RANGE ( UNIX_TIMESTAMP(inv_report_status_updated ))(
    PARTITION p0 VALUES LESS THAN ( UNIX_TIMESTAMP('2017-01-01
00:00:00') ),
    PARTITION p1 VALUES LESS THAN ( UNIX_TIMESTAMP('2017-05-01
00:00:00') ),
    PARTITION p2 VALUES LESS THAN ( UNIX_TIMESTAMP('2017-08-01
00:00:00') ),
    PARTITION p3 VALUES LESS THAN ( UNIX_TIMESTAMP('2017-10-01
00:00:00') ),
    PARTITION p4 VALUES LESS THAN ( UNIX_TIMESTAMP('2018-01-01
00:00:00') ),
    PARTITION p5 VALUES LESS THAN ( UNIX_TIMESTAMP('2018-02-01
00:00:00') ),
    PARTITION p9 VALUES LESS THAN (MAXVALUE)
);
```

Let's move on to the next option, which is LIST.

LIST partitioning

This option is very similar to RANGE partitioning, except partitions are selected on the basis of columns corresponding to a set of discrete values.

So, what is the main difference between RANGE and LIST? When dealing with list partitioning, rather than basing the partition definition and selection on a value from a group of interval values, it is based on a column value from one of the lists of value groups.

The PARTITION BY LIST (expression) option is used to achieve this, where the expression is a column value or an expression based on a column value. An integer value is returned; then, using VALUES IN (values_list), where value_list is a comma-separated list of values, each partition is defined.

The basic syntax for creating a partition with LIST is as follows:

```
PARTITION BY LIST(resto_id) (
    PARTITION p1 VALUES IN (v1,v2,v3..),
    PARTITION p2 VALUES IN (v1,v2,v3..),
    PARTITION p3 VALUES IN (v1,v2,v3..),
    PARTITION p4 VALUES IN (v1,v2,v3..)
```

Let's take the example that we used for RANGE:

```
CREATE TABLE employees (
    id INT NOT NULL,
    firstname VARCHAR(30),
    lastname VARCHAR(30),
    datehired DATE NOT NULL DEFAULT '1999-01-01',
    datefinished DATE NOT NULL DEFAULT '9999-12-31',
    job_id INT NOT NULL,
    resto_id INT NOT NULL
)
```

Suppose there are 17 restaurants divided between three franchises, as shown in the following table:

Region	Resto ID
R1	1, 2, 3, 5
R2	4, 7, 8, 9
R3	10, 22, 23, 13
R4	14, 12, 16, 17

The following shows how you can use the CREATE TABLE statement to have restaurants in the same region stored in the same partition in the table:

```
CREATE TABLE employees (
    id INT NOT NULL,
    firstname VARCHAR(30),
    lastname VARCHAR(30),
    datehired DATE NOT NULL DEFAULT '1999-01-01',
    datefinished DATE NOT NULL DEFAULT '9999-12-31',
    job_id INT NOT NULL,
    resto_id INT NOT NULL
)
PARTITION BY LIST(resto_id) (
    PARTITION pR1 VALUES IN (1, 2, 3, 5),
    PARTITION pR2 VALUES IN (4, 7, 8, 9),
    PARTITION pR3 VALUES IN (10, 22, 23, 13),
    PARTITION pR4 VALUES IN (14, 12, 16, 17)
);
```

This makes it easy to add or delete employee records from specific regions.

For example, suppose all restaurants in the pR3 region are sold to another company. In MySQL 8.0, all records pertaining to employees working in restaurants in that region can be deleted with the ALTER TABLE employees TRUNCATE PARTITION pR3 query, which can be executed much more efficiently than the equivalent DELETE: statement DELETE FROM employees WHERE resto_id IN (10, 22, 23, 13).

HASH partitioning

The concept behind this type of partitioning is to choose a partition according to the value returned by a user-defined expression that works on the column values of the records that are to be added to your table.

To use HASH partitioning on a table, a PARTITION BY HASH clause must be added to the CREATE TABLE command, where your expression is an expression that returns an integer.

The following command creates a table that uses the HASH on the resto_id column and is divided into four partitions:

```
CREATE TABLE employees (
    id INT NOT NULL,
    firstname VARCHAR(30),
    lastname VARCHAR(30),
    datehired DATE NOT NULL DEFAULT '1999-01-01',
    datefinished DATE NOT NULL DEFAULT '9999-12-31',
    job_id INT NOT NULL,
    resto_id INT NOT NULL
)
PARTITION BY HASH(resto_id)
PARTITIONS 4;
```

If you do not specify a PARTITIONS clause at the end of the command, the default number of partitions will be 1; otherwise, PARTITIONS without a subsequent number will result in a syntax error.

As you can see, the syntax side HASH command is quite simple.

KEY partitioning

KEY partitioning in quite like partitioning by HASH. This difference is that only one or more columns are provided for evaluation, and the HASH function is supplied by MySQL.

Using KEY is like CREATE TABLE ... PARTITION BY KEY and is similar to creating a table partitioned with HASH. The following are the main differences:

- KEY will be used rather than HASH
- Only lists of zero of more column names are accepted by KEY
- If the table has a primary key, some or all of it must be contained in columns used as a partitioning key
- If no column name is specified as the partitioning key, the primary key of the table is used as the default

Let's try the following example:

```
CREATE TABLE employees (
    id INT NOT NULL,
    firstname VARCHAR(30),
    lastname VARCHAR(30),
    datehired DATE NOT NULL DEFAULT '1999-01-01',
    datefinished DATE NOT NULL DEFAULT '9999-12-31',
    job_id INT NOT NULL,
    resto_id INT NOT NULL
)
PARTITION BY HASH(resto_id)
PARTITIONS 2;
```

If NOT NULL was not specified in the unique key column, this command will fail.

Using partitions

One of the most common reasons for using table partitioning is to separate data by date. Some RDBMSes support explicit date partitioning, which MySQL does not have in 8.0. However, it is very easy in MySQL to create partitioning based on DATE, TIME, or DATETIME columns.

Partition pruning

One of the best-known optimizations is **partition pruning**. The concept is relatively simple and is based on the principle: *"Do not analyze partitions where there can be no corresponding values"*. Let's assume you have a partitioned called employees, table defined by the following statement:

```
CREATE TABLE employees (
    id INT NOT NULL,
    firstname VARCHAR(30),
    lastname VARCHAR(30),
    datehired DATE NOT NULL DEFAULT '1999-01-01',
    datefinished DATE NOT NULL DEFAULT '9999-12-31',
    job_id INT NOT NULL,
    resto_id INT NOT NULL
)
PARTITION BY RANGE (resto_id) (
    PARTITION p0 VALUES LESS THAN (6),
    PARTITION p1 VALUES LESS THAN (11),
    PARTITION p2 VALUES LESS THAN (16),
    PARTITION p3 VALUES LESS THAN (21),
    PARTITION p4 VALUES LESS THAN (31),
    PARTITION p5 VALUES LESS THAN MAXVALUE);
```

Consider an example where you want to get the results of a SELECT command such as the following:

```
SELECT firstname, lastname, job_id, resto_id
FROM employees
WHERE job_id > 14 AND job_id < 17;
```

We need to look only in partitions p2 and p3 to find the corresponding lines.

In other words, partitioning with PRUNE can only be used with a WHERE condition to narrow the search with the following options:

```
partition_column = constante
```

```
partition_column IN (c1, c2, ..., cN)
```

When MySQL creates partition names itself (as in HASH and KEY partitions), the general model is p0, p1, ..., pN-1 (where N represents the number of partitions). Partition selection is supported for the majority of DELETE, UPDATE, INSERT, and JOIN-type operations.

So, you have learned in this case how partitioning in MySQL 8.0 works in different ways. You have also learned some tricks to increase your MySQL performance.

In the next section, we will explore how we can eliminate duplicate indexes and those we do not use.

Getting rid of unused and duplicate indexes

We all know now that indexes can mean the difference between a high-performance database and a slow query. Over time, indexes will need occasional maintenance to see whether you have indexes that are no longer useful or are duplicates.

MySQL 5.7.7, introduced a new schema called SYS. MySQL uses a set of objects found in this new schema to assist DBAs and developers in reading collected data from the performance schema. The objects that you'll find in the SYS schema can be used for typical cases of optimization and diagnostics. The objects in this scheme include the following:

- VIEWS that summarize schema performance data in a more convenient and easier form
- Stored procedures and stored functions that execute or query operations, such as configuring the performance schema and generating diagnostic reports, that will help you perform optimization

Unused indexes

In the SYS schema, it is quite easy to find useless indexes using the schema_unused_indexes view:

```
mysql> select * from sys.schema_unused_indexes;
+---------------+------------------+------------+
| object_schema | object_name      | index_name |
+---------------+------------------+------------+
| employees     | People           | LCode      |
| employees     | Language         | LCode      |
+---------------+------------------+------------+
2 rows in set (0.01 sec)
```

This view is based on the `performance_schema.table_io_waits_summary_by_index_usage` table, which requires the activation of the performance schema, and of the `events_waits_current` variable and other dependencies, such as `wait`, `io`, `table`, and `sql`. Please note that primary indexes (keys) will be ignored.

If you have not enabled variables, I suggest you run these queries:

```
update performance_schema.setup_consumers set enabled = 'yes' où name
= 'events_waits_current';

update performance_schema.setup_instruments set activé = 'yes' où name
= 'wait / io / table / sql / handler';
```

Before erasing an unhelpful index, I suggest you wait until you've observed this index and consider these important points:

- Do you have weekly tasks scheduled? Wait at least a week.
- Do you have monthly reports? Wait at least a month.
- Do you have any candidate applications that could use this index and have been stopped for a while? Research, and ask your colleagues.

Once you are sure the index is really useless, delete it.

Duplicate indexes

As already mentioned, MySQL now uses a new schema called **SYS**. To find duplicate indexes, you can use `view the schema_redundant_indexes` from the SYS schema.

`view schema_redundant_indexes` is easy to use once you have installed the SYS schema. The difference is that this view uses the `table information_schema.statistics`.

You can use the following statement to find duplicate indexes:

```
mysql> select * from schema_redundant_indexes\G
*************************** 1. row ***************************
            table_schema: employees
              table_name: Language
     redundant_index_name: LCode
  redundant_index_columns: LCode
redundant_index_non_unique: 1
       dominant_index_name: PRIMARY
    dominant_index_columns: LCode,Language
dominant_index_non_unique: 0
           subpart_exists: 0
            sql_drop_index: ALTER TABLE `employees`.`language` DROP
INDEX `LCode`
1 row in set (0.00 sec)
```

Again, if you're sure your indexes are duplicates, you can delete them.

Bonus – potentially missing indexes

The performance summary tables in the schema instructions have several interesting columns. In our case, two of them are important: NO_INDEX_USED (this will tell you which indexes have not been solicited) and NO_GOOD_INDEX_USED, if MySQL did not find a correct index for the query.

In the SYS schema, you will find a base view that points to the performance_schema.events_statements_summary_by_digest table and is very useful for this purpose via the statements_with_full_table_scans statement, which keeps all instructions that have performed a table analysis.

The following is an example:

```
mysql> select * from employees.language where lang = 'E';
56b204785fe7a5befa67b135c58gt655


746 rows in set (0.00 sec)

mysql> select * from statements_with_full_table_scans\G
*************************** 1. row ***************************
                query: select * from employees.language where lang = ?
                   db: employees
           exec_count: 1
        total_latency: 533.34 us
  no_index_used_count: 1
no_good_index_used_count: 0
   no_index_used_pct: 100
            rows_sent: 1743
        rows_examined: 946
       rows_sent_avg: 642
   rows_examined_avg: 946
           first_seen: 2018-02-05 20:44:33
            last_seen: 2018-02-05 20:44:33
               digest: ab627af0817666c891221bar39f24231
```

The preceding query does not use an index because there was no relevant index for MySQL to use. See the output of the execution plan, as follows:

```
mysql> explain select * from employees.language where lang = 'E'\G
*************************** 1. row ***************************
           id: 1
  select_type: SIMPLE
        table: language
         type: ALL
possible_keys: NULL
          key: NULL
      key_len: NULL
          ref: NULL
         rows: 946
        Extra: Using where
```

In our example, the language table does not contain an index on the lang column. The recommendation here, of course, would be to create an index on the lang column to make our query faster.

The most important query optimizations

Queries statements are used to retrieve data from a database. We can get the same results by writing different SQL queries for different needs. But using the optimal query is important when performance is considered for your business. So, you need to SQL query tuning based on this requirement. In this section, we will cover the most important queries importation with WHERE, GROUP BY, and ORDER BY.

Optimizing a query with the WHERE clause

Before we start looking at how to optimize a query with the WHERE clause, you need to know the optimization recipe that you have to apply to be efficient.

Here is an optimization recipe:

1. Identify the query that is slow
2. Run an EXPLAIN plan on this slow query
3. Identify what kind of slow problem your query is facing (for example, a full scan)
4. Run a SHOW CREATE TABLE on the tables that are part of the slow query
5. Identify whether the query uses the correct index and the order of the WHERE clause columns
6. Make the required corrections or modifications

Before turning to an example from the recipe, I'd like to explain how an index works in MySQL so that you can get an idea of the impact on your queries by using the WHERE clause.

First of all, MySQL uses by default what is called a **B-tree type index**. The operation that we can use with this index is an interval or equality. Here is an organization chart that demonstrates the logic of the B-tree type index:

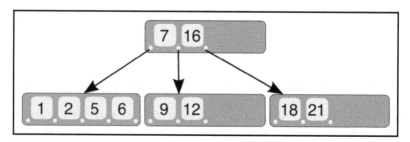

But what does *B-tree* mean?

A B-tree index contains internal nodes that can contain a number of child node variables in a predefined range. When data is inserted or deleted from a node, its number of child nodes changes automatically.

In the following example, we will use a WHERE clause with equality, and we will show you how MySQL uses the index to find the value.

Here is the query we want to execute:

```
select * from employees where employeeid = 12;
```

The following are the steps of the query in the context of the B-tree index:

1. Scan through the tree and go straight to the first branch
2. Stop searching, as the unique value has been found:

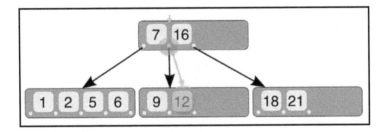

Assume now that we have many values!

```
select * from employees where employeeid in(6, 12, 18);
```

Perform the following steps:

1. Browse the tree
2. Find the values across the nodes
3. Stop when you know the unique values have been found:

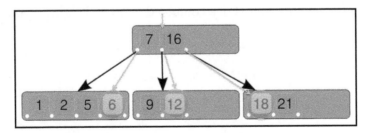

Now that you have a better understanding of a B-tree type index and also generally use default, let's use an example with the WHERE clause, and you will have a different viewpoint of our optimization recipe.

The following illustrates our optimization recipe:

```
SHOW CREATE TABLE employees (
    id INT NOT NULL,
    firstname VARCHAR(30),
    lastname VARCHAR(30),
    datehired DATE NOT NULL DEFAULT '1999-01-01',
    datefinished DATE NOT NULL DEFAULT '9999-12-31',
    job_id INT NOT NULL,
    resto_id INT NOT NULL
    Primary key (id),
    Key job_id (job_id) )as emp;


mysql> explain select * from employees where ID = 1;

+-------+-------+---------------+---------+---------+-------+------+------+
| table | type  | possible_keys | key     | key_len | ref   | rows | Extra|
+-------+-------+---------------+---------+---------+-------+------+------+
| emp   | const | PRIMARY       | PRIMARY | 4       | const | 1    |      |
+-------+-------+---------------+---------+---------+-------+------+------+

mysql> explain select * from employees where job_id = 33;

+-------+-------+---------------+---------+---------+-------+------+-------------+
| table | type  | possible_keys | key     | key_len | ref   | rows | Extra       |
+-------+-------+---------------+---------+---------+-------+------+-------------+
| emp   | ref   | job_id        | job_id  | 3       | const | 563  | Using where |
+-------+-------+---------------+---------+---------+-------+------+-------------+
```

In the context of our preceding example, MySQL will use the most performant index that's available for our query.

Now, let's look together in the context of a combined index as I showed you in the previous chapters.

The following is our table structure, but this time we have changed the `job_id`:

```
SHOW CREATE TABLE employees (
    id INT NOT NULL,
    firstname VARCHAR(30),
    lastname VARCHAR(30),
    datehired DATE NOT NULL DEFAULT '1999-01-01',
    datefinished DATE NOT NULL DEFAULT '9999-12-31',
    job_id char(3) NOT NULL,
    resto_id INT NOT NULL
    Primary key (id),
    Key job_id (job_id) )as emp;
```

For instance, let's start by adding a combined index:

```
mysql> alter table employees add key combine(job_id, resto_id, datehired),
drop key job_id;
```

```
mysql> explain select * from employees where job_id = 33 \G

********************** 1. row ******************

table: employees

type: ref

possible_keys: combine

key: combine

key_len: 3 <<--- Use the first column

ref: const

rows: 563

********************** ************************
```

`kry_len` is calculated as follows:
`Key_len = total size` (in bytes) of index parts used.
So, in our preceding example, we will have the following:
`combine(job_id, resto_id, datehired)`

Our first column is `job_id` with a CHAR (3) type; notice our `key_len` is 3.

And if I added another column, for example: `resto_id`, we would most likely have `key_len = 13` because the column is an integer.

Now let me show you a slightly more complex example:

```
explain select * from employees where resto_id = 33 and lastname like
'%Tremb%'\G

********************** 1. row ******************

table: employees

type: ALL

possible_keys: NULL

key: NULL

key_len: NULL

ref: NULL

rows: 1023

*****************************************************
```

As you will have noticed, because we do not use the first column of our index on the left precisely, we now have a full scan.

I hope that the explanations of the WHERE clause versus the indexes will allow you to optimize your queries in a more efficient way with our optimization recipe.

In our next section, we will see how we can optimize a GROUP BY clause.

Optimizing a query with a GROUP BY clause

One query that is generally considered slow is a query that is accompanied with the GROUP BY option. We will show you how to optimize and reduce the response time for this kind of query.

Group by example

Let's look at this simple example: a question about the number of employees in each restaurant:

```
SHOW CREATE TABLE employees (
    id INT NOT NULL,
    firstname VARCHAR(30),
    lastname VARCHAR(30),
    datehired DATE NOT NULL DEFAULT '1999-01-01',
    datefinished DATE NOT NULL DEFAULT '9999-12-31',
    job_id char(3) NOT NULL,
    resto_id INT NOT NULL
    Primary key (id));




mysql> Select max(id), job_id, resto_id from employees where job_id =
7 and resto_id > 10 group by datehired;



    ...
          type: ALL
 possible_keys: NULL
           key: NULL
       key_len: NULL
           ref: NULL
          rows: 5354
         Extra: Using where; Using temporary; Using filesort
```

When we look at the output, we can see that there is no indexes are used by MySQL (no proper ones are available). We do, however, notice Using temporary; Using filesort. MySQL will unfortunately have to create a temporary table to satisfy the GROUP BY clause and also the fact that it has to support four thousand records.

However, MySQL can use a **combined index** (as we learned from previous sections) to satisfy the GROUP BY clause and avoid creating a temporary table.

We create a combined index such as follows:

```
Alter table employees add index combine(job_id, resto_id, datehired);
```

The combined index works well if we have a `const` (where `DAYOFWEEK = N`). However, if there is a `range` scan in the `WHERE` clause, it will be be possible for MySQL to use an index and avoid a filesort. For example:

```
mysql> Select max(id), job_id, resto_id from employees where job_id =
7 and resto_id > 10 group by datehired, resto_id\G
...

         type: range
possible_keys: combine
          key: combine
      key_len: 2
          ref: NULL
         rows: 2443
        Extra: Using where; Using index; Using temporary; Using
filesort
```

In the next section, we will cover another option that impacts the ORDER BY performance, and we will explore the best approach we can take to optimize it. As you can see, we are back again to the combined index that has solved the performance problem of our GROUP BY clause.

Optimizing a query with the ORDER BY clause

In this section, we will learn how to optimize an ORDER BY which in general causes in many cases mentions in the EXPLAIN plan like filesort.

More often than not, the filesort operation in the example can be rather time-consuming (even if it does not require the creation of a file on disk). This is especially true if MySQL has a large number of records to sort.

Let's take our WHERE example and add an ORDER BY:

```
SHOW CREATE TABLE employees (
    id INT NOT NULL,
    firstname VARCHAR(30),
    lastname VARCHAR(30),
    datehired DATE NOT NULL DEFAULT '1999-01-01',
    datefinished DATE NOT NULL DEFAULT '9999-12-31',
    job_id char(3) NOT NULL,
    resto_id INT NOT NULL
    Primary key (id));



mysql> explain select * from employees where job_id = 100 order by
datehired\G
*********************** 1. row ***************************
          id: 1
 select_type: SIMPLE
       table: employees
        type: ALL
possible_keys: NULL
         key: NULL
     key_len: NULL
         ref: NULL
        rows: 345
       Extra: Using where; Using filesort
```

To optimize this query, we can use a combined index:

```
Alter combine(job_id, datehired);
```

We combine the job_id and datehired column because we use them in a WHERE and an ORDER BY, and we create our index with the columns in left order (WHERE clause) on the right (ORDER BY) in our query.

If we execute the same query again, we will see that the result is much better:

```
mysql> explain select * from employees where job_id = 100 order by
datehired\G
*************************** 1. row ***************************
id: 1
table: employees
type: ref
possible_keys: combine
key: combine
key_len: 3
ref: const
rows: 563
Extra: Using where;
```

Please note that the use of the LIMIT clause option is not a guarantee that your query will perform better, because the effect is to reduce the final result but not the number of records processed through sub-queries or join, for example.

In this section, you learned how to optimize an ORDER BY by optimizing it with a combined index.

In the next section, we'll see why temporary tables can slow MySQL's performance.

Temporary tables

In this section, we will talk about **temporary tables**. We will answer the question "*Why does MySQL need to create temporary tables with* GROUP BY, RANGE, ORDER BY, *and other expressions?*"

When using the EXPLAIN plan, you will notice that MySQL can create temporary tables when the query uses the following:

- GROUP BY
- RANGE
- ORDER BY
- Other expressions

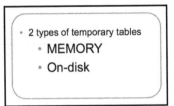

In the case of the creation of a temporary table, MySQL will always try to create a temporary table in memory at its the first attempt. Then, if MySQL cannot create this temporary table in memory, it will create it on disk, which is not desirable as far as performance is concerned.

MySQL uses the following variables in the configuration:

- `tmp_table_size`: This determines the maximum size for temporary tables in memory
- `max_heap_table_size`: This sets the maximum size for MEMORY tables

You can optimize MySQL to better manage the two previously mentioned variables by doing the following calculation:

1. Let's find the current value of `tmp_table_size`:

```
mysql> show global variables like 'tmp_table_size';
+------------------+-----------+
| Variable_name    | Value     |
+------------------+-----------+
| tmp_table_size   | 468435456 |
+------------------+-----------+
1 row in set (0.00 sec)
```

2. Let's find the percentage of tables created on disk:

```
mysql> show global status like 'created_tmp_disk_tables';
+-------------------------+--------+
| Variable_name           | Value  |
+-------------------------+--------+
| Created_tmp_disk_tables | 248551 |
+-------------------------+--------+
1 row in set (0.00 sec)

mysql> show global status like 'created_tmp_tables';
+--------------------+---------+
| Variable_name      | Value   |
+--------------------+---------+
| Created_tmp_tables | 1618533 |
+--------------------+---------+
1 row in set (0.00 sec)

La formule suivante vous aidera à déterminer le pourcentage:

Tmp_disk_tables=((created_tmp_disk_tables*100/(created_tmp_tables+crea
ted_tmp_disk_tables))
= ((248551*100/(1618533 + 248551))
= 13.31%
```

The ratio of the temporary tables of the created disk seems correct. With a ratio exceeding **25%**, increasing tmp_table_size is a possibility. If necessary, define it by the following command:

```
mysql> set global tmp_table_size=468435456;
Query OK, 0 rows affected (0.00 sec)
```

Keep in mind that tmp_table_size and max_heap_table_size should have the same value. The main goal in MySQL tmp_table_size optimization should be to avoid the creation of temporary tables to the greatest possible extent. Simply increasing tmp_table_size and max_heap_table_size allows slow queries and tables that are not properly indexed to respond quickly.

If the ratio of tables created on the disk is ever greater than 50%, start by checking your database indexing to ensure it is correctly set up for `JOIN` and `GROUP BY`. After adjusting the index, wait a few days and adjust the `tmp_table_size` if necessary.

In this section, you learned how to optimize or efficiently manage temporary tables in different situations and also we explained why temporary tables were created and needed.

In the next section, we will have a case study that will show you how to optimize a complex query.

Case study 1 – an example of how to optimize a complex query

We will explore in this case study a complex step-by-step query such as the following:

1. How to format a complex query
2. Run and analyze an execution plan
3. Optimize a complex query

When we have a query that runs in production and is complex, we need to format it so that we can have more clarity and can easily optimize it.

Here is our request (not formatted):

```
SELECT * FROM employees WHERE ((employees_id=59235 AND employees_flag1 = 1)  OR
(employees_division_employees_id=87459234 AND employees_flag2 = 1)) AND
(employees_id=59235 OR other_employees_id=59235) AND (employees_id <> 38465 AND
other_employees_id <> 38465)AND (employees_prop1 IS NOT NULL) AND
(employees_rangedate >= '2018-01-01') OR (employees_rangedate_min >
'2018-03-04' AND employees_rangedate_max < '2018-04-05') AND (NOT EXISTS (
SELECT 1 FROM employees_party WHERE fk_employeess_id = employeess.id AND
Important_id BETWEEN 1 and 4 AND diff_value BETWEEN 1 and 3));
```

Here is our formatted query:

```
SELECT * FROM employees
WHERE
      ((employees_id=59235 AND employees_flag1 = 1)
OR
      (employees_division_employees_id=87459234 AND employees_flag2 = 1))
AND
      (employees_id=59235 OR other_employees_id=59235)
AND
      (employees_id <> 38465 AND other_employees_id <> 38465)
AND
      (employees_prop1 IS NOT NULL)
AND
      (employees_rangedate >= '2018-01-01')
OR
      (employees_rangedate_min > '2018-03-04'
AND
      employees_rangedate_max < '2018-04-05')
AND
      (NOT EXISTS ( SELECT 1 FROM employees_party WHERE fk_employees_id =
employees.id AND
      Important_id BETWEEN 1 and 4 AND diff_value BETWEEN 1 and 3));
```

Here is the EXPLAIN plan:

```
*************************** 1. row ***************************
id: 1
select_type: PRIMARY
table: employees
type: ref
possible_keys: idx_employees_id,idx_division_employees_id,idx_prop1
key: idx_employees_id
key_len: 4
rows: 917943
Extra: Using where
*************************** 2. row ***************************
id: 2
select_type: DEPENDENT SUBQUERY
table: employees_party
type: subquery
possible_keys: PRIMARY,fk_employees_id
key: PRIMARY
key_len: 4
rows: 1
Extra: Using where
2 rows in set (0.01 sec)
```

Let's analyze the query together.

The first problem observed from the output of the execution plan is the following:

```
SUBQUERY DEPENDENT (NOT EXISTS ( SELECT 1 FROM employees_party WHERE
fk_employees_id = employees.id AND Important_id BETWEEN 1 and 4 AND
diff_value BETWEEN 1 and 3));
```

The solution is to rewrite the part of the SUBQUERY DEPENDENT as follows, in order to optimize our query:

```
SELECT E.* FROM EMPLOYEES E

LEFT JOIN employees_party ep

ON ep.fk_employees_id = employees.id

WHERE

ep.fk_employees_id IS NULL

AND

ep.important_id

BETWEEN 1 AND 4

AND

ep.diff_value BETWEEN 1 AND 3
```

Let's run the query again but this time with the following changes:

```
*************************** 1. row ***************************
id: 1
select_type: SIMPLE
table: ep
type: ref
possible_keys: idx_important_id_diff_value    (see note 1)
key: idx_important_id_diff_value
key_len: 4
ref: const
rows: 43844
Extra: Using where
*************************** 2. row ***************************
id: 1
select_type: SIMPLE
table: t
type: ref
possible_keys: PRIMARY
key: PRIMARY
key_len: 4
ref: ts.fk_employees_id
rows: 5
Extra: Using where
2 rows in set (0.01 sec)
```

 We have created a **combined index** (as we discussed in our previous sections) on the important_id and diff_value columns.

In conclusion, our optimization required four actions:

1. Formatting the query
2. Executing an EXPLAIN plan and analysis
3. Rewriting the query
4. Creating a combined index

In our next section, which is our second case study, we will see how to optimize a query with ranking indexes.

Case study 2 – how to optimize sort indexes

Did you know that performance problems are often due in particular to MySQL's ORDER BY and LIMIT?

Here's what you need to know about optimizing MySQL's ORDER BY and LIMIT to avoid problems.

MySQL's ORDER BY and LIMIT constitute the most common use of ORDER BY in web and enterprise applications, with large datasets that are sorted.

For example, on many websites, you will sort top tags, users who have recently subscribed, and so on, which requires using ORDER BY and LIMIT in the background on the server.

This type of ORDER BY generally does something like the following:

```
SELECT ... .. WHERE [conditions] ORDER BY [sort] LIMIT N1, M1
```

As I often recommend, you need to make sure that your queries use indexes. It is important to have an ORDER BY with LIMIT executed, without having to use a full scan and just as a full results filesort, is not recommended.

It is therefore important to use good indexes, which will help your selection and will execute your queries much faster.

For instance, if we had SELECT * FROM transactions ORDER BY date_created DESC LIMIT 10;, the best option if we want quick results would be to use an index on the date_created column.

Here is another example. What if we have SELECT * FROM where job_id = 5 ORDER BY date_created DESC LIMIT 10;?

In this case, indexing by date_created could possibly work. However, it might not be the most efficient index. If the category is rare, a large part of the table has to be scanned to find 10 records. So, a combined index on the columns (job_id, date_created) would be a better idea and more effective.

If you have a join with ORDER BY and LIMIT, you should try to have the columns that are mainly part of the primary table of this join. For example: if ORDER BY passes through a column in the table, that is not the first in the join order, and the index cannot be used.

Sometimes, this means not respecting normalization and duplicating the columns you will use in ORDER BY from another table.

Here is an example of when an ORDER BY is used in a second table that requires filesort, as well as the EXPLAIN plan:

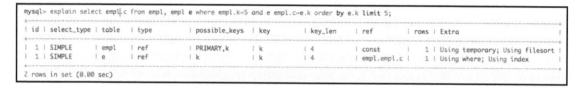

If our first table has a const or system type, this one is actually removed from the execution of the join (and replaced by constants), and ORDER BY can be optimized even if it is done by the second table:

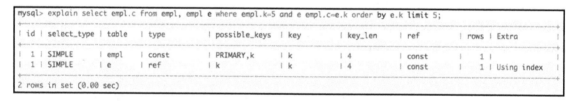

The difference between the two results is c, which is the primary key, while k is simply the column containing the indexes.

In our case study, we learned how to transform a filesort that affects the performance of our query by the use of one column that is the primary key and another that is in a ranking index.

In our next section, I will share some tips and techniques in the context of the concepts we learned about in this chapter.

Tips and techniques

The tips and techniques which I am sharing with you come from two decades of improving and optimizing MySQL performance in thousands of situations. These tips and techniques can help you better understand how to make your MySQL servers more efficient.

Partitions

Here are some tips:

- It is not recommended to use PARTITIONS until you know how it will help you
- Do not use PARTITIONS unless you have more than one million records
- Do not use more than 50 PARTITIONS on a table; otherwise, the performance will be impacted
- The PARTITION RANGE mode is the only method that is useful and perfect for your needs in general; it is also easy to manage
- SUB-PARTITIONS are not necessarily useful, except in specific cases
- The partition key should not be the first column of an index; otherwise, maintenance affects performance

Techniques:

It is wrong to claim that partitioning will solve performance problems. Partitioning divides a table into several small tables. However, the size of the table is rarely a performance problem. In general, the input and output time and the indexes are the problems.

By the way, version 8.0 of the data dictionary eliminates the usage of 50 partitions.

Use cases for partitioning are as follows:

- **Use case 1**: DROP PARTITION is much faster than DELETE when dealing with many records
- **Use case 2**: If the index of a table is too large to be cached, then it is better to use an index of a partition, because partitioning can keep the entire index in RAM, thus avoiding a lot of disk I/O

Optimization

Here are some tips:

- The use of `Using temporary` and filesort are often unavoidable in joins, `GROUP BY`, and `ORDER BY`. But as demonstrated in our previous sections, it is possible to make them disappear with certain conditions.
- Avoid using forced use of indexes (`USE/FORCE/IGNORE/STRAIGHT_JOIN`), as this shows that index strategies are not well planned or that you have too many indexes on the same columns.
- A CPU problem is usually a slow query problem that needs to be revisited.
- If you have to have more than 20% of records, in this case, a `FULL SCAN` table will be faster than using an `INDEX`.
- `SHOW CREATE TABLE` is more descriptive than `DESCRIBE` and is part of our optimization recipe, which has been explained in previous sections.

Techniques

If most records can be removed using an `INDEX`, the index will be the most effective way. If you cannot eliminate many of these records, the performance results between the index and the data in your table might be more expensive than using an index, and the solution would simply be to use a `FULL SCAN`. A good practice of the 20% use of the data seems to be the best value whether we use an index or not.

A typical use case: time series data

As already mentioned, partitions are commonly used when dealing with a dataset containing many records. These may include phone call records, invoices, subscriptions, and so on.

In general, we all want our reports to present new data, and unfortunately there will be old data to delete once they are out of date and not at all useful.

To illustrate how to deal with this problem, I will present the scenario of a company that uses two million records for a gas station network. We will be performing some common operations on the `metrics` table as it-is, and partitioning a copy of the table by `RANGE` to identify any potential differences.

The following example will have millions of records and two tables:

```
CREATE TABLE `metrics` (
  `metric_timestamp` datetime NOT NULL,
  `station_name` varchar(255) DEFAULT NULL,
  `gas1_mtsperhour` int(11) NOT NULL,
  `gas2_mtsperhour` int(11) NOT NULL,
  `gas_qty` int(3) NOT NULL,
  `rain_mm` decimal(5,2),
  `temperature` int(5),
  `humidity` int(5),
  `barometric_pressure` decimal(10,2) NOT NULL,
  `barometric_temperature` decimal(10,0) NOT NULL,
  `lux` decimal(7,2),
  `is_plugged` tinyint(1),
  `battery_level` int(3),
  KEY `metric_timestamp` (`metric_timestamp`)
) ENGINE=InnoDB DEFAULT CHARSET=latin1;
```

```
CREATE TABLE `partitioned_metrics` (
  `metric_timestamp` datetime NOT NULL,
  `station_name` varchar(255) DEFAULT NULL,
  `gas1_mtsperhour` int(11) NOT NULL,
  `gas2_mtsperhour` int(11) NOT NULL,
  `gas_qty` int(3) NOT NULL,
  `rain_mm` decimal(5,2),
  `temperature` int(5),
  `humidity` int(5),
  `barometric_pressure` decimal(10,2) NOT NULL,
  `barometric_temperature` decimal(10,0) NOT NULL,
  `lux` decimal(7,2),
  `is_plugged` tinyint(1),
  `battery_level` int(3),
  KEY `metric_timestamp` (`metric_timestamp`)
) ENGINE=InnoDB DEFAULT CHARSET=latin1;
```

We will alter the `partitioned_metrics` table so it has partitions, as follows:

```
ALTER TABLE `test`.`partitioned_metrics`
 PARTITION BY RANGE (YEAR(metric_timestamp)) (
    PARTITION to_metric_logs VALUES LESS THAN (2017),
    PARTITION to_metric_prev_year_logs VALUES LESS THAN (2018),
    PARTITION to_metric_current_logs VALUES LESS THAN (MAXVALUE)
 ) ;
```

Now let's assess the performance of our queries:

To do so, we will take both tables, run a series of common queries on them, and see how they line up. (The SQL-NO_CACHE keyword will be used to see the impact of the query without MySQL caching):

Here is the first execution:

```
SELECT SQL_NO_CACHE

COUNT(*)

FROM

test.metrics

WHERE

metric_timestamp >= '2018-01-01'

AND DAYOFWEEK(metric_timestamp) = 1;
```

Here is the second execution:

```
SELECT SQL_NO_CACHE

COUNT(*)

FROM

test.partitioned_metrics

WHERE

metric_timestamp >= '2018-01-01'

AND DAYOFWEEK(metric_timestamp) = 1;
```

Here is an observation:

It takes about half a second to return 122,157 records for both queries (partitioned and unpartitioned).

Note that both tables have an index on the `metric_timestamp` column; I expected this index to have a positive impact on the effectiveness of executed queries.

If I remove the indexes from both tables, I can see the impact of partitioning on `SELECT`:

```
ALTER TABLE `test`.`metrics`
DROP INDEX `metric_timestamp` ;
ALTER TABLE `test`.`partitioned_metrics`
DROP INDEX `metric_timestamp` ;
```

So, in conclusion, the execution of `SELECT` on the unpartitioned table takes about twice the time, compared to the same query on the partitioned table.

Example of a mass DELETE

Let's try a mass delete on older data and see how much time it requires. But, first, we will add an index to the `metric_timestamp` column:

```
ALTER TABLE `test`.`metrics`
ADD INDEX `index99` (`metric_timestamp`);
ALTER TABLE `test`.`partitioned_metrics`
ADD INDEX `index99` (`metric_timestamp`);
```

We like our tables with indexed data. Our next step is to perform a mass delete on the unpartitioned table:

```
DELETE
FROM test.metrics
WHERE metric_timestamp < '2017-01-01';
```

Roughly 0.8 seconds are required to delete 77,354 records. What happens if I execute a `DROP` partition command to get the same result in the partitioned table?

```
ALTER TABLE test.partitioned_metrics
DROP PARTITION to_metric_logs
```

It takes less than 0.05 seconds. Let's try to delete all data prior to 2018:

```
DELETE
FROM test.metrics
WHERE metric_timestamp < '2018-01-01';
```

Then, delete the equivalent data from the partitioned table:

```
ALTER TABLE test.partitioned_metrics DROP PARTITION
to_metric_prev_year_logs ;
```

Let's look at the results of each run:

Command	Output	Time
DELETE FROM test.metrics WHERE metric_timestamp < '2018-01-01'	866654 row(s) affected	54.13 sec
ALTER TABLE test.partitioned_metrics DROP PARTITION to_metric_prev_year_logs	0 row(s) affected Records: 0 Duplicates: 0 Warnings: 0	0.051 sec

As you can see, data deletion is much quicker when you have partitions when compared to the DELETE command.

In my experience, partitioning should be the last step in the optimization process. I would only do it after exhausting other alternatives, such as slow query optimization.

In general, partitioning works best when you process millions of records. In this case, I found that PARTITION RANGE was the most useful and the easiest to manage as well. The best use for RANGE is removing older data.

Before configuring partitions, remember that they impose several limitations—the way unique and primary keys are generated, and the fact that foreign keys are not allowed (except in MySQL 8.0).

Summary

In this chapter, I tried to demonstrate that partitioning is a solution that can be used when you have exhausted all other alternatives, such as optimizing your queries, configuration, and so on. That is applicable when you have several millions of records.

We have covered how to clean your indexes, and of course how to keep the necessary number of indexes needed for your application.

We've looked at how to optimize complex queries, using the proposed optimization recipe that we've discussed throughout.

We also looked at what was given to temporary tables, why these tables appear, and how they can be avoided.

Finally, we saw why we had filesort with `JOINS`, `GROUP BY`, and `ORDER BY`, and how we can improve this situation.

In the next chapter, we will cover advanced techniques for MySQL server settings and MySQL's data dictionary, in MySQL 8.0. We will also look at the different uses of the data dictionary, and much more.

5
MySQL Data Dictionary in MySQL 8.0

In previous chapters, you learned how to use indexes and optimize complex queries. Optimization will not be complete if we do not examine the MySQL server settings and the data dictionary. This chapter explains how to get optimal MySQL server 8.0 settings, and you will learn how to work with the MySQL data dictionary.

We will cover the following topics in this chapter:

- The MySQL data dictionary structure in MySQL 8.0
- The dictionary object cache
- Transactional storage of the data dictionary
- Different uses of the data dictionary
- Removal of file-based metadata storage
- Serialized Dictionary Information (SDI)
- Limitations of the data dictionary

MySQL data dictionary structure in MySQL 8.0

We have already discussed in Chapter 2, *MySQL 8's New Features*, the new features of the data dictionary. Now, we'll explore its structure and limitations.

Let's summarize the problems of the MySQL data dictionary before MySQL 8.0:

- The INFORMATION_SCHEMA is slow when questioned
- Because of the storage of non-transactional metadata, there are inconsistencies
- There are inconsistencies between metadata, InnoDB, and MySQL metadata

The big challenges in MySQL replication are these:

- It's almost impossible to extend
- The API is not uniform

The following diagram shows the structure of the data dictionary before MySQL 8.0:

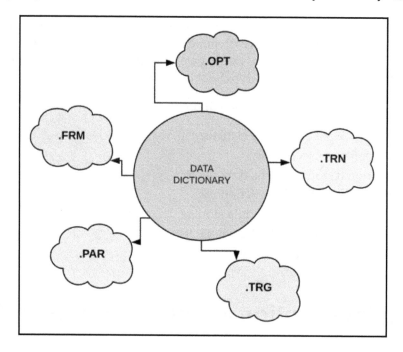

Let's look at the new concept of the transactional data dictionary in MySQL 8.0:

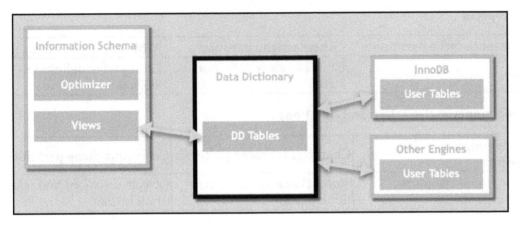

The benefits of the new MySQL 8.0 data dictionary structure include the following:

- It is based on standard SQL
- It has been improved so that updates are automated
- It is more flexible to new requirements

In this section, you have learned about the differences between the old and the new structures of the data dictionary and the benefits of the new approach for MySQL 8.0.

Dictionary object cache

As stated in the official documentation of MySQL, the **dictionary object cache** is a global cache shared by MySQL 8.0 that stores previously accessed data dictionary objects in memory to enable object reuse and minimize disk I/O.

It should be mentioned that the concept is similar to other caching mechanisms used by MySQL. The cache of dictionary objects uses a control strategy based on LRU to handle the least recently used memory objects.

It also includes cache partitions that store different types of objects. Some of the limits in the cache partition size are configurable, while others are integrated.

The following is the list of the tables from `information_schema`:

Tablespaces

Tablespace cache partition	Schema cache partition	table cache partition
Stores table definition of objects	Stores schema definition items	Stores table definition objects

Stored program, characters, and collations

Stored program cache partition	Character set cache partition	Collations cache partition
Stores stored program definition objects	Stores character set objects (limit of 256)	Objects collations and object (limit of 256)

I will not list all the tables from `INFORMATION_SCHEMA`, as it would take too long and you can always find them on the MySQL official website (`https://dev.mysql.com/doc/refman/8.0/en/`).

As you now know, we can execute read requests directly on tables and views of the `INFORMATION_SCHEMA`, which is now much more efficient because they get information from the tables of the data dictionary rather than by other slower means.

Transactional storage of the data dictionary

In the past, the MySQL data dictionary was stored in the file metadata and non-transactional tables, as already indicated in previous sections, but in MySQL 8.0 we now have a transactional data dictionary to store the information on the database objects.

The main difference between the tables MySQL system and data dictionary tables is that the system tables contain auxiliary data, such as time zone and help information, while the data dictionary tables contain the data required to perform SQL queries.

That said, the **transactional storage of the data dictionary** stores dictionary data in tables such as `InnoDB`, and not `MyISAM` as before. These tables of data dictionaries are located in the `mysql` schema with the other system tables.

The dictionary data is now protected by the same validation, restoration, and recovery after an incident that protects user data stored in `InnoDB` tables. This makes the management of objects based on the MySQL data dictionary more interesting and safer.

Applications of the data dictionary

In this section, we will explore and summarize the different uses of the data dictionary.

Previously, to prevent the creation and destruction of tables or databases:

- It was necessary to enable the `innodb_read_only` variable for protection, which impacted only the InnoDB engine. Now, with MySQL version 8.0, all storage engines are affected.
- One of the functionalities in MySQL 8.0 has been improved, the data dictionary tables are protected and not visible, and the `INFORMATION_SCHEMA` is more stable.
- The tables of `INFORMATION_SCHEMA` are now connected directly to the data dictionary. This allows the optimizer to use indexes continuously live, resulting in better performance.
- Before MySQL 8.0, we could use `mysqldump` and do a MySQL export scheme. This will now not be possible and the export action will be only on schemas and tables, and not systems with the option of `--all-databases`.
- Another option that has been changed is `--routines`, which required the `SELECT` privilege for the `proc` table. In MySQL 8.0, this table is no longer used; `--routines` requires global `SELECT` privilege replacement.
- Since MySQL 8.0, these headers are capitalized; the previous query results were generated with a header from `TABLE_NAME`. If necessary, a column alias can be used to obtain a different letter, for example:

```
SELECT TABLE_NAME AS 'table_name'
FROM INFORMATION_SCHEMA.TABLES;
```

Removal of file-based storage metadata

In previous versions of MySQL, the dictionary data was partially stored in the metadata file type. Frequently encountered problems of storage related to these files, based on the type metadata, included scans of very expensive files. Thus, vulnerability to bugs related to the filesystem, complex code to handle failures for data replication and disaster recovery, and a lack of scalability made it difficult to add metadata to new features and relational objects.

Remember, in our previous section on the MySQL data dictionary structure in MySQL 8.0, we saw a graph of the data dictionary before MySQL 8.0, where the data dictionary was surrounded by auxiliary files. Now, with MySQL 8.0, the following list of files will be removed and replaced with tables:

- `.frm`
- `.par`
- `.trn`
- `.trg`
- `.isl`
- `db.opt`

It is better to have metadata managed from tables than files, resulting in better and more stable performance.

Serialized Dictionary Information (SDI)

In this chapter, we'll look at the SDI and discuss its advantages and changes.

Many DBAs and developers prefer to copy table data and `.frm` files from the data dictionary and schedule some batch jobs that automatically recover these tables. This ability has also been used for disaster recovery, where people who are really familiar with `.frm` are able to rebuild the metadata in the `.frm` file when they want to.

In MySQL 8.0, the information is provided in the dictionary serialized objects for the dictionary. For `InnoDB` tablespaces, this information is added to the tablespace, so that the metadata and data are combined, again with performance in mind. For storage engines that do not support this feature, a `.sdi` file is written.

This is illustrated in the following diagram:

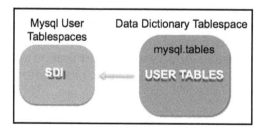

For MySQL tablespaces, InnoDB has an API type of tool to read the SDI information. The SDI information is in JSON format. Thus, the same ability to change the SDI that users have with .frm files for disaster recovery is also provided.

Limitations of the data dictionary

In this section, we will look at the limitations of the data dictionary.

As we saw in the previous sections, the data dictionary of previous versions of MySQL 8.0 had many performance problems because it was all managed from files instead of tables, as Oracle has built-in MySQL 8.0.

One limitation is the need to create manual database directories in the data directory (for example, with mkdir Linux). This is not supported by MySQL. Manually created database directories are not recognized by the MySQL server.

Another limitation is that DDL type operations take longer because of the need to write to storage, the cancellation of logs, and restoring logs instead of .frm.

Tips and techniques

As already mentioned, in MySQL 8.0, Oracle introduced a new concept called the **transactional data dictionary,** which changed the classic view files by passing the InnoDB table types.

MySQL 8.0 is very promising regarding performance, with the new concept of the transactional data dictionary.

Here is an example:

```
mysql> select count(*), engine from information_schema.tables where table_schema =
'mysql' group by engine;
+-----------+---------+
| count(*) | ENGINE|
+-----------+---------+
|        2  | CSV    |
|       30  | InnoDB |
+-----------+---------+
2 rows in set (0.00 sec)
```

Summary

The new transactional data dictionary in MySQL 8.0 is an incredible addition that opens the door to many future improvements in how MySQL handles DDLs, for example.

In this chapter, you have learned about the new structure of the data dictionary, with its improvements and its different uses and limitations. We must not forget that a new feature has been incorporated, called SDI, allowing for more openings toward new flexible and powerful options.

In the next chapter, we will cover all the following points by getting started with the most significant variables. We will then look at MySQL server optimization. We will discuss two important variables and introduce two case studies.

6

MySQL Server Settings

So far, in our previous chapters, you have learned how to use indexes and optimize complex queries. The optimization will not be complete if we do not examine the MySQL Server settings.

This chapter explains how to get optimal MySQL Server 8.0 settings.

Here are the topics covered in this chapter:

- Getting started with the most important variables
- MySQL server optimization
- The InnoDB Buffer Pool
- The thread cache
- Case study 1 – when MySQL uses more than 100% of a CPU
- Case study 2 – when MySQL swaps on disk

Let's get started!

Getting started with the most significant variables

During a performance investigation, it is of course necessary to try to optimize queries in the first place because often, as demonstrated, it is these that most affect the performance of MySQL, no matter which version we use on a server.

When we maximize our queries and our data model is well organized, we can look at the question of MySQL configuration and try to improve the most important variables that could help MySQL performance.

Keep in mind that you have to change one thing at a time, especially if you already have a solid configuration. If this is a new configuration, or if you have worked with the default configuration until now, do not implement all the changes at once. Take the time to monitor the server after each change.

So, let's explore the most popular variables that affect the overall performance:

- `innodb_buffer_pool_size`: The size in bytes of the memory buffer that InnoDB uses to cache data and indexes of its tables is the most important of all variables. This variable should never exceed 80% of your server's RAM, but the recommendation is to start with 60% and gradually increase by 5%.

- `innoDB_flush_method`: This parameter specifies how InnoDB opens and dumps log files and data files. This is another variable that is used most of the time for performance. Configuring `innodb_flush_method` with `O_DIRECT`, will prevent double buffering and will reduce disk swaps and improve performance.

- `tmp_table_size`: Maximum size of internal temporary tables in memory. The current limit is based on the minimum set for `tmp_table_size` and `max_heap_table_size`, which must be adjusted together.

- `max_heap_table_size`: This variable defines the maximum size allowed for memory tables created by you and needs to be adjusted with `tmp_table_size`.

- `query_cache_size`: The amount of memory allocated for caching the results of the query. The larger the size the more result sets can be cached. Thus, the result of an SQL query whose result set has already been cached will be served from memory and the response time will be very fast. For a medium-sized database, you must set it between 16 MB and 32 MB.

- `query_cache_type`: This variable defines the type of query cache. The recommended cache type is set to `1`. If you set it to `0`, it means the cache will be disabled. So, for an active query cache, `query_cache_type` should be `1` and `query_cache_size` should be a reasonable size.

- `query_cache_limit`: This variable defines the size of the cache. Do not cache results that are too big. You can set it with 1 MB or 2 MB, which will be perfect for the normal use of your DB.

- `table_open_cache`: This is the number of open tables for all threads in memory. Increasing this value will increase the number of file descriptors required by the `mysqld` service. You can check whether you need to increase the table cache by taking a look at the `Opened_tables` variable.

If the value of `Opened_tables` is large and you do not use `FLUSH TABLES` often (which simply forces all tables to be closed and reopened), then you should increase the value of the `table_open_cache` variable (but be aware of the limits of your system).

The MySQL system type variables mentioned here are mainly used to help of MySQL performance. Always check those variables that are the most important of MySQL that are correctly configured. What value these variables must have depends on many factors, and this is on a case by case basis.

In the next section, we will see how we can optimize the MySQL server for better performance.

MySQL server optimization

Of course, it's important to keep in mind that there are different settings that work better for some servers with light and predictable loads, compared to servers running at almost full capacity all the time or those experiencing high activity variations.

In the following sections, we will discuss the the main optimization steps you can perform.

Control the types of data change operations

When operations such as `INSERT`, `UPDATE`, and `DELETE` are run on a table, the values of the indexed columns are often in unsorted order, and this will require input/output; updating the secondary indexes included will adversely affect performance.

However, InnoDB caches (in memory) the changes made to secondary index entries when the corresponding page is not in the memory pool, thus avoiding expensive input/output operations by not immediately reading the page from the disk. The stored changes are in this case merged when the page is loaded into this memory pool and the updated page is then flushed to disk.

Enabling the adaptive hash indexing function

You can enable and disable the adaptive hash indexing function by using the `innodb_adaptive_hash_index` option. This option allows InnoDB to work more like a database in memory on systems with the appropriate workload and memory for the memory pool, without sacrificing any transactional functionality, integrity, or reliability.

This feature is enabled by the `innodb_adaptive_hash_index` option, or disabled in the MySQL `my.cnf` configuration file.

Set a limit on the number of concurrent threads

Setting a limit on the number of simultaneous threads InnoDB processes is a great opportunity to use hardware or virtual resources when the server is in a bottleneck or overloaded.

To limit the number of concurrent threads, we use the `innodb_thread_concurrency` configuration parameter.

Controlling the amount of InnoDB preloading

When the system has unused input/output capacity, early reading can improve the performance of your queries. On the other hand, too much early reading can lead to periodic drops in performance on a heavily loaded system.

Increasing the number of background threads

Increase the number of background threads for read or write operations, if you have a high-end input/output subsystem that is not fully used by default values.

Did you know that you can configure the number of background threads that maintain read/ write I/O on data pages by using the configuration parameters named `innodb_read_io_threads` and `innodb_write_io_threads`?

They are very effective on almost all platforms. You can set or change the values for these parameters in the MySQL options file (`my.cnf` or `my.ini`); you can't change the values dynamically, unfortunately.

The main goal of these configuration options is to make MySQL more scalable on busy systems. Each background thread can handle up to 256 pending I/O requests, so these options are mostly to be considered when you have an SSD.

Controlling InnoDB input/output performance in the background

You can control InnoDB I/O in the background, especially when you observe periodic performance declines; in this case, you can reduce this setting to improve performance.

Taking advantage of multicore processors

A lot of InnoDB mutexes and rw-locks are reserved for a short time. On a server with multiple cores, you will have more advantages if a thread is constantly checking whether it can acquire a mutex or rw-lock for a while before going to sleep.

You can control the maximum delay in this case between testing a mutex and an rw-lock by using the `innodb_spin_wait_delay` parameter.

For example, on a server where all processors share a fast cache, you can reduce the delay or disable the busy loop completely if you change the `innodb_spin_wait_delay` variable to 0, which will help to improve the performance of your database.

Preventing punctual operations

Preventing one-off operations such as table scans from interfering with frequently used data stored in the InnoDB cache can substantially improve the performance of your DB.

InnoDB uses an internal way to minimize the amount of data that will be used in the memory pool. The purpose of this InnoDB technique is to ensure that the most accessed pages stay in this memory pool, even if previous reads and full table scans bring new data blocks that may or may not be accessed later on.

Configuring the number and size of instances

For systems with memory pools that have a lot of RAM, separating the memory pool into divided independent instances can improve the load by reducing contention when different threads read and write in cached pages.

These divided memory pool instances are configured with the `innodb_buffer_pool_instances` variable and you can also adjust the `innodb_buffer_pool_size` value if needed.

Prior to MySQL 8.0, each memory pool was protected by its own mutex memory pool. In MySQL 8.0 and later, the memory pool mutex has been replaced by several lists and hash mutexes to reduce conflicts.

The InnoDB buffer pool

The first variable that we intuitively use in our optimization is `innodb_buffer_pool_size`. You may think that, by increasing the value of this variable, we will have higher performance. I am going to disappoint you by telling you that it is not by increasing its value that will get you higher performance.

In fact, the acceptable maximum that you can allocate is 80% of the size of your RAM; you must keep a minimum of 20% for the operating system. From a good-practice point of view, when we start with MySQL, it is recommended to use 60% and increase by 5% over time if we need to. But before changing the value of the `innodb_buffer_pool_size` variable, you need to know who the users of your RAM memory are. In a typical MySQL server, it is understood that there is a list of applications or services that use your service's RAM; together, we will look at this list; it is not necessarily complete, but I think that it describes the large areas that a MySQL server might consume.

The following is a short list of these areas:

- **Operating system**: Kernel, running threads, system cache, and so on
- **MySQL**: Query cache, InnoDB buffer size, connections, join buffer, sort buffer, and so on
- **MySQL replication**: Binary log cache, replication connections, relay logs, and so on
- **All other services hosted on the same server**: web server, mail server, cache server, and so on

Again, the `Innodb_buffer_pool_size` variable is the most important when it comes to helping the performance of MySQL and InnoDB. But, it must be tuned in a way that takes into account the needs of other server services, to prevent the swap from coming into play and degrading your performance quickly; you may think that you are increasing the performance of your MySQL, but in fact you impair the entire server because other services use the disk swap.

However, as a general rule, I would say that the 70% rule is a good value, a rule that will help get fast performance result to help MySQL work better. Let's say that we don't know what is causing the load on the server, but we know that this server is dedicated to MySQL; the question is, How might our 70% rule help?

The following is an example:

Total server RAM	Buffer pool with 70% rule	Remaining RAM
4G	2.8G	1.2G
16G	11.2G	4.8G
64G	44.8G	19.2G

If your MySQL servers have under 64 GB of RAM, the 70% rule seems pretty reasonable. However, when we have servers with more hardware resources, it starts to seem less obvious. To make the rule true, the memory usage increases in proportion to the required size of the buffer pool, but this is not always the case.

Suppose our server has 1 TB of RAM and probably does not need 205 GB to handle things such as connections and queries (MySQL probably could not handle as many connections and active queries anyway).

The rule that I propose will permit you to adjust the `innodb_buffer_pool_size` using no more than 70% and will also avoid using the swap when the server runs the production workload. Fortunately, as of version 5.7, we can adjust `innodb_buffer_pool_size` dynamically, which will avoid restarting MySQL to apply these adjustments.

In this section, you learned the general rule for adjusting the important `innodb_buffer_pool_size` variable, and its impact.

In the next section, we will look at another important variable, which is the thread cache.

The thread cache

How does MySQL use memory?

MySQL has three actions to help improve the performance of database operations: allocate, reserve some buffers, and cache. The default configuration allows a MySQL server to boot a server with a minimum of 512 MB of RAM. You can improve the performance of MySQL by increasing the values of some system variables related to caches and buffers, as I mentioned in the previous sections.

Suppose your MySQL 8.0 has the following values when running commands:

- `SHOW GLOBAL STATUS LIKE 'max_used_connections';` gives 200
- `SHOW GLOBAL STATUS LIKE 'Threads_created';` gives 200
- `SHOW GLOBAL STATUS LIKE 'connections';` gives 400

The common question that arises is, Do I have to increase the `thread_cache_size` variable?

This is often subject to the following context: "I'm running `SHOW PROCESSLIST`, I see open connections (most of them are sleeping). Do you have to change the `thread_cache_size`? If the size of the pool is greater than 250, do you think that is a good or bad value? Will it be better to set the `thread_cache_size` variable to 250+? Does it have a lot of impact on the processor and memory a?"

In the following example, we will find the highest number of concurrent connections the `mysqld` service has by using these three important variables: `Connections`, `Threads_created`, and `Max_used_connections`.

We could execute the following commands:

- `SHOW GLOBAL STATUS LIKE 'Connections';`
- `SHOW GLOBAL STATUS LIKE 'Threads_created';`
- `SHOW GLOBAL STATUS LIKE 'Max_used_connections';`

And of course, by performing the calculation with the following elements, we get an indicator value:

`Threads_created/Connections`

If this indicator value is greater than `0.01`, `thread_cache_size` must be increased. At a minimum, `thread_cache_size` must be greater than `Max_used_connections`.

In this section, we have seen how to improve the MySQL cache with a formula.

In the next two sections, we will see two common MySQL problems that you have probably experienced; the first is that a MySQL server uses 100% of a processor, and the second, which is so popular, is the cause of disk swap operations.

Case study 1 – when MySQL uses more than 100% of a CPU

As you know, web applications nowadays use majority based database. We all need MySQL to be a popular open-source database server for those applications that are also open-source, but we have seen that it can have long-term performance issues.

The cause of performance issues with MySQL databases is that they get bigger and its tables become fragmented over time. This helps to create workloads for MySQL. Protecting a server against MySQL processor problems requires monitoring and periodic optimization.

Apart from the possibility that the performance problem may be caused by traffic directed to your web application, normally we must analyze whether MySQL has reached the limits of its configuration, as indicated several times in previous chapters. A revision of SQL queries should be made in advance before changing anything in the configuration of your MySQL server. But, assuming that you have maximized these queries, let's try to see how we can detect and investigate in a case where MySQL continues to use 100% or more of your processors.

How to detect high usage of the MySQL processor

Very often, DBAs or developers think that a high workload in MySQL is because of the high use of processors. This is not always true. The workload in a server may increase due to bottlenecks caused by any resource.

The main reason for MySQL server load is due to the depletion of memory or input/output usage. If the bottleneck is at the CPU level, the output of the `top` command (Linux system) will look as follows:

```
top - 8:45:35 up 53 days, 12:8, 1 user, load average: 25.35, 17.43, 26.03

Tasks: 68 total, 6 running, 62 sleeping, 0 stopped, 0 zombie

Cpu(s): 89.8%us, 0.4%sy, 0.0%ni, 12.5%id, 0.0%wa, 0.2%hi, 0.5%si, 0.0%st

Mem: 2975930k total, 1118314k used, 1857616k free, 267407k buffers
```

If it is an input/output-induced bottleneck, `%wa` (called **wait average**) will have the highest-percentage CPU. On the other hand, if it is a charge caused by the memory, `free` memory will be limited to a few MB.

Correcting the use of the MySQL CPU

If the server load is indeed related to high CPU utilization, we can analyze and apply the following corrections:

- As already mentioned, optimizing database queries should be your first task. Some applications often use complex queries to display information on the site. These queries might take a long time to execute and cause a load on the server. Grabbing these queries from the slow query log will be a good idea, and reduce the number of joins and other table manipulations under a single query if possible, as we have already seen.
- If your MySQL is open to the public, block abusive processes. When a website is attacked (such as with DoS, spam, and so on), an unusually high number of connections can load your server in a short time. Use PROCESSLIST in MySQL to identify the main users and block access to abusive connections.
- Another potential solution is to enable persistent connections. If you have only one application that receives a lot connections, let's say per hour, enabling persistent MySQL connections can improve performance drastically. If your server has multiple applications running, unfortunately this may not work.

How to prevent MySQL from using high CPUs

Server and database traffic increases over time. The problems of the high CPU user by MySQL can be avoided, if the database server is monitored and tuned for performance:

- MySQL uses different caches and buffer memory to execute all queries. As the number of records and the complexity of queries change over time, server settings must be tweaked or adjusted for better performance.
- If your web applications are badly coded, no optimization of the database can solve the problem on an overloaded server. Monitor the MySQL slow query log and reduce the number of joins to gain performance.

In this section, you learned how to solve a common problem with MySQL, using 100% use of a processor. There is no miracle cure unfortunately, but you have learned the steps to detect and remedy this problem at the optimization level.

Case study 2 – when MySQL swaps on disk

What does disk swapping mean?

We can define a disk swap as the system moving data from memory to a special area on the disk called the **swap space**. The process is called an exchange or swap, depending on the direction in which it occurs.

The system halts when it makes the decision to free physical memory (RAM) and retrieve data from disk. It interfaces when an application needs to access the data that has been exchanged.

I believe you'll have guessed by now that the swapping between memory and disk will have a negative impact on the performance of MySQL.

The most important step to prevent disk swaps is to make sure that the MySQL database, and not any other application, uses all available memory. Generally, I would say that it is a common and recurring problem and this situation happens when we have our web server sharing the same server as MySQL; these two neighbors are constantly fighting for hardware resources and this causes the disk swapping problem.

One of the solutions that is often discussed is to zero the `vm.swappiness` variable in your Linux system; usually this variable contains a default value of `60`.

The following is an example of a Linux server:

```
sysctl vm.swappiness

vm.swappiness = 60
```

And to prevent your server from swapping, do the following:

```
sysctl -w vm.swappiness=0

vm.swappiness = 0
```

This changes the parameter at the command level. To extend the change to system reboots, simply add `vm.swappiness = 0` as a separate line in the `/etc/sysctl.conf` file.

Tips and techniques

The following is a list of variables, parameters, or simply comments to improve a particular situation or context:

- Use `innodb_flush_method=O_DIRECT` to avoid a double buffer when writing.
- Setting `innodb_buffer_pool_size` to load the entire InnoDB data into memory can help to avoid reading from the disk.

- Do not make `innodb_log_file_size` too high; with faster disks, flushing often is not bad and lowers the recovery time during crashes from your server.
- Avoid mixing these two variables: `innodb_thread_concurrency` and `thread_concurrency`. This will have a better impact on MySQL performance.
- Allocate only `max_connections`. When we use too many connections, the impact is that MySQL will use a lot of your RAM and needlessly slow down your MySQL server.
- Keep `thread_cache` at a relatively high setting; a minimum of 16 should be good enough to prevent slowness when opening connections.
- Use `skip-name-resolve` to remove DNS lookups.
- Use a query cache if your queries come back often and your data does not change too much.
- Another solution is to increase `temp_table_size` to prevent disk writes.
- By increasing `max_heap_table_size`, you prevent disk writes.
- Do not set your `sort_buffer_size` too high, because this variable is configured per connection and can use all of your memory very quickly.
- Setting `innodb_flush_log_at_trx_commit = 0` can improve the performance.

Summary

In this chapter, I tried to show you that, in optimization, the most important MySQL variables could have a better impact on performance. However, be aware that optimization is not an exact science but rather a step-by-step recipe with one change at a time, using monitoring and analysis.

Of course, no matter which version of MySQL you have, with 8.0 you will still have to monitor your database for performance and adjust it in line with your business's growth. Keep in mind that the two most important variables are InnoDB Buffer Pool and thread cache.

In the next chapter, we will look at how to configure high availability with MySQL global replication.

7
Group Replication in MySQL 8.0

In the previous chapter, we focused on tuning MySQL variables to achieve maximum performance. In this chapter, we are going to focus on an important topic—high availability. With this feature, we will be able to create a very powerful, reliable, and highly available replication infrastructure.

In this chapter, we will be looking into the following topics:

- The journey of MySQL replication mechanisms
- Types of replication method in MySQL
- Group replication
- How group replication works
- The installation, configuration, and management of group replication

You do not require any prior knowledge. If you have prior knowledge of high availability requirements and MySQL replication mechanisms, then you may jump directly to the group replication basics.

High availability and requirements

Any system or service should be accessible when a user wants to perform any action. If a user cannot perform the desired action, it is said to be unavailable or down. So, high availability acts as a very basic requirement for each system or service. In the era of online business, where the internet connects business to millions of customers, a downtime can cause loss of revenue, exacerbate customer relationships, lessen competitive advantages, incur legal obligations, and lower the industry's reputation and investor confidence. An analysis of downtime risk helps businesses to understand the maximum time that an IT-based business process can be down before the organization starts to suffer unacceptable consequences. For a system running a stock exchange, this time in regular business hours is zero, or close to zero.

Another very important aspect of any organization or business process is data. Businesses need to identify the maximum amount of data an IT-based business may lose before causing harming the organization. Imagine a stock exchange where millions of dollars' worth of transactions occur every second; it cannot afford to lose any data. In fact, the transactions that are inflight should also be preserved for some advanced requirements and analytics.

Scaling

Let's focus on some aspects of applications. Where you can predict the application load depends on the application type, or it can be completely unknown. In the cloud era, we need to make sure that when the workload is high, an application and its infrastructure should **scale up**, **scale out**, and **scale down** as required.

For many use cases, scaling up infrastructure might not be sufficient. To withstand workloads, an application needs to understand its database requirements.

Scaling a database means scaling database reads, database writes, or the database size. In some applications, in order to scale, data is divided across geographies. For example, Facebook stores data related to a user in its geography. This can help the user to access data faster, and it can help Facebook to scale its application; then Facebook can manage its workload based on time and the amount of data with minimal latency. To make sure the data is disaster-proof, it could be backed up and kept available in stand-by mode in case a specific geography fails. Sometimes, it is also necessary to keep user data in specific geographies based on local legal and compliance issues. Scaling can be achieved using clustering in databases. We can achieve that via two architectures: **shared-disk** and **shared-nothing**.

In **shared-disk**, only disks are shared; each processor can cache data from the disk. To ensure that consistency, a distributed lock management capability is required as multiple nodes can ask to update the same data. This is used when it is difficult to partition the data.

In a **shared-nothing** environment, a message is routed to the system that owns the resource. What is important to note the following is that we need to partition the data to achieve maximum scalability in a shared-nothing environment.

Further to database scaling operations, an application needs to be written and designed in such a way that read-only transactions are separated with read-write transactions. We can use some of the advanced techniques such as database partitioning, where we can divide our data using the strategy that works best for a given use case. Partitioning can be looked at on multiple levels. For example, Facebook can divide its data based on a user's geography and store it in a separate database; this technique is called a **shard**. In another use case, a user's table can be divided to a store user's information based on the first letter of the user's first name. Here, we are talking about partitioning at a table's row level. Sharding helps us to scale out rather than scale up. In sharding, data is partitioned across multiple schemas. We can get the benefit of processing power over multiple servers. The disadvantage is that it requires more resources, and querying for aggregating data is hard. If one shard goes down, the data on that shard will not be accessible. So, we require **replication** to achieve high availability, in the case of failure.

Replication

Replication is defined as:

> *"The process of generating and reproducing multiple copies of data at one or more sites."*

> *- Thomas M Connolly, Carolyn E Begg, 2002.*

When a database instance fails, the service it provided must be available through another route. This requires process redundancy. In a database, either only one processor can process all transactions, or there can be multiple processors. When there is a single process managing all transactions, we should have a standby process available, in the case of failure, for an active one. It is also necessary to make sure that this fail-over is seamless and the process itself can detect the failure.

Data redundancy is also required for high availability. Data redundancy can be achieved either by having a storage subsystem that maintains redundancy while presenting the data to DBMS processes as a single copy, or having the DBMS explicitly maintain multiple copies of the data.

Group replication

Group replication is a MySQL server plugin. It helps us create a replication topology that has the following attributes:

- **Elasticity**: On-demand resource allocation/reallocation
- **Fault tolerance**: Ability to withstand up to n failures
- **High availability**: Systems or services will be available for a longer period of time without failures, or, in some cases, available for a longer period of time, which is more than the agreeable time without failures

It achieves this by implementing **Paxos protocol** (Mencius) to support the multi-master facility, which allows applications to write on all servers of the same group at the same time while maintaining consistency through conflict detection and resolution mechanisms. It achieves this by implementing replicating databases with state machine fundamentals. It has built-in modules to support distributed recovery across all platforms. It also achieves fault tolerance with a built-in fail over mechanism. It is a shared-nothing replication scheme, as each server has an entire copy of the data.

The plugin has implemented the distributed state machine, as it satisfies the following criteria:

- On change, multiple servers agree on the state of the system and the data
- All need to progress as one single database
- They all eventually converge to the same state

The preceding explanation sounds exciting, and we are going to understand everything in detail.

The following diagram shows the **Group Replication topology**:

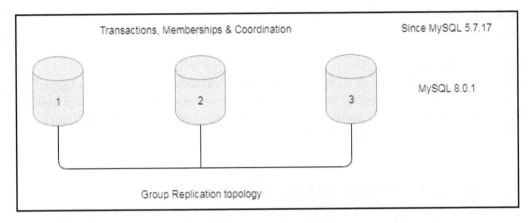

Group Replication topology

This plugin also allows you to upgrade to group replication from an existing replication. This can ensure a highly available MySQL service distributed across *n* instances. It can also take care of your scaling burning issues and eliminates the need for manual intervention to achieve fault tolerance:

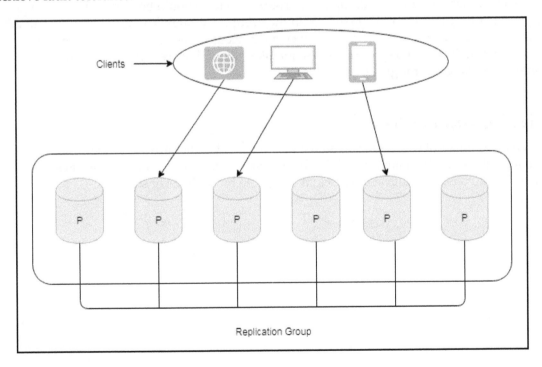

There are two types of transaction we execute on any of the replicas of the database:

- Read-only
- Read-write

Read-only transactions can be run on any servers and do not require any kind of communication amongst the group members. Read-only transactions are also not logged in a binary log, as they are not changing the state of the data or not changing the membership of the group. If you want to write read-only transactions, you can enable a general query log. Use the `general_log` variable to enable a general query log.

Use cases for group replication

MySQL's group replication feature provides a way to build a highly available MySQL service, as long as the group has the majority of the servers functioning. We can achieve this because it replicates the same state of the system to all members in a group. A majority of the group's members should agree on the change of the state of MySQL members, message delivery, and state updates. Group replication has a built-in service for failure detection, which maintains a view of members subscribed to the group. At any given point when a member server leaves or joins the group, the view should be updated after the approval of the majority of the members in the group. Although MySQL is highly available as a service, if clients connected to a node crash, it needs to re-establish the connection to some other node. Group replication does not take care of that scenario. Let's figure out some of the use cases for group replication.

Elastic replication

When the number of servers has to adjust the workload, either growing or shrink, dynamically with little pain if possible, this is a valid use case for a lot of websites, for example: university results at a particular date/time for millions of students.

The following diagram shows an example of an elastic replication:

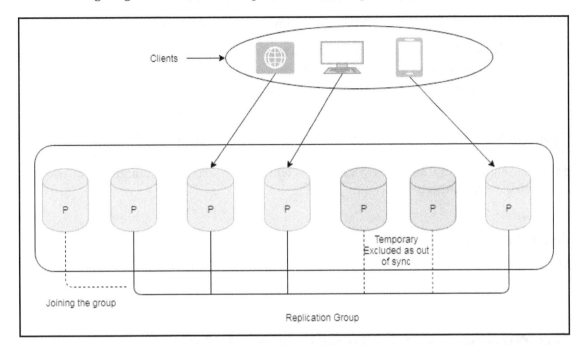

As you can see, the first node is trying to join the group, whereas the nodes colored red are temporarily excluded from the group for being out of sync, until they catch up with all the updates.

When a server tries to join a group, its state is updated as recovering. Once it catches up with the rest of the group, it state gets transitioned to online, and once the server becomes online, it can start accepting live traffic.

Highly available shards

Group replication has a limitation: it can work with, at most, nine servers in a group. So, if you have a higher requirement for resources, then it can be a problem. So, you can breakdown your schema in multiple shards, and each shard itself can represent a group.

Sharding is a popular approach to achieving write scale-out. Users can use MySQL group replication to implement highly available shards, and each shard can map into a replication group. This way, you can infinitely scale your system. In this case, multiple shards are responsible for taking care of the disjoint dataset.

Alternative to master – slave replication

With a single master server replication, the following can be potential issues:

- Automatic primary/secondary role assignment
- Automatic new primary election on primary failures
- Automatic setup of read/write modes on primary and secondaries
- Globally consistent view of which server is the primary

If you use the group replication mechanism, these issues are taken care of automatically, and no manual intervention is required. It is a very strong use case, as it can reduce downtime significantly, and fail over happens within milliseconds, although clients need to re-establish fresh connections.

Autonomic systems

MySQL's group replication can be deployed for automation built into the replication protocol.

An overview of MySQL's database replication

As group replication is built on top of existing replication framework, let's revisit how replication works in MySQL traditionally. MySQL has provided a replication feature in its management service and utilities. It is usable with all kinds of storage engines, despite their differences. We configure a topology of two nodes to replicate the data, from one node to the other node. The one that accepts client connections is called a master. The one to which data is being copied is called a slave.

The following diagram shows the **MySQL Database Replication Overview**:

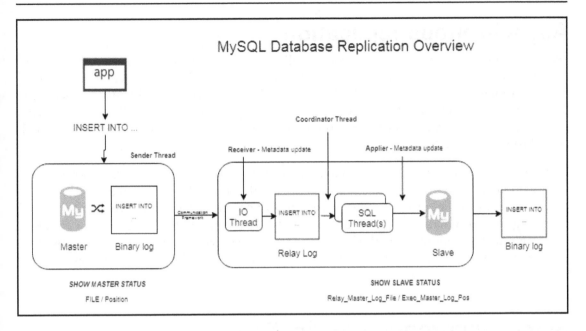

As shown in the preceding diagram, the clients connect to a single database instance called **Master**, where the **Master** is responsible for running all transactions. It is also responsible for recording all of the events that can change the state of MySQL database (DML or DDL) in a binary log. It has two modes: **row-based logging** or **statement based logging**. In row-based logging, MySQL identifies the rows that are required to be changed and logs them. In statement-based logging, only MySQL statements are being logged, which serves two purposes:

- Shipping the logs to the slave server helps recreate the same state
- **For point-in-time recovery**: When restoring backups, we can replay the events that happened after we have taken the backup

The **Binary log** is then shipped to a **Slave** server via the communication framework, established between the **Master** and the **Slave**. The **Slave** contains an **IO** thread, which is responsible to for recreating **Relay Log** as shown in the diagram. The coordinator threads receive the **Relay Log,** and they provide necessary work to the SQL worker threads, which are responsible to executing the changes on the slave database. On executing statements or applying row-level changes to the slave database, it also generates the **Binary log** the same way the master generates it. MySQL replication can be useful for taking backups, dividing read-write workloads and to create redundancy if the primary or the master server fails/dies. Though MySQL was not providing any built-in mechanism for automatic failover. System architects need to switchover and allow the standby to become active manually.

Asynchronous replication

When we configure a server as a slave, the replication is initiated by the slave process itself, by communicating with the master server. The slave process will ask the active server to provide updates since the last update it received. The master process will be responsible to logging the events on every state change. It doesn't stop executing transactions if the slave is lagging behind or even if the slave is not reachable. Thus, this type of replication is called **asynchronous replication**.

In earlier releases of MySQL asynchronous replication, you could not deny the loss of transactional data on slaves, even if you were using the InnoDB engine and setting sync_binlog to 1. For example, we use the InnoDB engine and issue a COMMIT after executing certain statements; it records every detail to the binary log, synchronizes it, and then commits the transaction to the InnoDB table. If the server crashes in between those two operations, the transaction done on InnoDB would be rolled back upon server restart but still exists in the binary log.

Semi-synchronous replication

This plugin was introduced in MySQL 5.5. The plugin needs to be installed on both the **Master** and **Slave**. Once enabled, a thread on the **Master** that performs a transaction commit is getting blocked, which is depicted in the following diagram:

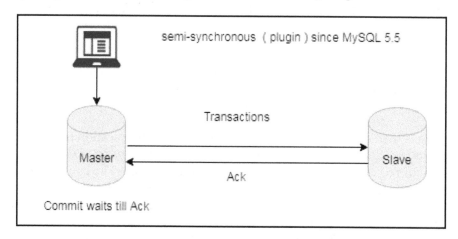

It is interesting to note here that the transaction on the **Master** gets committed, but the client thread and is blocked until it receives an answer from at least one **Slave** server. The **Slave** acknowledges that it has received all events for a transaction and is written to relay the log, as well as written to disk, but not necessary executed on the **Slave**.

This mechanism also does not protect against data loss.

Delayed replication

From MySQL 5.6, MySQL developers have come up with a new replication mechanism called **delayed replication**, where a slave deliberately doesn't execute the events received from MySQL master for a set number of seconds. The MySQL variable for this is as follows:

```
> CHANGE MASTER TO MASTER_DELAY = N;.
```

Where N specifies the number of seconds.

Use cases

- To protect the slave against a developer's mistake on the master for N seconds
- To test how the system behaves when there is a lag
- If the delay is longer, DBA has the ability to compare the current state of the master

From MySQL 8.0.1, for every **global transaction identifier (GTID)**-based transaction, a replication lag can be determined by the difference between the timestamp of the transaction committed on the master versus the timestamp of the transaction committed on the immediate master. For more information, you can look at the `mysqlbinlog` output for a specific GTID.

Global transaction identifier-based replication

To serve advanced MySQL topologies, MySQL has included global transaction identifier-based replication. It adds a unique identifier to each transaction committed on the server of origin called the master. By introducing GTID-based replication, you can identify the origin of the transaction and the order in which the transaction needs to be executed if all servers are part of the same group.

A GTID is represented as a pair of coordinates, separated by a colon (:), as shown here:

```
GTID =source_id:transaction_id
```

Where the `source_id` is the server's UUID specified in the configuration. `transaction_id` is a sequence number determined by the order in which the transaction was committed on this server.

The state of the slave database server is maintained in an InnoDB table and updates to the state are recorded within the same transaction as a state of database operation. In the case of a slave failure, it can start crash recovery and make sure that the replication starts from the position where it stopped. The slave database keeps track of the current position in a system table named `mysqld.gtid_slave_pos`.

There are two ways of generating GTIDs:

- **Automatic**: In this mechanism, the transaction is assigned and automatically generates an ID.
- **Assigned**: Before the transaction starts, the transaction ID can be set using a value we can get via `SET GTID_NEXT` in the transaction. In multi-primary mode, all nodes are assigned a block of GTIDs:

  ```
  group_replication_gtid_assignment_block_size ( Default value is 1
  million )
  ```

This technique is used in the MySQL group replication plugin.

Multi-source replication

As shown in the previous diagram, in this replication mechanism more than one master can replicate data to a single slave in parallel. One slave receives all the transactions at the same time. It is not compatible with a file-based replication mechanism, but we can configure GTID-based replication or binary log-based replication in masters. The slave maintains table repositories for master information and relay log information.

Use cases for multi-source replication include the following:

- Backing up multiple servers to a single server
- Merging table shards
- Consolidating data

In a multi-source replication mechanism, there is no in-built conflict detection or resolution when applying transactions from multiple sources. In this case, there are chances the application owners need to take care of the same.

The following diagram represents **Multi Source Replication**:

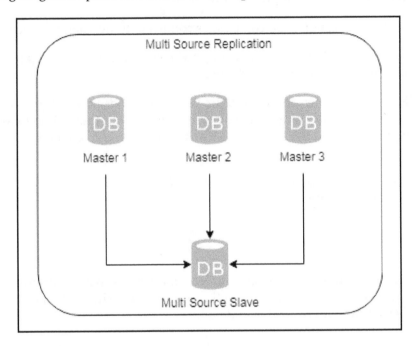

So far, we have learned about the different replication mechanisms available in MySQL. Enterprises had to be dependent on third-party database solution providers to get automatic failover, elasticity, and fault tolerance, for example: Percona XtraDB and Galera. We will try to understand how group replication has achieved the same result. Let's go through some of the key changes to group replication.

MySQL's group replication architecture

The MySQL group replication plugin architecture is layered with the following components, and it is responsible for how it works overall. The plugin depends on binary log, row-based logging, GTID-based transaction identification, performance schemas, and the infrastructure.

At the heart of the plugin are the following components:

- **Capture**: Keeps track of currently executing transactions
- **Applier**: Execute remote transactions
- **Recovery**: To keep all replicas up-to-date

On top of these, the replication protocol handles conflict detection and transaction delivery.

The plugin provides the API for the capture, apply, recovery life cycle. It separates the group replication plugin from the MySQL core.

During the life cycle of MySQL and the plugin, the server sends notifications for the server start, stop, recover, ready to accept connections or committing a transaction to the group replication plugin. However, the plugin also instructs the server to commit a transaction or abort a transaction.

And the final layer is the group communication system API and the implementation of the group communication engine.

Group

A set of servers forms a replication group. Servers can join or leave the group at any time. The status of the group can be queried from the performance schema. In the group membership section, we will cover this in detail.

Writeset

The writeset of a transaction is a set of hashes that identify each row in the database changed by it. It contains the hash for the row's primary keys that are changed, and in some cases, the hashes of foreign keys or other dependencies that need to be captured. (for example, non-null unique keys; writesets are generated during the execution of a transaction and are used to parallelize transactions that modify disjoint sets.

We demonstrate the **Write set parallelism** in the following diagram:

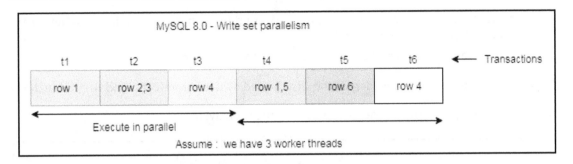

Writesets are used by group replication to detect which read-write transactions can run in parallel among member servers using the certification mechanism. The same idea is also used in each member to detect which transactions can be applied in parallel for already-accepted transactions irrespective of the commit order:

To enable WRITESET parallelization:

```
On primary > SET binlog_transaction_dependency_tracking = WRITESET;
On replica > SET slave_parallel_workers = 3
slave_parallel_type = LOGICAL_LOCK;
```

For some of the applications, it is required to run transactions in the same order as the master. For them, you need to set slave_preserve_commit_order = 1. This will preserve the commit order for transactions. And you might not get the benefit of parallelization. A binlog_transaction_dependency_tracking variable has been introduced to control this new behavior. This can take three values:

- COMMIT_ORDER: The default setting.
- WRITESET: Allows for better parallelization. The master or primary starts storing information from written transactions in the binary log.
- WRITESET_SESSION: Ensures that transactions will be executed in order on the slave or the secondary. Problems with a slave seeing a database state never before seen on the master are eliminated. Though this reduces parallelization, the obtained throughput is still often better than with the default settings.

How group communication works

To allow multiple servers to execute writes in parallel, consistency should be maintained. There are three roles for each member:

- Proposers, who suggest values for consideration by the acceptors

- Acceptors, who consider the value proposed by proposers and decide whether to accept or reject the proposal
- Learners, who learn the value chosen by the acceptors

The task is to deliver a message across the distributed system atomically and in total order.

The following diagram shows the group communication system:

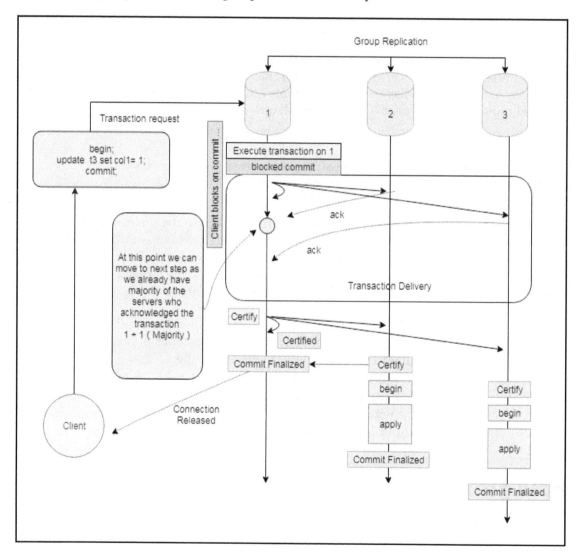

As shown in the preceding diagram, we have three servers configured to operate in a multi-primary mode. The **Client** asks to execute a transaction, the **Client** connects to one of the servers, and the server executes the transaction. Before it commits the transaction, the majority of the group members need to come to an agreement on the state change. **Group Replication** initiates transaction delivery to other members in the group. As soon as the master server gets an acknowledgement from the majority of the servers in the group, it can move to the next step, where it will again ask the group members to certify this transaction. The other members of the group inspect the writesets of the different and concurrent transactions, in a process called certification. Once a majority of the servers certifies the transaction, the primary server finalizes the commit, commits the transaction, and releases the client connection. It is important to note that the certification process does not execute the transaction on the other members. Once the transaction is certified, the transaction gets a commit order and will be present in the relay log for the SQL threads to proceed further. In this example, server 1 is playing the role of a proposer, and other nodes are performing the role of an acceptor. Once they accept, they will apply and perform the role of a learner.

Certification process

This process determines whether the write transaction can be committed. Based on the yet-to-be-applied transactions, such conflicts must come from other members. It happens to every member, and its deterministic acknowledgement may not be necessary at the same time from all members of the group.

Total order delivery

To maintain the same state on all of the members of the group, it is very important that execution of the transaction happens in the same order. As shown in the previous diagram, server 1 is executing a transaction first, but the transaction that is executed on server 5 gets certified first, and that will be queued first. The same order of the transactions will be preserved and followed by the slaves. For advanced users, the execution of threads on slaves can be parallelized for transactions with the disjoint sets of the writeset.

The following diagram represents the ordered delivery of certified transactions:

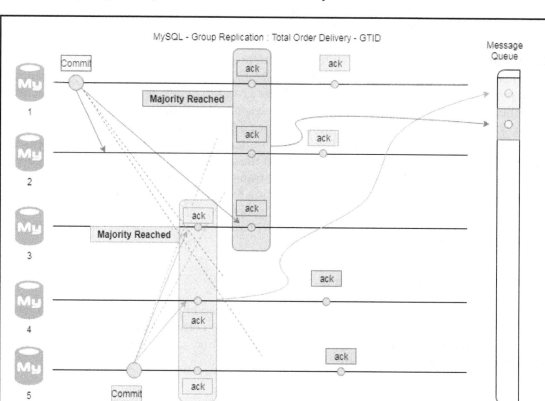

Detecting failure

Group membership is a service as part of the group replication plugin. It maintains a view of a group, which contains a list of all the members of the group, channels, member IDs, their hostname, port, state, role, and MySQL Version. The view is consistent across all members of the group.

For any state change in any members, voluntarily or not, a group reconfiguration event is triggered. All members need to agree upon is to allow a server to join or leave the group and trigger the change of view. If a member suddenly becomes unavailable, then the failure detection mechanism realizes the fact and reconfiguration of the group is proposed, without the failed member. For any change, the majority of the group's members should be able to agree upon the proposal. If the majority of members do not come to an agreement, then it blocks to prevent a split-brain situation. At this point, the administration team needs to step in and fix it.

Network partitioning

A group replication plugin assumes that we have deployed group members on a great network. But networks are fragile. Let's look at an example. In our group replication topology, we have five servers:

```
mysql> SELECT MEMBER_ID,MEMBER_HOST,MEMBER_PORT,MEMBER_STATE  FROM
performance_schema.replication_group_members;
+---------------------------------------+-------------+-------------+--------
--------
| MEMBER_ID | MEMBER_HOST | MEMBER_PORT | MEMBER_STATE|
+---------------------------------------+-------------+-------------+--------
--------
| 2322f8f4-2bbg-34w4-hh64-21i311123i98 | 127.0.0.1 | 19002 | ONLINE |
| 2312f7b4-2bbg-34w4-hb59-21i311123i98 | 127.0.0.1 | 19001 | ONLINE |
| 2327v9q2-2bbg-34w4-bb21-21i311123i98 | 127.0.0.1 | 19000 | ONLINE |
| 2321n8s3-2bbg-34w4-hae4-21i311123i98 | 127.0.0.1 | 19003 | ONLINE |
| 2872s612-2bbg-34w4-heg1-21i311123i98 | 127.0.0.1 | 19004 | ONLINE |
+---------------------------------------+-------------+-------------+--------
--------
```

For an unexpected reason, three nodes out of five become UNREACHABLE:

```
mysql> SELECT MEMBER_ID,MEMBER_HOST,MEMBER_PORT,MEMBER_STATE FROM
performance_schema.replication_group_members;
+---------------------------------------+-------------+-------------+--------
--------+
| MEMBER_ID | MEMBER_HOST | MEMBER_PORT | MEMBER_STATE |
+---------------------------------------+-------------+-------------+--------
--------+
| 2322f8f4-2bbg-34w4-hh64-21i311123i98 | 127.0.0.1 | 19002 | UNREACHABLE |
| 2312f7b4-2bbg-34w4-hb59-21i311123i98 | 127.0.0.1 | 19001 | ONLINE |
| 2327v9q2-2bbg-34w4-bb21-21i311123i98 | 127.0.0.1 | 19000 | ONLINE |
| 2321n8s3-2bbg-34w4-hae4-21i311123i98 | 127.0.0.1 | 19003 | UNREACHABLE |
| 2872s612-2bbg-34w4-heg1-21i311123i98 | 127.0.0.1 | 19004 | UNREACHABLE |
+---------------------------------------+-------------+-------------+--------
--------+
```

In this case, the group membership needs to be tested. That might be possible for servers 2 and 3, but servers 1, 4, and 5 are unreachable. But it might also be possible that they are online and they can access one another. If they are online and can access one another, they can technically create a quorum and reach an agreement to execute state changes. In this case, they are the group.

In the other case, if they are not reachable, we are left with two servers: server 2 and server 3. Now, as a original group had five members, these two alone cannot execute any state changes, as the majority is not formed. In this case, we need to force the reconfiguration of the group membership:

```
mysql>SET GLOBAL
group_replication_force_members="127.0.0.1:19000,127.0.0.1:19001"
```

This needs to be handled with care. In this case, the other servers needs to be in the shutdown state, they are forced out of the group, and they are not online.

In a case where we have forced servers two and three to be part of a group and if the other three servers are online and they can access one another, technically, we have created an artificial split-brain situation. So, you need to ensure that other servers are in the shutdown state before forcing members or re-configuring groups via this method.

Traditional locking versus optimistic locking

Group replication uses optimistic locking. In a traditional locking mechanism, if two transactions are updating the same tuple, the second transaction waits to read the value until the first transaction commits. In a group replication mechanism, those two transactions are happening on separate machines. Group replication optimistically assumes there will be no conflicts across nodes, and in this phase, no communication happens among nodes. Cluster-wide conflict resolution happens only at commit, during the certification process.

Distributed first commit wins rule

The following diagram shows an error: modifying the same tuple across primary at the same time:

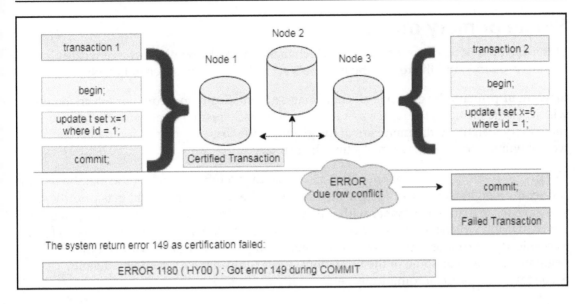

The system return error 149 as certification failed:

As you can see from the previous diagram, **transaction 1** started execution on **Node 1**, and **transaction 2** on **Node 3**. Both of them are updating the same tuple in this case. The certification process has detected this, allowed the first transaction to make the change, and failed the other.

Drawbacks of optimistic locking

As shown in the diagram, a transaction that got distributed first could update the tuple. It also means that the chances of conflict in applications writing on multiple members with large transactions and long running transactions are high.

Modes of group replication

The modes of group replication are as follows:

- Single primary mode
- Multi primary mode

Single primary mode

This is the default configuration mode, which makes a single member act as a writeable master (primary), and the rest of the members act as hot-standbys (secondaries):

Election of primary the group itself coordinates automatically to figure out which member will act as the primary, through a primary election mechanism. For advanced users, you can specify weights to the members of the group. Upon loss of the primary member, the weight will be considered when electing the primary.

Use `group_replication_member_weight` to set the weight for each of the members. You can set the weight from `0` to `100`. The member with the maximum weight gets priority. If you have more than one member with the same weight, then the algorithms sort based on the UUID, and whichever member comes at the top is elected as the primary. This is closer to classic asynchronous replication setups, and is simpler to reason about from the beginning and avoids some of the limitations of the multi-primary mode by default. Secondary servers are automatically set to `read_only` as `ON`.

To identify the current primary node in a group, you can execute the following query:

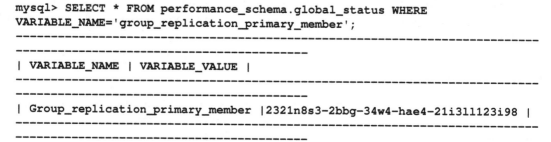

```
mysql> SELECT * FROM performance_schema.global_status WHERE
VARIABLE_NAME='group_replication_primary_member';
---------------------------------------------------------------------
---------------------------------------------
| VARIABLE_NAME | VARIABLE_VALUE |
---------------------------------------------------------------------
---------------------------------------------
| Group_replication_primary_member |2321n8s3-2bbg-34w4-hae4-21i311123i98 |
---------------------------------------------------------------------
---------------------------------------------
```

The following diagram represents the **Single Primary Mode**:

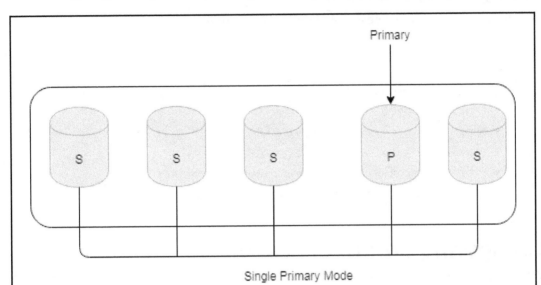

Multi-primary

This is an update-everywhere replication mechanism. While setting up, we need to set the setting option: `--group_replication_single_primary_mode = OFF`.

Two transactions on different servers can write at the same time.

If there is a conflict, then the transaction that gets an acknowledgement from the majority of the group members gets first commit rights. The other one fails.

Group replication requirements

For group replication to work, the following the list of infrastructure requirements:

- **IPV4 network**: Plugin-only support IPV4
- **Network performance**: Network latency and bandwidth can impact
- **InnoDB storage engine**: Transaction engine with **atomicity consistency isolation and durability (ACID)** guarantee required
- **Primary keys**: Tables that need to be replicated will not need a null unique key

Configuring the server

The following options must be enabled on MySQL config:

- `--log-bin`
- `--log-slave-updates`
- `--binlog-format=ROW`
- `--gtid-mode=ON`
- `--master-info-repository=TABLE`
- `--relay-log-info-repository=TABLE`
- `--transaction-write-set-extraction=XXHASH64`
- `--slave-preserve-commit-order=1 ( Optional )`

Configuring group replication

In this step, we are going to configure MySQL group replication step by step. For demonstration purposes, I am going to run three instances of a MySQL 8.0.13 server on a single machine. We are also going to deploy a single primary mode of group replication.

I have downloaded MySQL 8.0.13 Community Edition and extracted it to `C:\mysql-8.0.13`. Open the Command Prompt, and execute the following command to create three directories under `C:\mysql-8.0.13\data`, that is, `server1`, `server2`, and `server3`:

```
---------------------
C:\>cd mysql-8.0.13
C:\mysql-8.0.13>cd data
C:\mysql-8.0.13\data>mkdir server1
C:\mysql-8.0.13\data>mkdir server2
C:\mysql-8.0.13\data>mkdir server3
C:\mysql-8.0.13\data>cd..
C:\mysql-8.0.13\>cd bin
C:\mysql-8.0.13\bin>mysqld --initialize-insecure --basedir=c:/mysql-8.0.13
--datadir=c:/mysql-8.0.13/data/server1
C:\mysql-8.0.13\bin>mysqld --initialize-insecure --basedir=c:/mysql-8.0.13
--datadir=c:/mysql-8.0.13/data/server2
C:\mysql-8.0.13\bin>mysqld --initialize-insecure --basedir=c:/mysql-8.0.13
--datadir=c:/mysql-8.0.13/data/server3
c:\mysql-8.0.13\bin>cd ..
c:\mysql-8.0.13>mkdir socket
```

```
c:\mysql-8.0.13>mkdir extra_conf
```

Let's create the configuration file for each of the servers, starting with `server1`.

I am saving the following configuration for `server1`, under the `C:\mysql-8.0.13\extra_conf\server1.cnf` file. We will start a MySQL instance with this file:

 Do not forget to change the path according to your platform and directory structure.

```
[mysqld]
# server configuration
datadir='C:\\mysql-8.0.13\\data\\server1'
basedir='C:\\mysql-8.0.13'
port=24801
socket=C:/mysql-8.0.13/socket/s1.sock
```

The preceding configuration offers the following:

- `basedir`: Defines the base directory for MySQL installation
- `datadir`: Defines where the data will be stored
- `port`: Server will listen on the port specified for client connections

We have specified the `port`, because in the same server, we are going to run three instances. By default, it runs on port `3306`.

The following settings are related to replication framework-related settings. Append the following settings to the same file:

```
server_id=1
gtid_mode=ON
enforce_gtid_consistency=ON
binlog_checksum=NONE
```

The preceding settings define the server's unique identifier as number `1`.

The second line is specified to allow the execution of only statements that can be safely logged using a GTID, and the last line disables writing a checksum for the events written to the binary log.

Before we can use group replication, we need to make sure that the plugin is installed or enabled in MySQL.

Let's start our first MySQL database instance with the options file that we have created:

```
C:\mysql-8.0.13\bin>mysqld --defaults-
file=c:\mysql-8.0.13\extra_conf\server1.cnf
```

Login to MySQL server using following command:

```
C:\mysql-8.0.13\bin>mysql -P 24801 -u root
```

This should log you in to the MySQL prompt.

In order to verify if the plugin is loaded, you can run the following query:

```
mysql> select * from mysql.plugin;
Empty set (0.01 sec)
```

You can also verify this by using one more query: `Mysql> show variables like '%group%';`.

Once run, the previous query will list all of the variables related to the `group_replication` plugin. If it is not installed, you will not see them. The variable name starts with `group_replication_*`. If you do not find them, then please install the group replication plugin using the following command:

```
mysql > INSTALL PLUGIN group_replication SONAME 'group_replication.dll';
```

For other platforms, you have to change the preceding query to the following:

```
mysql> INSTALL PLUGIN group_replication SONAME 'group_replication.so';
```

Once again, verify whether the plugin is loaded now. Once done, stop the MySQL service and add the following variables to the `server1.cnf` file.

It is important to note that alternatively you can skip the installation process of the group replication plugin. Use `plugin-load = group_replication.dll` in the config file, and the plugin will be loaded while starting MySQL. Now you just need to make sure that all of the `group_replication_*` variables are after the `plugin-load` variable. Otherwise, MySQL might not start and may throw error such as "`unknown-variable...`".

The following section adds settings related to group replication:

```
transaction_write_set_extraction=XXHASH64
group_replication_group_name="aaaaaaaa-aaaa-aaaa-aaaa-aaaaaaaaaaaa"
group_replication_start_on_boot=off
group_replication_local_address= "localhost:24901"
group_replication_group_seeds=
"localhost:24901,localhost:24902,localhost:24903"
group_replication_bootstrap_group=off
binlog-rows-query-log-events=ON
log_bin=binlog
log_slave_updates=ON
binlog_format=ROW
master_info_repository=TABLE
relay_log_info_repository=TABLE
disabled_storage_engines="MyISAM,BLACKHOLE,FEDERATED,ARCHIVE"
transaction-isolation = 'READ-COMMITTED'
group_replication_recovery_get_public_key=ON
```

Replace the `localhost` with your hostname, which resolves to an IP address.

The following is a description of the variables:

- The `Transaction_write_set_extraction` variable instructs the server that, for each transaction, it has to extract the writeset and encode it as a `HASH` using the `XXHASH64` hashing algorithm. This is the default setting from MySQL 8.0.2.
- The `group_replication_group_name` variable defines the group's name. And it must be a valid UUID.
- The `group_replication_start_on_boot` variable is set to `OFF` initially, as we want to configure the server first. Once configured, we will set this to `ON`, so that group replication starts as soon as the server boots up.
- The `group_replication_local_address` variable is used for the server that is getting initialized. The `ip:port` combination will be used to communicate with the members of the group. This `ip:port` is only used for internal group-related communication. For member-to-member communication group replication uses the XCOM protocol. Client connections are not accepted here.
- The `group_replication_group_seeds` variable specifies members of the group called `seeds`.
- The `group_replication_bootstrap_group` instructs the plugin whether to bootstrap the group or not.

The other variables are added as they were specified in the requirements for group replication.

Save the file, and again start the server using the following command on the Command Prompt:

```
C:\mysql-8.0.13\bin>mysqld --defaults-
file=c:\mysql-8.0.13\extra_conf\server1.cnf
```

Now log in to MySQL using the following command:

```
C:\mysql-8.0.13\bin>mysql -P 24801 -u root
```

To achieve recovery for a server who joins the group, one user who has permission to set up the member-recovery replication channel is required. Group replication relies on the group_replication_recovery channel to transfer transactions from an existing group member (it acts as a donor) to a recently joined member. The user requires the "REPLICATION_SLAVE" privilege.

Right now, we are setting up the user, and the queries related to that can be logged in the binary log and later on can be played on other members who join the group. Run the following command to disable the binary logging on the server1 instance of MySQL:

```
mysql> SET SQL_LOG_BIN=0;
mysql> CREATE USER rplication_user1@'%' IDENTIFIED BY
'replication_password1';\
mysql> GRANT REPLICATION SLAVE ON *.* TO rplication_user1@'%';
mysql> FLUSH PRIVILEGES;
mysql> SET SQL_LOG_BIN=1;
mysql>CHANGE MASTER TO MASTER_USER='rplication_user1',
MASTER_PASSWORD='replication_password1' FOR CHANNEL
'group_replication_recovery';
mysql> SET GLOBAL group_replication_bootstrap_group=ON;
 mysql> START GROUP_REPLICATION;
 mysql> SET GLOBAL group_replication_bootstrap_group=OFF;
mysql> SELECT * FROM performance_schema.replication_group_members\G;
*************************** 1. row ***************************
CHANNEL_NAME: group_replication_applier
MEMBER_ID: 46e7375a-f661-11e8-91ff-00ff461ae7f1
MEMBER_HOST: 127.0.0.1
MEMBER_PORT: 24801
MEMBER_STATE: ONLINE
MEMBER_ROLE: PRIMARY
MEMBER_VERSION: 8.0.13
1 row in set (0.00 sec)
```

We will create a database and add one table to it. Later on, when we configure and add more servers, we will be able to verify a lot of concepts that we studied earlier in our theory section:

```
mysql> CREATE DATABASE test_group_replication;
Query OK, 1 row affected (0.45 sec)
mysql> use test_group_replication;
Database changed
mysql> CREATE TABLE first_table (first_column INT PRIMARY KEY,
second_column TEXT NOT NULL);
Query OK, 0 rows affected (0.56 sec)\
mysql> INSERT INTO first_table values (1,'Albert');
Query OK, 1 row affected (0.07 sec)
mysql> select * from first_table\G;
*************************** 1. row ***************************:
first_column: 1
second_column: Albert
1 row in set (0.01 sec)
```

Adding the second Instance

Add the following config file and save it
to `C:\mysql-8.0.13\extra_conf\server2.conf`:

```
[mysqld]
basedir=C:/mysql-8.0.13
datadir=C:/mysql-8.0.13/data/server2
port=24802
socket=C:\mysql-8.0.13\socket\s2.sock
server_id=2
gtid_mode=ON
enforce_gtid_consistency=ON
binlog_checksum=NONE
transaction_write_set_extraction=XXHASH64
plugin-load=group_replication.dll
group_replication_group_name="aaaaaaaa-aaaa-aaaa-aaaa-aaaaaaaaaaaa"
group_replication_start_on_boot=off
group_replication_local_address= "localhost:24902"
group_replication_group_seeds=
"localhost:24901,localhost:24902,localhost:24903"
group_replication_bootstrap_group=off
binlog-rows-query-log-events=ON
log_bin=binlog
log_slave_updates=ON
binlog_format=ROW
master_info_repository=TABLE
relay_log_info_repository=TABLE
disabled_storage_engines="MyISAM,BLACKHOLE,FEDERATED,ARCHIVE"
```

```
transaction-isolation = 'READ-COMMITTED'
group_replication_recovery_get_public_key=ON
```

Only the highlighted lines have changed. Use the following command to start the second instance of MySQL:

C:\mysql-8.0.13\bin>mysqld.exe --defaults-file=c:/mysql-8.0.13/extra_conf/server2.cnf --console

Once you have finished, run the following commands to start group replication on the second node:

C:\mysql-8.0.13\bin>mysql -u root -P 24802

```
mysql> SET SQL_LOG_BIN=0;
mysql> CREATE USER rplication_user1@'%' IDENTIFIED BY
'replication_password1';
mysql> GRANT REPLICATION SLAVE ON *.* TO rplication_user1@'%';
mysql> FLUSH PRIVILEGES;
mysql> SET SQL_LOG_BIN=1;mysql>CHANGE MASTER TO
MASTER_USER='rplication_user1', MASTER_PASSWORD='replication_password1' FOR
CHANNEL 'group_replication_recovery';
mysql> START GROUP_REPLICATION;
mysql> SELECT * FROM performance_schema.replication_group_members\G;
*********************** 1. row ***********************
CHANNEL_NAME: group_replication_applier
MEMBER_ID: 46e7375a-f661-11e8-91ff-00ff461ae7f1
MEMBER_HOST: 127.0.0.1
MEMBER_PORT: 24801
MEMBER_STATE: ONLINE
MEMBER_ROLE: PRIMARY
MEMBER_VERSION: 8.0.13
-------------------------------2.row-------------------------------
-------------
CHANNEL_NAME: group_replication_applier
MEMBER_ID: 55e7375a-f661-11e8-91ff-00ff461bdf81
MEMBER_HOST: 127.0.0.1
MEMBER_PORT: 24802
MEMBER_STATE: ONLINE
MEMBER_ROLE: SECONDARY
MEMBER_VERSION: 8.0.13
```

Let's verify that the table we had created is present in the second server.

```
mysql> show databases;
+-----------------------+
| Database |
+-----------------------+
```

```
| test_group_replication |
+-------------------------+
1 rows in set (0.01 sec)

mysql> use test_group_replication;
Database changed
mysql> show tables;
+-----------------------------------+
| Tables_in_test_group_replication |
+-----------------------------------+
| first_table |
+-----------------------------------+
1 row in set (0.01 sec)

mysql> select * from first_table;
+---------------+----------------+
| first_column | second_column |
+---------------+----------------+
| 1 | Albert |
+---------------+----------------+
1 row in set (0.00 sec)
```

You can follow the same steps and add one more member to the group. You will need to change the bold lines given in the server2.cnf and create server3.cnf and change the relevant values.

Once you have finished, there will be three servers configured and running the group replication. Once all three servers are configured, you can test whether the database tables that were created on the primary server have been replicated:

```
mysql> SELECT * FROM performance_schema.replication_group_members;
+------------------------------+---------------------------------------------+--------
-------+--------------+----------------+---------------+-----------------+
| CHANNEL_NAME | MEMBER_ID | MEMBER_HOST | MEMBER_PORT | MEMBER_STATE |
MEMBER_ROLE | MEMBER_VERSION |
+------------------------------+---------------------------------------------+--------
-------+--------------+----------------+---------------+-----------------+
| group_replication_applier | 23b6644a-f6eb-11e8-9d31-00ff461ae7f1 |
localhost | 24801 | ONLINE | PRIMARY | 8.0.13 |
| group_replication_applier | 30b1afea-f6eb-11e8-8019-00ff461ae7f1 |
localhost | 24802 | ONLINE | SECONDARY | 8.0.13 |
| group_replication_applier | 3dec75f0-f6eb-11e8-bd27-00ff461ae7f1 |
localhost| 24803 | ONLINE | SECONDARY | 8.0.13 |
+------------------------------+---------------------------------------------+--------
------+--------------+----------------+---------------+-----------------+
3 rows in set (0.00 sec)
```

The state of the members should be online. And you should be able to verify the table we created on the secondary databases.

For multi-primary deployment, for the bootstrap node use the `group_replication_single_primary_mode=OFF` variable and repeat the same procedure.

Monitoring group replication

To monitor the group replication progress, MySQL has provided several views that provide a lot of built-in statistics so that we can monitor the health of the group replication across members.

Replication_group_members

This view contains all members currently part of the replication group. For any member to get information about all group members, we can query this table for up-to-date information.

It contains the following information related to a member:

- Channel name
- ID
- Host
- Port
- State (`ONLINE`, `RECOVERING`, `ERROR`, `UNREACHABLE`)
- Role (`PRIMARY`, `SECONDARY`)
- Version (MySQL version)

replication_group_member_stats

This table contains statistics for two processes: `certifier` and `applier`. It is helpful to maintain flow control for group replication for every member in the group. The stats related to the transactions, which are checked for conflict, need to be applied helps the `certifier` process to manage its workload. As well as transactions that are certified but need to be executed on local helps `applier` process to manage workloads.

For each member of the group, it tries to keep the following information:

- `Count_transactions_in_queue`
- `Count_transactions_checked`
- `Count_conflict_detected`
- `Count_transactions_rows_validating`
- `Transaction_committed_all_members` (periodic update)
- `Last_conflict_free_transaction`
- `Count_transactions_remote_in_applier_queue`
- `Count_transactions_remote_applied`
- `Count_transactions_local_proposed`
- `Count_transactions_local_rollback`

This information is used to decide the flow control for group replication. This can also help us decide whether any member is applying the changes very slowly, and then all the members can agree to remove the member from the group until it recovers so that the whole group doesn't get slowed down.

Replication_connection_status

This table keeps track of transactions received from the group, but it still needs to apply: `received_transaction_set` keeps track of them.

Replication_applier_status

This table also has similar information to `replication_connection_status`. This table also keeps the data if transactions need to be retried. And, if there is any delay, which is specified for the applier.

Server state

The following show the status of the server:

- `ONLINE`: The member is fully up-to date and ready to execute transactions.
- `RECOVERING`: The member is currently going through a recovery process. Once it gets all the updates, it goes online
- `OFFLINE`: The plugin loaded by the member does not belong to any group

- ERROR: If there is an error during the recovery phase, the server goes to this state
- UNREACHABLE: Local failure detector detects whether it is crashed or unreachable

Limitations of group replication

The following is a list of limitations for group replication:

- Group replication works on top of a GTID-based replication, and it depends on transactions. So, we need tables with the InnoDB storage engine, which has transaction support.
- CREATE TABLE...SELECT statements are not allowed, because the binlog_format maybe different on the master and slave. If the format is set to STATEMENT, the binary log will have one transaction with one GTID. If the format is set to ROW, the CREATE_TABLE..SELECT statement would result as two transactions with two GTIDs.
- When the binary log format is set to STATEMENT, the creation of temporary tables and dropping temporary tables cannot be used inside transactions, functions, or triggers when we use GTID-based replication with auto commit set to 1. From MySQL 8.0.13, if the binary log format is set to ROW or MIXED, we can use these statements.
- All of the statements which can cause GTID-based replication to fail need to be prevented from execution. To do that, just set the --enforce-gtid-- consistency option.
- Skipping the transactions on the slave is not supported while using GTID-based replication.
- When GTIDs are enabled for the mysql_upgrade, do not enable binary logging.
- Replication event checksums should be set to none, as this is one of the design limitations.
- The certification process cannot take into account gap locks, table locks, and named locks. As details about it are only available to the server on which it is running, the transaction and it cannot be accessed outside InnoDB.
- When you use the SERIALIZABLE isolation level, group replication refuses to commit the transaction; thus, it is not supported in multi-primary groups by default.
- There is a risk of using concurrent DML and DDL statements for the same object on different servers.

- If concurrent writes are happening to multiple members of the group, there are chances of conflict for those tables for which we have defined CASCADING foreign key constraints.
- If a transaction cannot be copied between group members within a span of five seconds, then it fails, so we should avoid large transactions.
- In multi-primary mode, the SELECT For...Update statement can become deadlocked, as the locks are not shared across the members.
- Global replication filters risk getting to a consistent state. So, it is advised that they should not be used.

Group replication security

To secure a group of members, we have three options:

- Whitelisting IP addresses of members
- Communicating over SSL
- Operating group replication over a **virtual private network (VPN)**

IP address whitelist

A group replication plugin has a configuration option group_replication_ip_whitelist. If you set this option on server 1, then when server 2 is establishing a connection to server 1, it accepts/rejects the connection. By default, it sets the whitelist to the private networks that the server has interface on. We can specify host names, IP addresses, and **Classless Inter-Domain Routing (CIDR)** notation, separated by a comma. IPV6 addresses and hostname resolving to IPV6 addresses are not supported:

```
mysql> SET GLOBAL group_replication_ip_whitelist="1.1.1.2/24";
```

When we have set a specific IP addresses on a whitelist, we need to take care when a reconfiguration of the group happens, as, generally, we whitelist IP addresses on the bootstrap machine. When the bootstrap machine itself is down, we need to make sure to change the whitelist accordingly.

SSL

To make sure that the connections on which members of the group communicate, we can set up SSL certificates to make it secure. We can do so by setting the following variables. Group communication connections as well as recovery connections are secured using SSL. At the time of joining the group while set up, or in recovery process, we set up a user who has InnoDB REPLICATION SLAVE permission. We have to set up the user for SSL using the following commands:

```
mysql> SET SQL_LOG_BIN=0;
mysql> CREATE USER 'rec_ssl_user'@'%' REQUIRE SSL;
mysql> GRANT replication slave ON *.* TO 'rec_ssl_user'@'%';
mysql> SET SQL_LOG_BIN=1;
```

On the server which is joining the group:

```
mysql> SET GLOBAL group_replication_recovery_use_ssl=1;
mysql> SET GLOBAL group_replication_recovery_ssl_ca='../cert.pem';
mysql> SET GLOBAL group_replication_recovery_ssl_cert='../client-cert.pem';
mysql> SET GLOBAL group_replication_recovery_ssl_key='../client-key.pem';
```

And by configuring the recovery channel to use the credentials of the user that requires the secure connection:

```
mysql> CHANGE MASTER TO MASTER_USER="rec_ssl_user" FOR CHANNEL
"group_replication_recovery";
mysql > START GROUP_REPLICATION;
```

The Group_replication_ssl_mode variable accepts the following:

- DISABLED
- REQUIRED
- VERIFY_CA
- VERIFY_IDENTITY

Here is a sample set of the configurations for SSL:

```
[mysqld]
ssl_ca = "cacert.pem"
ssl_capath = "/.../ca_directory"
ssl_cert = "server-cert.pem"
ssl_cipher = "DHE-RSA-AEs256-SHA"
ssl_crl = "crl-server-revoked.crl"
ssl_crlpath = "/.../crl_directory"
ssl_key = "server-key.pem"
group_replication_ssl_mode= REQUIRED
```

VPN

As group replication relies on an IPV4 socket to establish connections among servers, we can operate our group replication on a VPN and secure it.

Operations on an online group

There will be times when we will require to run and manage an online group. It can be due to a maintenance activity or to an unscheduled downtime. We can make changes to the online group while it is serving the live traffic, and we can do so using a set of user defined functions that are packaged and installed with the group replication plugin, and the prerequisite is that all members of the group must be running MySQL 8.0.13 or later.

To use **user-defined functions** (**UDFs**), we need to connect to a member of the running group and issue the UDF with the SELECT statement. The plugin will process the action and its parameters and the coordinator sends it to all members that are visible to the member where we have issued the UDF. If the action is accepted, all members execute the action and send a termination message when completed. Once all members declare the action as finished, the function returns to the client. The following are some important things you should take care with while running UDFs:

- You can issue the configuration operations on any group member
- All members must be in the ONLINE state
- No member can join during a configuration change
- There can be only one configuration at once
- You cannot use configuration functions on mixed-version groups

Changing groups primary members on a single primary group; you can set the following:

```
mysql> SELECT issue group_replicaiton_set_as_primary( member_uuid ) ;
```

When you are setting a server as primary you need to take care about the asynchronous channel; if that is running on the server, no switch is allowed until that is stopped.

You can also check progress by issuing the following:

```
Select event_name, work_completed, work_estimated FROM
performance_schema.events_stages_current WHERE event_name LIKE
"%stage/group_rpl%" \G;
--------------------------------------------------
Event_name|stage/group_rpl/primary election:Waiting for members to turn on
super_read_only |
|Work_completed | 3 |
|Work_estimated | 5 |
```

Changing the group mode

We can switch from single-primary to multi primary and vice versa. Use the `grop_replication_switch_to_single_primary_mode()` UDF to change a group running in multi-primary mode to `single_primary_mode`:

```
mysql> SELECT group_replication_switch_to_single_primary_mode(Optional
UUID);
```

If we do not pass any argument, the election of the primary will happen based on weights assigned to the members or the UUID lexicographic order. And if you want a specific member to be primary, then you need to specify the UUID of the member.

Use the `group_replication_switch_to_multi_primary_mode()` UDF to change a group running in single-primary mode to `multi_primary_mode` by issuing the following command:

```
mysql> SELECT group_replicaiton_switch_to_multi_primary_mode()
```

Tuning recovery

When a member joins the group, there can be two scenarios: either it's a new member or it's a member connecting after some time. In both of these cases, the new member might lag behind the other members. The newly joined member is assigned a state RECOVERING, and it tries to select a server from existing online members in the group called a donor. The recovery process now has been extended to detecting the following:

- **Purged data scenario**: If the donor contains purged data that is required for recovery, it throws an error and tries to elect a new donor

- **Duplicated data**: If the server joining the group already contains data that the data is coming from the donor during the recovery process, it
    - throws an error
    - **Other errors**: If the
- recovery thread itself fails or any other error occurs

Use `group_replication_recovery_retry_count` to specify the number of retries. It applies for each donor it connects to.

Use `group_recplication_recovery_reconnect_interval` to make the recovery process sleep between donor connection attempts. This interval applies once the joining servers tries all of the donors in the view.

Combining group replication versions

In a scenario where we have multiple versions of MySQL installed on members, there are some constraints for the group replication to work, and all versions should be compatible in the same group.

You can identify the members and their MySQL version in the same member view:

```
mysql> select MEMBER_HOST, MEMBER_PORT, MEMBER_VERSION from
performance_schema.replication_group_members;
+---------------+---------------+-----------------+
| member_host   | member_port   | member_version  |
+---------------+---------------+-----------------+
| slavedb.com   | 3306          | 8.0.13          |
+---------------+---------------+-----------------+
```

There are some rules when different major MySQL versions are used:

- You cannot join a member to a group when it is running a major version than the major version older that the existing group members are running. For a group member running MySQL version 8.0.13, you cannot add another member with MySQL 5.7 installed on it.
- You can join a member to a group if it is running a major version newer than the major version that the existing group members are running. If group members are running MySQL 5.7, you can add a member running MySQL version 8.0. But that member will be running in read-only mode. It is not advisable to keep the newer major version MySQL in read-write mode when writing is also allowed on an older major version.

For a minor version difference, it is OK to set up a multi-primary replication group.

Performance tuning

Group communication is a plugin. One of the key components of a group replication plugin is **group communication thread** (**GCT**), which runs in loop when the plugin is loaded. It handles messages from members of the group as well as the plugin, and it is responsible for failure detection tasks, keeping tasks alive, and transaction delivery in and out from/to the server/group. The thread waits for incoming messages in a queue. When there are no messages, the GCT waits.

Use the `group_replication_poll_spin_loops` option to make the active thread wait. This makes the thread loop; it does nothing relevant for the configured number of loops, before actually polling the queue for the next message:

```
mysql> SET GLOBAL group_replication_poll_spin_loops = 10000;
```

Configuring this wait to be a little longer (doing an active wait) before actually going to sleep may prove to be beneficial in some cases. This is because the alternative is for the operating system to switch out the GCT from the processor and do a context switch.

Message compression

The network plays a very important role, both in terms of latency and bandwidth. Message compression is a feature of the group communication system API, where we can specify the ratio of the message compression. It can provide up to 30-40% throughput improvement at the group communication level. It is required because group replication topology is a TCP peer-to-peer interconnection between *n* participants on the group who send and receive the same amount of data *n* times.

Compression happens in a group communication engine. Before the data is handed over to a GCT, it happens within the context of the MySQL session thread. Transaction payloads may be compressed before being sent out to the group and decompressed when received. By default, compression is enabled.

LZ4 is the algorithm used for compression. Compression is enabled by default with a threshold of 1,000,000 bytes.

Use `group_replication_compression_threshold` to set the compression threshold:

```
mysql> STOP GROUP_REPLICATION;
mysql> SET group_replication_compression_threshold = 2097152;
mysql> START GROUP_REPLICATION;
```

To disable compression, set it to 0.

Flow control

For consistency, a majority of the servers should agree on a state change for any given data. In that case, it might happen that some servers lag behind a lot, and it has to continuously play the game of syncing transactions from other servers, which are serving transactions very fast. Due to the slowness of some of the servers, the entire cluster may be slow. To make sure that this situation doesn't occur, group replication has come up with a flow control mechanism.

In this mechanism, the servers that can execute more quickly reduce their speed to allow the slow servers to catch up quickly, rather than burdening them continuously. When the group replication flow control mode is set to QUOTA, and when the faster node realizes that one of the servers is lagging behind and has reached a threshold, new transaction writes get throttled based on a QUOTA that is calculated based on the number of transactions completed in the last second and that is reduced by subtracting the over-the-quota message from last period.

In group replication, every member sends statistics about the `applier` queue and the `certifier` queue:

```
Flow Control - configuration variables:
group_replication_flow_control_applier_threshold - 25000
group_replication_flow_control_certifier_threshold - 25000
group_replication_flow_control_hold_percent - 10
group_replication_flow_control_max_quota - 0
group_replication_flow_control_member_quota_percent - 0
group_replication_flow_control_min_quota - 0
group_replication_flow_control_min_recovery_data - 0
group_replication_flow_control_mode - QUOTA
group_replication_flow_control_period - 1
group_replication_flow_control_release_percent - 50
```

The following diagram shows the flow control on writers:

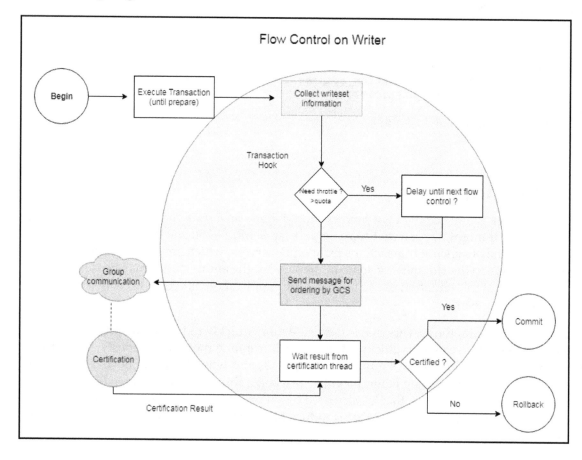

The following diagram shows the flow control on all members:

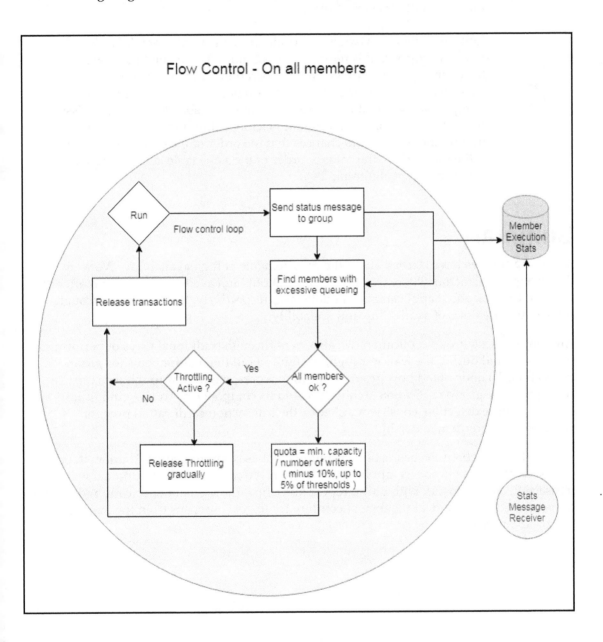

It is not advisable to run DDL statements on multiple servers at the same time in a multi-primary group.

Caution: Although MySQL has come up with atomic data definition statement support, it is referred to as atomic DDL. It combines data dictionary updates, storage engine operations, and binary log writes associated with DDL operation into a single, atomic transaction. For example, say we want to add two columns to a table. For that, if we issue two statements from two different machines simultaneously in a multi-primary mode, there are chances that the order of the execution will not be the same. Thus, the column order of the same table across different servers might be different.

Summary

In this chapter, we have learned about the requirements of high availability. We went through external factors where we need to think about high availability first, and after that, we need to think about applications and databases respectively. We also went through some of the use cases of availability and scalability.

After introducing group replication, we also went through traditional ways of performing replication, and during the walk-through, we figured out the requirements for group replication. To understand how group replication works, we went through the core concepts of the group replication architecture and its components: group communication systems, failure detection, consistency checks, the transaction certification process, writesets, and group membership.

We also learned about the basics of distributed database requirements and understood components such as proposer, applier, and learner. We compared the traditional ways transactions used to work with group replications, how they remain optimistic and execute transactions locally, and, at the time of commit, try to get consensus from the majority of the group members.

We discussed group replication performance tuning, and security as well, and we went through flow control in detail, where, if one of the servers lags, flow control helps the lagging server recover and throttles transactions on write. We went through how to configure, manage, and monitor the group replication topology, and we highlighted commands to run and manage group replication topology members and how to change deployment modes from single-primary mode to multi-primary mode.

During the course of the chapter, we went through various MySQL system variables that can help configure MySQL in a high-performance way. Finally, we also checked the limitations of using group replication and GTID-based replication.

I hope this chapter has provided sufficient insights regarding MySQL's group replication plugin and enough information regarding managing a high-availability cluster. In the next chapter, we will learn about the InnoDB cluster in MySQL 8.

InnoDB Cluster in MySQL 8.0

8

In the previous chapter, we learned about MySQL Group Replication. We discussed Group Replication internals and also looked at its step-by-step configuration. We went through all of the important MySQL variables that can be used to fine-tune the performance of Group Replication. In this chapter, we shall focus on MySQL InnoDB, concentrating on the following topics:

- What InnoDB cluster is
- InnoDB cluster requirements
- Creating a MySQL InnoDB cluster
- Routers in InnoDB cluster
- Managing InnoDB cluster
- InnoDB cluster limitations
- Storage engines

We highly recommend that you refer to Chapter 7, *Group Replication in MySQL 8.0*, before proceeding with this chapter, to have a thorough understanding of Group Replication.

What is InnoDB cluster?

InnoDB cluster is a complete, high-availability solution provided by MySQL. InnoDB cluster uses a Group Replication mechanism at its heart to replicate data; on top of that, InnoDB cluster provides a built-in failover mechanism, as illustrated in the following diagram:

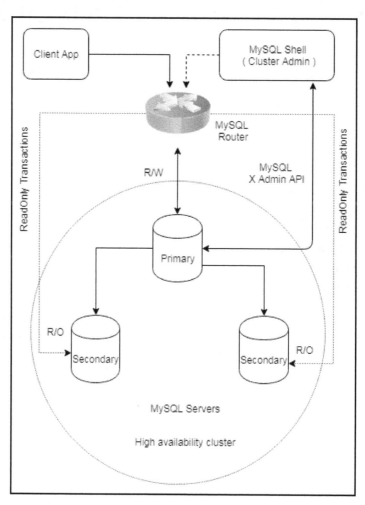

To ensure high-availability, a seamless failover mechanism and the ability to load-balance are essential. MySQL provides this with MySQL Router. The router is an important component in InnoDB cluster but is a separate component that needs to be downloaded and installed. The router acts as middleware that provides routing between clients and servers. InnoDB cluster can operate in multi-primary mode or single-primary mode. In the case of primary server failure, applications do not need to manage the failover logic, as it is automatically taken care of by MySQL Router. It acts as lightweight middleware that routes READWRITE and READONLY transactions, as well as appropriately routing data requests to either primary or slave servers. This functionality can help to achieve scalability at the MySQL level.

MySQL Router should be installed near to applications or on the same host as applications. After installation, MySQL Router fetches the metadata or configuration from InnoDB cluster and caches it locally. If the availability of servers on InnoDB cluster changes, router updates its local data to reflect any changes where necessary.

Application connections that are shut down are disconnected from the MySQL server and then moved to a closed state. Note that applications are required to reconnect, to re-establish the connection, as the router will not take care of such a failover.

MySQL Router 8.0 supports both MySQL 5.7 and MySQL 8.0. If you are using an older version, such as 2.0 or 2.1, you must upgrade to MySQL Router 8.0.

MySQL Shell is an advanced client and code editor for MySQL server. You can install MySQL Shell separately. Refer to the official documentation of MySQL Shell for more information.

In addition to existing SQL functionality, MySQL Shell provides scripting capabilities for JavaScript and Python. Shell also uses X DevAPI, which is helpful for developers who want to use MySQL as a document store or RDBMS. Shell also includes X AdminAPI for architects who want to manage MySQL InnoDB cluster and do not want to configure and manage everything manually.

By using X AdminAPI, we can do the following:

- Configure, create, and check the status of groups
- Configure, add members, and remove members
- Create sandbox environments for testing

Shell also provides us with a way to configure colors, to customize the look and feel of an application.

Let's now deep dive into these programs and explore which APIs will be useful for us going forward.

By now, you should have downloaded the latest versions of MySQL server, MySQL Shell, and MySQL Router. Let's first try to configure a sandbox environment before going through the production setup. We'll start with identifying cluster requirements.

InnoDB cluster requirements

InnoDB cluster uses **Group Replication** to replicate data across various machines, so we need to make sure that our server instances meet the minimum requirements necessary; they are as follows:

- Python Version 2.7 or higher is required for MySQL Shell to work, and is required for all machines that are part of a group; for Windows, MySQL Shell bundles Python
- MySQL Router, MySQL Shell, and MySQL server should already be downloaded and installed on the servers before configuring InnoDB cluster
- InnoDB must be used as a storage engine for all tables

Please refer to `Chapter 7`, *Group Replication in MySQL 8.0*, for more information on the preceding requirements.

Let's now configure a testing scenario to understand these components and how they work.

Installing MySQL Shell

First, download the zip file for MySQL Shell for Windows (Windows X86, 64-bit) from the official MySQL website, `http://dev.mysql.com/downloads/shell/`. Extract it, and you should see the `mysqlsh.exe` file in the `bin` folder. Configure the environment and path variables so that they can access `mysqlsh.exe` from the command prompt.

For Linux distributions, either the MySQL APT repository or the MySQL Yum repository is required. Make sure you select MySQL 8.0 as the release. Please follow the official MySQL documentation for more details.

You can install MySQL Shell with the following command:

```
sudo apt-get update
sudo apt-get install mysql-shell
```

If you already have a MySQL APT Repository configuration, use the following commands:

```
> sudo apt-get update
> sudo apt-get install mysql-apt-config
```

Make sure you choose MySQL 8.0 as the release series before running the following command:

```
> sudo apt-get install mysql-shell
```

For Yum repositories, use the following command. Configure the MySQL Yum repository with the new release package, `mysql80-community-release`. Once complete, run the following command:

```
> sudo yum install mysql-shell
```

How to use MySQL Shell

You can use the `mysqlsh` command to initiate MySQL Shell, provided you have configured the environment and path variables on Windows. If not, you can open the command prompt and navigate to the `bin` directory after the Shell download has been extracted.

MySQL Shell provides two ways for connecting to a MySQL server, one of which includes the use of the **X Protocol**.

Some of the most important commands that you will use to interact with MySQL Shell are as follows:

Command	Alias	Description
\help	\h or \?	This prints help about Shell
\quit	\q or \exit	Exits MySQL Shell
\js		JavaScript execution mode
\py		Python execution mode
\sql		SQL mode
\connect		Connects to the MySQL server
\use		Switches to schema
\source		Executes a script
...	...	...

Note that if you use `mysqlsh` as a command, it will simply open a window with a prompt.

As seen in the preceding table, the `help` command can be used in a number of different scenarios. The command is divided into hierarchies, to provide you with specific information. The main categories are as follows:

- **AdminAPI**: This is a DBA global object and cluster administration API
- **Shell commands**: These list the available shell commands
- **ShellAPI**: This contains the global shell and UTIL objects, as well as the MySQL module
- **SQL syntax**: This offers syntax help with SQL commands
- **X DevAPI**: This is a `mysqlx` module that uses MySQL as a document store

When the shell starts, you will see the following global objects, already initialized and available for interaction in both `js` and `py` mode:

GLOBAL OBJECTS For "js" mode and "py" mode	
dba	Used for InnoDB cluster administration.
mysql	Support for connecting to MySQL servers using the classic MySQL protocol.
mysqlx	Used to work with X Protocol sessions using the MySQL X DevAPI.
shell	Gives access to general purpose functions and properties.
sys	Gives access to system specific parameters.
util	Global object that groups miscellaneous tools like upgrade checker and JSON import.

The commands available include the following:

- The DBA global object and the classes available with AdminAPI
- The `mysqlx` module and the classes available with DevAPI
- The MySQL module and the global objects and classes available with ShellAPI
- The functions and properties of the classes exposed by the APIs
- The available shell commands
- The command line, which invokes built-in shell functions without entering interactive mode

Try out the following commands and then check the output yourself in the interactive shell:

```
MYSQL JS>\status

MYSQL JS>\? AdminAPI

MySQL JS>\? dba.checkInstanceConfiguration
```

You should now understand how to use MySQL Shell and how to browse the API, available functions, and global objects and their properties. Feel free to play around with the commands for greater understanding. These commands will help you when configuring an InnoDB cluster.

To connect to an existing, and running, MySQL server from MySQL Shell, use the following command while initializing the MySQL Shell:

```
> mysqlsh --mysql -u username -h host
```

This is classic MySQL protocol:

```
> mysqlsh --uri myuser@localhost:4406 --user overriddenuser
```

The preceding command uses the X Protocol to connect to MySQL. Parameters passed in the URI will be taken as base, and any extra parameters will override the parameters provided in the URI string.

If you require a database connection when programming in JavaScript, use the following command:

```
MYSQL SQL>\js
```

To switch to JavaScript mode, input the following:

```
MYSQL JS> var
session_x=mysqlx.getSession('javascriptuser@mysql.domain.com:4406', '');

MYSQL JS> session_x

<Session:javascriptuser@mysql.domain.com:4406>
```

The preceding command uses the `mysqlx` global object and the X Protocol to connect you to the MySQL server.

The following example shows you how to create a `ClassicSession`:

```
MYSQL JS> var
session_classic=mysql.getClassicSession('javascriptuser@mysql.domain.com:44
06', '');
 MYSQL JS> session_classic
 <ClassicSession:javascriptuser@mysql.domain.com:4406>
 MYSQL JS>
```

Also in JavaScript mode, you can use the following command to connect to MySQL:

```
MYSQL JS> shell.connect('mysqlx://javascriptuser@mysql.domain.com')
Creating an X protocol session to 'javascriptuser@mysql.domain.com'
Please provide the password for 'javascriptuser@mysql.domain.com':
Save password for 'javascriptuser@mysql.domain.com'? [Y]es/[N]o/Ne[v]er
(default No): no
Fetching schema names for autocompletion... Press ^C to stop.
Your MySQL connection id is 13 (X protocol)
Server version: 8.0.13 MySQL Community Server - GPL
No default schema selected; type \use <schema> to set one.
<Session:javascriptuser@mysql.domain.com:4406>
```

You should now understand how to use MySQL Shell, something that will come in handy for JavaScript and Python developers.

Installing an InnoDB cluster

Before we move on to production setup, we need to test an InnoDB cluster in a sandbox environment. Fortunately, MySQL provides easy-to-follow ways of doing this. We can test an InnoDB cluster locally and figure out how everything works before using it. In this section, we will cover both types of installations: sandbox and production.

MySQL InnoDB cluster for a sandbox environment

We have MySQL Server and MySQL Shell installed on one machine. We have ensured that MySQL Shell is able to connect to MySQL Server. So, in this section, we will create an InnoDB cluster in a sandbox environment.

Here, we will use XAdminAPI, which has built-in features that configure an InnoDB cluster on a local machine, allowing us to set up and play around with the program. Note that this method should not be used to create a production environment.

First, we need to use DBA as a global variable from the MySQL Shell AdminAPI, as follows:

```
> mysqlsh
MYSQL JS > dba.deploySandboxInstance( 4410 )
```

A new MySQL sandbox instance will be created on this host in C:\Users\john\MySQL\mysql-sandboxes\4410.

> The sandbox instances are only suitable for deploying and running on your local machine for testing purposes; they are not accessible from external networks.

Please enter a MySQL root password for the new instance:

1. Deploy a new MySQL instance
2. Instance mysql.domain.com:4410 successfully deployed and started
3. Use shell.connect('root@mysql.domain.com:4410'); to connect to the instance

Make sure that MySQL binary is accessible to MySQL Shell. If not, configure the relevant PATH variables. By default, the sandbox is created in a directory named $HOME/mysql-sandboxes/port on Unix systems. For Microsoft Windows systems, the directory is %userprofile%\MySQL\mysql-sandboxes\port.

When the preceding command executes, it asks for a password. Use the same password throughout for simplicity when deploying a test environment. For a production environment, remember to use a dedicated username and password for each MySQL Server instance.

Let's now create two more sandbox instances with the following commands:

```
mysql-js> dba.deploySandboxInstance(4420)
mysql-js> dba.deploySandboxInstance(4430)
```

The preparation is complete, and we have the three required machines set up and running, so let's now configure an InnoDB cluster using MySQL Shell.

To do so, we need to use the first machine as a seed machine to initiate a cluster. So, let's connect and create one cluster with the following commands:

```
MYSQL JS> shell.connect('root@mysql.domain.com:4410')

Creating a session to 'root@mysql.domain.com:4410'
```

```
Please provide the password for 'root@mysql.domain.com:4410':
Save password for 'root@mysql.domain.com:4410'? [Y]es/[N]o/Ne[v]er (default
No): no
Fetching schema names for autocompletion... Press ^C to stop.
Your MySQL connection id is 11
Server version: 8.0.13 MySQL Community Server - GPL
```

As no default schema is selected, type \use <schema> to set one and input the following:

```
<ClassicSession:root@mysql.domain.com:4410>
MYSQL JS> var cluster = dba.createCluster('myFirstCluster')
```

A new InnoDB cluster should now have been created on the instance
'root@mysql.domain.com:4410':

```
Validating instance at mysql.domain.com:4410...
Instance detected as a sandbox.
Please note that sandbox instances are only suitable for deploying test
clusters for use within the same host.
This instance reports its own address as <HOSTNAME>
Instance configuration is suitable.
Creating InnoDB cluster 'myCluster' on 'root@mysql.domain.com:4410'...
Adding Seed Instance...
```

The cluster has now been successfully created! Use Cluster.addInstance() to add
MySQL instances. Remember that at least three instances are needed for the cluster to be
able to withstand up to one server failure.

If you run the following command, you will get the cluster's configuration description:

```
MySQL [localhost ssl] JS> cluster.describe()
{
"clusterName": "myFirstCluster",
"defaultReplicaSet": {
"name": "default",
"topology": [
{
"address": "mysql.domain.com:4410",
"label": "mysql.domain.com:4410",
"role": "HA"
}
]
}
}
```

You can also use the following command:

```
MySQL [localhost ssl] JS> cluster.status()

{
"clusterName": "myFirstCluster",
"defaultReplicaSet": {
"name": "default",
"primary": "mysql.domain.com:4410",
"ssl": "REQUIRED",
"status": "OK_NO_TOLERANCE",
"statusText": "Cluster is NOT tolerant to any failures.",
"topology": {
"mysql.domain.com:4410": {
"address": "mysql.domain.com:4410",
"mode": "R/W",
"readReplicas": {},
"role": "HA",
"status": "ONLINE"
}
}
},
"groupInformationSourceMember": "mysql://root@mysql.domain.com:4410"
}
```

Now let's add two more instances to the same cluster with the following command:

```
MYSQL JS> cluster.addInstance('root@mysql.domain.com:4420')
```

Here, a new instance will be added to the InnoDB cluster. Depending on the amount of data on the cluster, this might take anything from a few seconds to several hours:

```
Adding instance to the cluster ...
Please provide the password for 'root@mysql.domain.com:4420':
Save password for 'root@mysql.domain.com:4420'? [Y]es/[N]o/Ne[v]er (default
No): no
Validating instance at mysql.domain.com:4420...
Instance detected as a sandbox.
Please note that sandbox instances are only suitable for deploying test
clusters for use within the same host.
This instance reports its own address as <Hostname>.
Instance configuration is suitable.
The instance 'root@mysql.domain.com:4420' was successfully added to the
cluster.

MySQL [localhost ssl] JS> cluster.status()
{
"clusterName": "myCluster",
```

```
"defaultReplicaSet": {
"name": "default",
"primary": "mysql.domain.com:4410",
"ssl": "REQUIRED",
"status": "OK_NO_TOLERANCE",
"statusText": "Cluster is NOT tolerant to any failures.",
"topology": {
"mysql.domain.com:4410": {
"address": "mysql.domain.com:4410",
"mode": "R/W",
"readReplicas": {},
"role": "HA",
"status": "ONLINE"
},
"mysql.domain.com:4420": {
"address": "mysql.domain.com:4420",
"mode": "R/O",
"readReplicas": {},
"role": "HA",
"status": "ONLINE"
}
}
},
"groupInformationSourceMember": "mysql://root@mysql.domain.com:4410"
}
```

Currently, the cluster cannot tolerate failure. To amend this, we need to add one more instance to the cluster, as follows:

```
MYSQL JS> cluster.addInstance('root@mysql.domain.com:4430')
{
"clusterName": "myCluster",
"defaultReplicaSet": {
"name": "default",
"primary": "mysql.domain.com:4410",
"ssl": "REQUIRED",
"status": "OK",
"statusText": "Cluster is ONLINE and can tolerate up to ONE failure.",
"topology": {
"mysql.domain.com:4410": {
"address": "mysql.domain.com:4410",
"mode": "R/W",
"readReplicas": {},
"role": "HA",
"status": "ONLINE"
},
"mysql.domain.com:4420": {
"address": "mysql.domain.com:4420",
```

```
  "mode": "R/O",
  "readReplicas": {},
  "role": "HA",
  "status": "ONLINE"
},
  "mysql.domain.com:4430": {
  "address": "mysql.domain.com:4430",
  "mode": "R/O",
  "readReplicas": {},
  "role": "HA",
  "status": "ONLINE"
}
}
},
  "groupInformationSourceMember": "mysql://root@mysql.domain.com:4410"
}
```

As you can see in the preceding output, our cluster's status is now ONLINE and it is able to tolerate one failure.

Let's now move on and test our installation. At this point, you should see the following command prompt:

```
MYSQL [localhost ssl] JS>\sql
MYSQL [localhost ssl] SQL> create database my_first_database;
Query OK, 1 row affected (0.3625 sec)
```

At the moment, we are connected to an instance running on 4410. Let's connect to a second database to see whether this database is present, using the following code:

```
MYSQL [localhost ssl] SQL>\js
MYSQL JS> shell.connect('root@mysql.domain.com:4420')
MYSQL JS>\sql
MYSQL SQL> show databases;
+-------------------------------+
| Database |
+-------------------------------+
| information_schema |
| my_first_database |
| mysql |
| mysql_innodb_cluster_metadata |
| performance_schema |
| sys |
+-------------------------------+
6 rows in set (0.0032 sec)
```

As you can see from the preceding snippet, `my_first_database` has been replicated:

```
MySQL [localhost ssl] SQL> select * from
performance_schema.replication_group_members;
+-------------------------+-------------------------------------+-------
-------+-------------+---------------+-------------+-----------------+
| CHANNEL_NAME | MEMBER_ID | MEMBER_HOST | MEMBER_PORT | MEMBER_STATE |
MEMBER_ROLE | MEMBER_VERSION |
+-------------------------+-------------------------------------+-------
-------+-------------+---------------+-------------+-----------------+
| group_replication_applier | 657632bc-fd99-11e8-8c11-00ff461ae7f1 |
mysql.domain.com | 4420 | ONLINE | SECONDARY | 8.0.13 |
| group_replication_applier | 7831bde5-fd99-11e8-a73c-00ff461ae7f1 |
mysql.domain.com | 4430 | ONLINE | SECONDARY | 8.0.13 |
| group_replication_applier | cf0519f6-fd98-11e8-a9a4-00ff461ae7f1 |
mysql.domain.com | 4410 | ONLINE | PRIMARY | 8.0.13 |
+-------------------------+-------------------------------------+-------
-------+-------------+---------------+-------------+-----------------+
```

Our InnoDB cluster is now online! In `Chapter 7`, *Group Replication in MySQL 8.0*, we configured all of the settings manually, but now the API is making our lives a lot easier.

Let's now try to create a table in the same prompt with the following command:

```
MySQL [localhost ssl] SQL> use my_first_database;
Default schema set to `my_first_database`.
Fetching table and column names from `my_first_database` for auto-
completion... Press ^C to stop.
MySQL [localhost ssl/my_first_database] SQL> create table test(t1 int);
ERROR: 1290 (HY000): The MySQL server is running with the --super-read-only
option so it cannot execute this statement
```

Oops! As you can see from the preceding output, we tried to write to a secondary server that can only accept read-only transactions. This is because the default sandbox configuration deploys the instances in single primary mode automatically. If we had run this on the first server, which is running on `4410`, it would have been successful.

We have now had a play around with MySQL Shell and Group Replication in a sandbox environment. In the next section, we are going to look at deploying an InnoDB cluster in a production environment using Admin API, as well as how to configure the router.

Note that there is an alternative way of deploying a sandbox environment—using Docker images. You can easily find Docker images for MySQL Shell, MySQL Router, and MySQL server.

InnoDB cluster in a production environment

In a production environment, there are usually separate instances or virtual machines in a connected IPV4 environment where Group Replication is configured among the servers. Before we jump into using AdminAPI to configure InnoDB cluster ourselves, however, we first need to set up the necessary components of MySQL.

Let's assume that we want the minimum cluster requirements in InnoDB, which is at least three nodes. To configure and manage the cluster, we need to install MySQL Shell on one of the boxes that have access to all three MySQL instances. We also need to configure the MySQL Router component to load-balance data requests. As it is advised that we install Router with the application server, we will use one router server in this example.

The following table illustrates the components of each server and lists which virtual machine they have been assigned to:

Role	IP	Host	OS	MySQL username
Router	201.200.199.1	Router	CentOS7	router
Shell	201.200.199.2	Shell	CentOS7	admin
Primary Node 1	201.200.199.3	primaryone	CentOS7	firstnodeuser
Primary Node 2	201.200.199.4	primarysecond	CentOS7	secondnodeuser
Primary Node 3	201.200.199.5	primarythird	CentOS7	thirdnodeuser

As we are using any service discovery mechanism in this example, let's now add /etc/hosts entries for the routers and MySQL nodes so they can route requests to each other. Complete the following steps:

1. On all of the servers, add the following entries to /etc/hosts. Note that we will exclude MySQL Shell:

   ```
   201.200.199.1 router
   201.200.199.3 primaryone
   201.200.199.4 primarysecond
   201.200.199.5 primarythird
   ```

2. Disable SELinux on all nodes. Edit /etc/selinux/config and set SELINUX=disabled. Save the file and reboot the instances.

3. Install mysql80-community-release on each host with rpm -Uvh https://dev.mysql.com/get/mysql80-community-release-el7-1.noarch.rpm.

4. Install MySQL Sserver 8.0 on node1, node2, and node3 with yum install mysql-community-server -y.

5. Start the MySQLd service on `primarythird`, `primarysecond`, and `primaryone` with `service mysqld start`.

6. Once started for the first time, MySQLd will generate a temporary password in the log files of primarythird, primarysecond, and primaryone, as follows:

```
> grep "temporary password" /var/log/mysqld.log
> A temporary passwordis generated for root@localhost: 12qtN2X0_B4
```

7. Copy the password.

8. Now connect to the MySQL instance using the root user and with the password, we used in the previous step.

9. Create an admin user, which will be used to set up Group Replication and administer an InnoDB cluster. Perform the following command:

```
primaryone> create user 'cluster_admin'@'%' identified by
'xxxxxxxxx' ;
Query OK, 0 rows affected (0,03 sec)
primaryone> grant all privileges on *.* to 'cluster_admin'@'%' with
grant option;
Query OK, 0 rows affected (0,07 sec)
primaryone> flush privileges;
```

10. Then, repeat this step for `primarysecond` and `primarythird`.

11. Next, stop the service on all three nodes and configure `my.cnf` for each of them. For `primaryone`, use the following input:

```
/etc/my.cnf
[mysqld]
datadir=/var/lib/mysql
socket=/var/lib/mysql/mysql.sock
log-error=/var/log/mysqld.log
pid-file=/var/run/mysqld/m
ysqld.pid
# Replication part
server_id=1
gtid_mode=ON
super-read-only=OFF
persisted_globals_load=ON
enforce_gtid_consistency=ON
master_info_repository=TABLE
relay_log_info_repository=TABLE
binlog_checksum=NONE
log_slave_updates=ON
log_bin=binlog
binlog_format=ROW
# Group replication settings
```

```
transaction_write_set_extraction=XXHASH64
loose-group_replication_group_name="aaaaaaaa-bbbb-cccc-dddd-
eeeeeeeeeeee"
loose-group_replication_start_on_boot=off
loose-group_replication_local_address= "primaryone:43061"
loose-group_replication_group_seeds=
"primaryone:43061,primarysecond:43061,primarythird:43061"
loose-group_replication_bootstrap_group=off
[mysql]
prompt=primaryone
```

For `node2`, change the following lines from the preceding snippet, keeping the other variables as they are:

```
server_id=2
loose-group_replication_local_address= "primarysecond:43061"
```

For `node3`, change the following lines from the preceding snippet, keeping the other variables as they are:

```
server_id=3
loose-group_replication_local_address= "primarythird:43061"
```

12. Now save the files and restart the `mysqld` service on `primaryone`, `primarysecond`, and `primarythird` with `root@localhost > service mysqld restart`.
13. Install MySQL Router on the router host with `yum install mysql-router -y`.
14. Install MySQL Shell on the shell host with `Yum install mysql-shell -y`.

We now have all of the required components installed on all of our machines. Next, we will connect to MySQL Shell and start configuring an InnoDB cluster!

First, we need to start `mysqlsh` on the host where we have installed MySQL Shell, using the following command:

```
[root@shell ~]# mysqlsh
MYSQL JS>
```

Let's now check all of the instances, and their configuration, using AdminAPI, as follows:

```
MYSQL JS> dba.checkInstanceConfiguration("cluster_admin@primaryone:3306")
Please provide the password for 'cluster_admin@primaryone:3306': *
Validating MySQL instance at primaryone:3306 for use in an InnoDB
cluster...
```

The specific address reported by the preceding instance is `primaryone`. By default, this address will be used for communication with different clients and other cluster members. In any other scenario, the necessary changes should be made to the `report_host` MySQL system variable:

```
Verifying compliance of existing tables with Group Replication
requirements...
No incompatible tables detected
Verifying instance configuration...
Compatibility of instance configuration with InnoDB cluster confirmed
The 'primaryone:3306' instance is now valid for InnoDB Cluster usage.
{
"status": "ok"
}
```

Repeat the same command for `primarysecond` and `primarythird`; as seen in the preceding snippet, the status should be `ok`.

Whatever configuration changes we create on MySQL nodes using AdminAPI, we need to persist them to local configuration files. The following command helps us to achieve that. If the server restarts before persisting any changes made on the InnoDB cluster, it can lose the configuration, and on a restart, the server may not join the correct group:

```
MySQL JS > dba.configureInstance("cluster_admin@primaryone:3306")
Please provide the password for 'cluster_admin@primaryone:3306': *
Configuring MySQL instance at primaryone:3306 for use in an InnoDB
cluster...
```

The specific address reported by this instance is `primarysecond`. By default, this address will be used for communication with clients and other cluster members. In any other scenario, the necessary changes should be made to the `report_host` MySQL system variable.

The `primaryone:3306` instance is now valid for InnoDB cluster usage. Repeat the same process for `primarysecond` and `primarythird`.

Now, to configure Group Replication, we can use `primaryone` as a seed member, as follows:

```
MySQL JS > shell.connect("cluster_admin@primaryone:3306")
Please enter password for 'cluster_admin@primaryone:3306': *
Launching a session to 'cluster_admin@primaryone:3306'
Fetching schema names for autocompletion... To stop, press ^C.
Your MySQL connection id is 13
Server version: 8.0.13 MySQL Community Server - GPL
```

No default schema has been selected, so type \use <schema> to set one:

```
<ClassicSession:cluster_admin@primaryone:3306>
```

Now use the following command to create the InnoDB cluster:

```
MySQL primaryone:3306 ssl JS > cluster =
dba.createCluster("myProductionCluster")
```

The preceding command will create the cluster and show you a detailed message. You can check the status of the cluster using the following command:

```
MySQL primaryone:3306 ssl JS > cluster.status()
```

Once you have checked the output, you need to add primarysecond and primarythird as additional instances using the following code:

```
MySQL node1:3306 ssl JS >
cluster.addInstance("cluster_admin@primarysecond:3306")
MySQL node1:3306 ssl JS >
cluster.addInstance("cluster_admin@primarythrid:3306")
MySQL node1:3306 ssl JS > cluster.status()
```

The preceding command will show an output similar to that seen in the sandbox environment after three instances have been added. The only difference, in this case, is that it will be a multi-primary cluster, as we have added super-read-only=OFF to the my.cnf configuration file.

Configuring the router configuration

Let's now connect to our host router and start configuration. Input the following command:

```
[root@router ~]# mysqlrouter --bootstrap cluster_admin@primaryone:3306 --
directory /opt/router
```

Please enter the MySQL password for the root; after which, you should see the following output:

```
Bootstrapping MySQL Router instance at '/opt/router'...
```

The configuration of MySQL Router is now complete, allowing you to connect to the InnoDB cluster. The following connection credentials provide more detail.

The typical MySQL protocol connections to `myCluster` are as follows:

- Read/write connections: `localhost:6446`
- Read-only connections: `localhost:6447`

The X protocol connections to `myProductionCluster` are as follows:

- Read/write connections: `localhost:64460`
- Read-only connections: `localhost:64470`

To display the configuration of a router file that has been modified after the `bootstrap` command, input the following code:

```
[root@router router]# cat /opt/router/mysqlrouter.conf
```

The file you receive should contain metadata about `mycluster`, the routing strategy for read/write connections and read-only connections, and the routing policy.

We can now move on and start `router` with the following command:

```
/opt/router/start.sh
```

Now use the following command to connect to MySQL, using MySQL Router:

```
> mysql -u root -p -h 201.200.199.1
Welcome to the MySQL monitor. Your commands should end with ; or \g.
Your MySQL sign-in ID is 35
Server version: 8.0.13 MySQL Community Server - GPL
Copyright (c) 2000, 2018, Oracle and/or its affiliates. All rights
reserved.
Oracle is a registered trademark of Oracle Corporation and/or its
affiliates. Other names may be trademarks of their respective owners.
For help, type 'help;' or '\h'. To clear the current input statement, type
'\c'.
mysql>
```

We now need to select a `hostname` to understand where we are connected. So, check the current active RW node with the following code:

```
mysql> select @@hostname;
+--------------------+
| @@hostname |
+--------------------+
| primaryone |
+--------------------+
1 row in set (0.00 sec)
```

Let's now come out of the connection and try to connect from MySQL Router once more, using the following command:

```
> mysql -u root -p -h 201.200.199.1
```

Let's select the hostname once again to understand where we are connected. Check the current active RW node with the following command:

```
mysql> select @@hostname;
+---------------------+
| @@hostname |
+---------------------+
| primarysecond |
+---------------------+
1 row in set (0.00 sec)
```

The router comes with the following routing policies and algorithms.

Routing-strategy algorithms are assigned by default, depending on the following routing modes:

- Primary mode uses the **first-available** mechanism and picks up the first writer node
- Read-only mode uses the **round-robin** mechanism, splitting the read traffic among all servers

Some additional routing strategy algorithms are as follows:

- **next-available** is similar to first-available, except it marks failing nodes as crashed, which are then unable to return to the rotation
- **round-robin-with-fallback** is the same as round-robin but also includes the ability to route traffic to the primary mode, as well as read-only

You can now play around with creating databases and tables on one instance, and ensure they are replicated and available on other nodes. We have also learned how to configure multi-primary InnoDB clusters, so you can write on any of the instances available.

Managing clusters

To manage an InnoDB cluster successfully, you will need to familiarize yourself with the following commands.

Getting details of a cluster

The following command provides details of a cluster:

```
MySQL primaryone:3306 ssl JS > cluster =
dba.getCluster("myProductionCluster")
```

Removing instances from a cluster

The following command will remove an instance from a group and then update the view:

```
MySQL primaryone:3306 ssl JS >
cluster.removeInstance("cluster_admin@primarysecond:3306")
```

Adding instances to a cluster

This command will add an instance to a group with the status RECOVERING. Once recovered, it will be moved to an online state, where it can start accepting live traffic:

```
MySQL node1:3306 ssl JS > cluster.addInstance("cluster_admin@node2:3306")
```

Restoring a cluster after quorum loss

Sometimes, in the case of a failure, one or more instances fail to re-join a group. In this situation, the instances lose the ability to vote in a new primary election. If we want to force the instances, we can use cluster.forceQuorumUsingPartitionOf("myhost:4410").

Rebooting a cluster after a major outage

In a complete outage scenario, we can re-configure the cluster with dba.rebootClusterFromCompleteOutage().

Rescanning a cluster

If we have manually added or removed an instance during Group Replication, an InnoDB cluster metadata might not have updated the cluster. To update an InnoDB cluster metadata, we use the cluster.rescan() method.

Checking instance states

If you want to verify that an instance is good enough to join a cluster, you can use the `cluster.checkInstanceState()` function. This function validates a GTID and compares it to GTIDs already processed by a cluster. It also checks whether an instance that has processed transactions can be added to a cluster:

```
mysql-js> cluster.checkInstanceState('cluster_admin@node4:3306')
```

The output of the preceding function can be any of the following:

- **OK new**: Where the instance has not executed any GTID transactions, and cannot conflict with the GTIDs executed by the cluster
- **OK recoverable**: Where the instance has executed GTIDs that do not conflict with the executed GTIDs of the cluster seed instances
- **ERROR diverged**: Where the instance has executed GTIDs that diverge with the executed GTIDs of the cluster seed instances
- **ERROR lost_transactions**: Where the instance has more executed GTIDs than the executed GTIDs of the cluster seed instances

Dissolving an InnoDB cluster

If you ever need to dissolve an InnoDB cluster, connect to one of the primary servers and use the following `cluster.dissolve()` command:

```
mysql-js> session
<ClassicSession:root@localhost:3310>
mysql-js> cluster.dissolve({force:true})
```

The cluster should now be successfully dissolved, meaning all metadata and configuration associated with the cluster has been removed, Group Replication has been disabled, and any data stays put.

InnoDB cluster limitations

As InnoDB cluster uses Group Replication, the limitations of Group Replication are also important to understand. Refer to the limitations of Group Replication in Chapter 7, *Group Replication in MySQL 8.0*, for more information.

When we fire commands using MySQL Shell, the configuration is not always persisted to the disk. If so, when the machine restarts, any configuration is lost and the machine in question cannot re-join the group. In such a scenario, we cannot use the `dba.rebootClusterFromCompleteOutage()` command, as the configuration is not persisted. The machine, therefore, returns to its original state, causing the replication to stop responding and the command to time out.

We recommended that you use `dba.configureInstance()` before adding instances to a cluster to persist the configuration changes.

Note that the `--defaults-extra-file` (https://dev.mysql.com/doc/refman/8.0/en/server-options.html#option_mysqld_defaults-extra-file) is not supported in InnoDB cluster server instances.

Storage engines

Storage engines allow you to store data. The right storage engine is chosen according to the use-case at hand, and the customer's needs. If you are running MySQL and want to see which engines are available, you can use the `show engines` command for guidance. In this section, we are going to cover the basics of a number of storage engines and will learn why Oracle chooses InnoDB as the default storage engine for MySQL 8.0:

```
mysql> show engines;
+--------------------+---------+------------------------------------------------
--------------------+--------------+-------+------------+
| Engine | Support | Comment | Transactions | XA | Savepoints |
+--------------------+---------+------------------------------------------------
--------------------+--------------+-------+------------+
| MEMORY | YES | Hash based, stored in memory, useful for temporary tables
| NO | NO | NO |
| MRG_MYISAM | YES | Collection of identical MyISAM tables | NO | NO | NO |
| CSV | YES | CSV storage engine | NO | NO | NO |
| FEDERATED | NO | Federated MySQL storage engine | NULL | NULL | NULL |
| PERFORMANCE_SCHEMA | YES | Performance Schema | NO | NO | NO |
| MyISAM | YES | MyISAM storage engine | NO | NO | NO |
| InnoDB | DEFAULT | Supports transactions, row-level locking, and foreign
keys | YES | YES | YES |
| BLACKHOLE | YES | /dev/null storage engine (anything you write to it
disappears) | NO | NO | NO |
| ARCHIVE | YES | Archive storage engine | NO | NO | NO |
+--------------------+---------+------------------------------------------------
--------------------+--------------+-------+------------+
9 rows in set (0.00 sec)
```

Setting a storage engine

In a `CREATE TABLE` statement, you can add the `ENGINE` table option to reference a storage engine, as follows:

```
CREATE TABLE table1 (i INT) ENGINE = INNODB;
CREATE TABLE table2 (i INT) ENGINE = CSV;
CREATE TABLE table3 (i INT) ENGINE = MEMORY;
```

MyISAM storage engine

The **MyISAM** storage engine was the default MySQL storage engine for many years. MyISAM files are an extension of the **Indexed Sequential Access Method (ISM)** but feature additional optimizations such as advanced caching and indexing. The engine also includes a compression feature for increased speed.

The MyISAM storage engine is mainly used in applications where data needs to be retrieved quickly. It is particularly popular in LAMP Stack.

The following is a list of features provided by the MyISAM storage engine:

- B-tree indexes
- Full-text search
- Backup (with point-in-time recovery)
- Compression
- Replication
- Query cache
- Geospatial data type and indexing
- Encryption
- Updated statistics to the data dictionary

The MyISAM storage engine has a storage limit of 256 TB, and also provides table-level locking to support concurrent operations.

Each MyISAM table is stored in the following files on the disk:

- `.frm`: stores the table format
- `.MYD`: stores the data
- `.MYI`: stores the index

The MyISAM storage engine is reliable but can sometimes corrupt file formats, and thus tables, in the following potential scenarios:

- Unexpected shutdown of the MySQL service while it has yet to complete writing
- Disk or hardware failure
- Machine shutdown
- Multiple processes trying to update a table

The MEMORY storage engine

When we need to retrieve frequently-used data quickly, we can use the MEMORY storage engine. The MEMORY storage engine stores data via an in-memory table, so it is faster to retrieve information. As the data in this table is in-memory, however, it is only valid until a database service is restarted; on shutdown, data is lost. The MEMORY storage engine is often used when needing to retrieve static data that is hardly changed, such as the properties of an application or zip code data.

Some of the features of the MEMORY storage engine include:

- Storage is limited to RAM capacity
- B-tree indexes
- Backup (PTR)
- Replication support
- Query cache support
- Table-level locking for concurrency
- Hash indexes
- Encryption
- Updated statistics for data dictionary

The CSV storage engine

The CSV storage engine stores data in a text file, in fields separated by a comma. In this engine, the server creates a .frm file for the table, and the data is stored in a CSV format. The CSV storage engine does not provide indexing support, so it is often impractical in use-cases with a large amount of data. All columns of a CSV table should strictly follow the NOT NULL attribute.

The ARCHIVE storage engine

The ARCHIVE storage engine is designed to store a large amount of un-indexed data. Think of it as a place for data that is seldom used or will be stored for a long time. Use cases include application and security logs. The ARCHIVE storage engine does not provide indexing support, but compression support is included.

The only features the ARCHIVE storage engine provides are compression, encryption, the geospatial data type, and indexing.

The BLACKHOLE storage engine

The BLACKHOLE storage engine acts as a "black hole" that accepts data but does not store it. For example, even if you insert data into a table created with the BLACKHOLE storage engine, it will appear empty. If a binary log is enabled, however, the engine will write SQL statements and rows to the logs.

The MERGE storage engine

The MERGE storage engine is a collection of identical MyISAM tables (where identical column and indexes are in the same order), which can be used as the same table. This is an interesting storage engine. When we have a large amount of data but want to store it in smaller chunks, it's best to use the MERGE storage engine. The MERGE storage engine usually only applies to large databases. Note that a DROP table only deletes a merge specification—original tables are not altered:

```
CREATE TABLE alldata (no INT NOT NULL, student_name CHAR(40)) ENGINE =
MERGE UNION = (data1, data2, data3) INSERT_METHOD = LAST;
Query OK, 0 rows affected (0.09 sec)
```

In the preceding command, assume that data1, data2, and data3 all have the same definition.

The FEDERATED storage engine

The FEDERATED storage engine is designed to create a single reference from multiple MySQL database systems without using replication or cluster technology. Querying a federated table automatically pulls data from remote tables. No data is stored on local tables:

```
CREATE TABLE federated_table (
 no INT(3) NOT NULL AUTO_INCREMENT,
 name VARCHAR(42) NOT NULL DEFAULT '',
 Age INT(3) NOT NULL DEFAULT '0',
 PRIMARY KEY (no),
 INDEX name (name)
 )
 ENGINE=FEDERATED
 DEFAULT CHARSET=latin1
 CONNECTION='mysql://connctinguser@remotehost:3306/mydb/test_table';
```

InnoDB engine

InnoDB engine is a general-purpose storage engine that balances high reliability and high performance. It became a default engine from MySQL 5.7. Oracle has gone through several attempts to make robust, high-performance storage engines for MySQL, but InnoDB has been chosen as the default engine, as it matches the requirements of most of the use-cases. This engine was originally not part of MySQL, but part of a company called InfoBase. InnoDB engine is fully **Atomicity, Consistency, Isolation, Durability (ACID)**-compliant and accepts foreign key constraints.

InnoDB Engine provides the following features:

- Multi-version concurrency control
- B-Tree
- Full-text search engine
- Index cache
- Backup (PTR)
- Transactions
- Geospatial data type and indexing
- Clustered indexes
- Compression
- Replication

- Query caching
- Data caching
- Encryption of data
- Foreign key support
- Locking granularity at a row level
- Updates statistics to the data dictionary

Advantages of the InnoDB engine include the following:

- Excellent performance when processing large data volumes
- DML operations (adding, updating, and deleting data) are ACID-compliant, with transactions supporting commits, rollbacks, and crash-recovery capabilities that help protect user data
- Concurrency at row-level locking allows systems with increased multi-user concurrency and performance; data is written to disk only on transaction completion (during commit or rollback)
- Maintains data integrity using foreign key constraints, which provides high consistency
- Tables arrange data on disk to optimize queries based on primary keys
- Allows data queries using a join query from multiple database engine tables
- `AUTO_INCREMENT` support, which improves scalability and performance

So, to achieve maximum concurrency and consistency with isolation and durability, Oracle decided to go ahead with InnoDB engine.

Migrating from master-slave replication to MySQL InnoDB cluster

The MySQL InnoDB cluster is increasingly popular thanks to its high-availability features, so it's important that we look at how to migrate your replication mechanism from master-slave to InnoDB cluster.

First, you will need to have read through and understood Chapter 7, *Group Replication in MySQL 8.0*. Make sure that you understand Group Replication, the impact of using the MySQL database, and the pros and cons of each scenario.

There are several changes required in database table design that need to be followed carefully. Two important points to remember are as follows:

- InnoDB engine is a must for all tables
- All tables should have a primary key, not a null unique key

To list each table that does not use InnoDB Engine, use the following command:

```
SELECT table_schema, table_name, engine, table_rows,
(index_length+data_length)/1024/1024 AS sizeMB
 FROM information_schema.tables WHERE engine != 'innodb'
 AND table_schema NOT IN ('information_schema', 'mysql',
'performance_schema');
```

If your table does not use any primary keys, it should behave as follows:

```
mysql> create table no_primary_key (id int, name varchar(10));
mysql> insert into no_primary_key values (1,'test');
ERROR 3098 (HY000): The table does not comply with the requirements by an
external plugin.
```

In the error log, we should be able to see the reason for failure, as follows:

```
[Error] Plugin group_replication reported: Table no_primary_key does not
have any PRIMARY KEY.
```

If you want to know any tables that don't comply with the Group Replication design, use the following command:

```
information_schema.tables and information_schema.statistics
```

Once you have identified all the tables, you will need to add primary keys to each of them.

Let's assume that we have master-slave replication, where there is one master and one slave server. To move to the InnoDB cluster, GTID replication should be on MySQL 5.6 or later. In the upcoming sections, we will refer to the master as node1 and the slave as node2.

Now let's configure two more MySQL instances to be a part of InnoDB cluster. Here, we will refer to them as `node3` and `node4` (in MySQL 8.0). Note that Group Replication between MySQL versions 5.7 to 8.0 is compatible. After installing MySQL Shell on `node3`, we need to prepare `node3` and `node4` and install the latest version of MySQL. Make sure you follow the correct MySQL configuration file, as shown in `Chapter 7`, *Group Replication in MySQL 8.0*.

From `node1`, you can take a backup and restore it on `node3` and `node4` with the following command:

```
[node1 ~]# mysqlbackup --host=localhost --backup-dir=/usr/backup --
user=<username> --password=<password> backup-and-apply-log
```

In this example, we are using a physical backup method, but you can also use `mysqldump`.

Now, transfer the backup files to `node3` and `node4` using `scp` as follows:

```
[node1 ~]# scp -r /usr/backup node3:/tmp
[node1 ~]# scp -r /usr/backup node4:/tmp
```

Once transferred, restore the backup in both `node3` and `node4`. Make sure that the `mysqld` service has stopped, as follows:

```
[node3 ~]# systemctl stop mysqld
[node4 ~]# systemctl stop mysqld
```

Restore the backup on `node3` and `node4` with the following code:

```
[node3 ~]# mysqlbackup --backup-dir=/usr/backup --force copy-back
[node3 ~]# rm /var/lib/mysql/mysql*-bin* # just some cleanup
[node3 ~]# chown -R mysql. /var/lib/mysql
```

Now we only need to add `node3` as a slave to `node1`, as an asynchronous replicated database, as follows:

```
[mysqld]
 server_id=3
 enforce_gtid_consistency = on
 gtid_mode = on
 log_bin
 log_slave_update
```

Once finished, we then identify the latest GTID executed from backup. We can find out that out by searching the log file `backup_gtid_executed.sql`, as follows:

```
[node3 ~]# cat /tmp/backup/meta/backup_gtid_executed.sql
```

Once we have the latest GTID, we need to issue the following command on a slave if GTIDs are enabled:

```
SET @@GLOBAL.GTID_PURGED='44451222-3xe8-12e7-99x3-45672718d718:1-1001';
# Use the following command if you want to use the GTID handshake
protocol:
# CHANGE MASTER TO MASTER_AUTO_POSITION=1;
```

Next, on `node3`, execute the following commands:

```
mysql> CHANGE MASTER TO MASTER_HOST="node1",
 MASTER_USER="repl_async", MASTER_PASSWORD='imslave',
 MASTER_AUTO_POSITION=1;
 mysql> RESET MASTER;
 mysql> SET global
gtid_purged="44451222-3xe8-12e7-99x3-45672718d718:1-1001";
 mysql> START SLAVE;
```

Make sure that the credentials used in the preceding command are also present in `node1`.

Now use the following command to check whether the replication is working:

```
mysql> SHOW SLAVE STATUS;
```

At this point, we have added one more slave (`node3`) to the existing master-slave (`node1` | `node2`) replication topology, and we have also enabled asynchronous replication on `node3`.

It's now time to start creating a new InnoDB cluster on `node3` using MySQL Shell. Input the following command:

```
MYSQL JS> dba.checkInstanceConfiguration('cluster_admin@node3:3306')
```

If the configuration is fine, it will send a message that all is OK. If not, it can present which values need to be changed.

We can use the following command to auto-configure the suggested changes required if necessary:

```
mysql-js> dba.configureLocalInstance()
...
Do you want to modify this file? [Y|n]: y
Validating instance...
...
```

Here, we used `dba.configureLocalInstance()`, which is required if we ever need to restart the `mysqld` service when changing some of the MySQL variables:

```
[node3 ~]# systemctl restart mysqld
mysql-js> dba.checkInstanceConfiguration('cluster_admin@node3:3306')
 Please provide the password for 'cluster_admin@node3:3306':
 Validating instance...
The instance 'node3:3306' is valid for Cluster usage
 {
 "status": "ok"
 }
```

```
mysql-js> cluster = dba.createCluster('replicationCluster')
Please specify, your clustername here. Use cluster.status() to verify
mysql-js> cluster.status()
{
"clusterName": "replicationCluster",
"defaultReplicaSet": {
"name": "default",
"primary": "node3:3306",
"status": "OK_NO_TOLERANCE",
"statusText": "Cluster is NOT tolerant to any failures.",
"topology": {
"node3:3306": {
"address": "node3:3306",
"mode": "R/W",
"readReplicas": {},
"role": "HA",
"status": "ONLINE"
}
}
}
}
```

Now let's add one more instance (node4) to our cluster. As we have restored the MySQL backup, we just need to start the service with the following command:

```
[node4 ~]# systemctl start mysqld
```

We will use MySQL Shell on node3 to add node4 as an additional instance to the group. Once again, we'll check the instance configuration using the following command:

```
mysql-js> dba.checkInstanceConfiguration('cluster_admin@node4:3306')
```

Once complete, configure the instance before saving the configuration and restarting the MySQL service on node4. We will use the same purged GTIDs as we did previously (in /tmp/backup/meta/backup_gtid_executed.sql), as follows:

```
mysql-js> \c cluster_admin@node4:3306
 mysql-js> \sql
 mysql-sql> RESET MASTER;
 mysql-sql> SET global
gtid_purged="44451222-3xe8-12e7-99x3-45672718d718:1-1001";
mysql-js> dba.checkInstanceConfiguration('cluster_admin@node4:3306')
...
The instance 'node4:3306' is valid for Cluster usage
 {
 "status": "ok"
 }
```

Now connect MySQL Shell to node3, and then to MySQL, to find out the status of the cluster. Use the following code:

```
mysql-js> \c cluster_admin@node3:3306
  Creating a Session to 'cluster_admin@node3:3306'
  Enter password:
  Your MySQL connection id is 13
  Server version: 8.0.13-log MySQL Community Server (GPL)
  No default schema selected; type \use <schema> to set one.
  mysql-js> cluster = dba.getCluster()
  <Cluster:replicationCluster>
```

Now check the state of node4 by issuing the following command:

```
mysql-js> cluster.checkInstanceState('cluster_admin@node4:3306')
  . .
  {
  "reason": "recoverable",
  "state": "ok"
  }
```

Once we see that its state is ok, we're ready to add node4 to the cluster with the following command:

```
mysql-js> cluster.addInstance("cluster_admin@node4:3306")
```

We follow the same procedure for node2; however, we do not need to restore a backup, as data is already available. Note that we *do* need to stop slave operations. Check the configuration of node2 using the checkInstanceConfiguration() method and configureInstance(). Remember to save the configuration, restart the mysqld service, and add node2 as the third member of the group.

If you do not know how to change and save a configuration, you can install MySQL Shell on each server and use dba.configureLocalInstance().

Now you can install MySQL Router on the application server and bootstrap it with the following command:

```
[root@application1 ~]# mysqlrouter --bootstrap node3:3306 --user
mysqlrouter
```

Once done, restart MySQL Router with the following command:

```
[application1 ~]# systemctl start mysqlrouter
```

Remember to ensure that a user has the rights to connect to node3.

Now all that's left to do is test the system from MySQL Router to node3, including read/write and read-only connections. Before you test read/write transactions, break the current master-slave asynchronous replication so InnoDB cluster is ready for your application to accept connections. Do this by pointing your application to use the correct router and IP port combination.

Summary

In this chapter, we concentrated on the different storage engines available in MySQL and also looked at why InnoDB was chosen to achieve high availability. We also covered MySQL Shell and MySQL Router, and their roles in achieving high availability. We also checked out AdminAPI and how to configure an InnoDB sandbox cluster, as well as a production environment. We also went through how to manage clusters in production and discussed various scenarios and methods relevant to cluster management.

Finally, we covered how you can migrate from a master-slave replication mechanism to an InnoDB cluster, and how to make your system highly available as well as fault tolerant. In the next chapter, we will explore the best tools for monitoring your large distributed databases.

9
Monitoring Your Large Distributed Databases

Whenever we collect, store, and access data electronically, it's called a database. Databases can be stored in various forms and under different architecture. SQL uses tables to store data over the servers and to access it. Another very popular format is the JSON architecture to store data. Now, all of these databases are accessed by database management systems. For example, MySQL 8.0 or SQLite are database management systems that use the SQL language. Google Firebase or MongoDB are database management systems that use JSON.

Database management systems, such as MySQL 8.0, aren't enough for monitoring the real-time changes and updates in the database on a live server.

In order to monitor these changes, there are various database monitoring tools available. Of all of the database monitoring tools out there, in this chapter, we're going to understand and compare the top three monitoring tools for your large distributed databases. We'll look at the following tools:

- MONyog
- Datadog
- Navicat

Let's get started by discussing these tools one by one.

MONyog

MONyog is the MySQL-based database monitoring tool and is the product of a company called Webyog. Webyog was acquired on April 18, 2018 by the tech giant IDERA, Inc. Webyog is a leader in the category of database tools and the key component is to manage and monitor MySQL servers. It serves over 35,000 companies, with up to 2.5 million users worldwide. Webyog also has another quite successful product called SQLyog. It's the company's flagship product, being used for query profiling and migration. Synchronization and backups are also something SQLyog is primarily being used for.

MONyog is the company's database monitoring tool, designed to offer real-time insights. MONyog may have some room for improvement but shows some great promise. The design has some really different and innovative architectural decisions that help it to stand apart from other MySQL database monitoring tools. The tool also claims to provide assistance in finding and fixing issues that might create a problem at a later stage or limit the scalability.

It'll help you to manage more than one database server in an effective way. As it monitors enterprise environments, the tool is also able to advise on low security or how to optimize the performance of MySQL powered systems, making sure that they face minimum downtime. In other word, it's like having a DBA in a monitoring tool, as demonstrated in the following screenshot:

Pros

There are some solid reasons you might want to use MONyog as your database monitoring tool. Most of the MySQL monitoring and advisory tools will require you to install some kind of agent on every server you would like to monitor and it would need another server collecting data from all of these agents but **MONyog has agentless monitoring**.

There's no external PHP or Java agents being used to connect with MySQL. MONyog uses an API in the C language and interacts directly with MySQL without the need of any agent. This has made the deployment of MONyog much easier, as you won't have to install anything on each and every MySQL server you plan to monitor. MONyog just uses the MySQL client to connect and fetch information from the database.

MONyog uses JavaScript and has it embedded in the system. The website states that the entire MONyog application logic is handled by JavaScript objects. From defining the values of thresholds to the performance metrics, everything is handled by JavaScript. What's even more attractive is that the complete code of these JavaScript objects is available and you can customize it according to your needs.

MONyog can also display system statistics, such as CPU usage if you're monitoring Linux servers. All you need to do is specify the SSH login information.

It also has SNMS traps, email, slack, and other such notification services. A notification service is provided so that you can receive notifications if anything is wrong with your server without having to sit in front of the monitor all of the time.

There's an installer available for Windows as well, which makes it a fairly easy process to install MONyog on the system.

Cons

The number one drawback for MONyog has to be its pricing, as these services and tools are out there and they cost nothing. Even with the features it has, relatively speaking, it has some very high pricing. Drawbacks also include the lack of support for all operating systems. You can clearly see that MONyog features Windows and there's still a lack of proper documentation for the Linux platform. The documentation in general is inadequate and you may encounter a number of difficulties in setting up the tool properly.

One further drawback of MONyog is the load when there's no SSH connection available. Private SSH keys for each and every server have to be entered in order to monitor them, as demonstrated in the following screenshot:

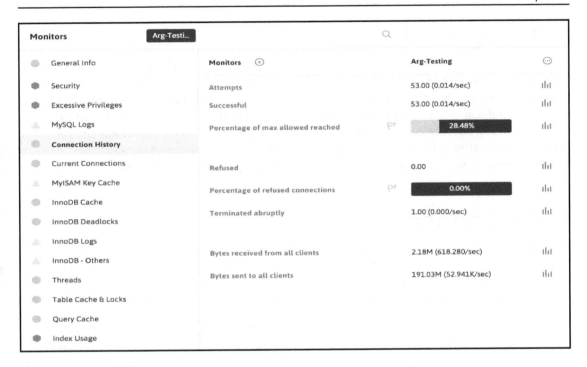

Conclusion

MONyog, as a tool, has some great and innovative features and has a lot of potential for growth. One thing that might be stopping it's the extreme pricing, which makes it ideal for only the enterprise level. The agentless model has simplified the tool and we have to accept that it's pretty effective. The representation of data is seamless, including all of those beautiful charts, graphs, and logs but the only major added advantage MONyog has is the agentless model it works on. The feature has been implemented successfully and works just like the tools that need any kind of agent installed on the server.

Datadog

The infrastructure management and network monitoring service, Datadog, is delivered in a **Software as a Service (SaaS)** wrapper with agents and you can install it on a lot of platforms. Datadog has some features that can perform high-end analysis successfully. It also enables the ability to customize with the help of Application Programming Interfaces (APIs). Datadog isn't the topmost player in the market but comes close and has proven itself to be a worthy contender. Datadog also has the ability to connect through alert and teaming services, such as Atlassian HipChat, Slack, and other such services.

Getting started

You can get started with Datadog by first creating an account on the Datadog website. The website will ask you about your requirements and you'll have to choose a pricing plan. However, there's a demo and a free plan available if you want to try your hand at Datadog. After this, the installation and configuration of a software agent is required.

The website has clear documentation and a detailed step-by-step procedure of how to set up these agents across various platforms. Some of the platforms for which the agent is available include Apple macOS X, Chef, Microsoft Windows, Ubuntu, Red Hat Fedora, and others. The Windows agent has its own installer to make the process easier.

The installer requires the API key from the account created online. After the installation and the connection to your Datadog account has been made, you can easily log in and start monitoring, as demonstrated in the following screenshot:

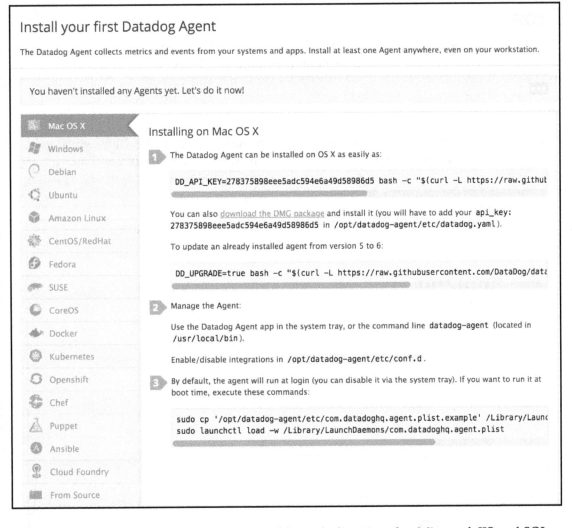

Install your first Datadog Agent

The Datadog Agent collects metrics and events from your systems and apps. Install at least one Agent anywhere, even on your workstation.

You haven't installed any Agents yet. Let's do it now!

| Mac OS X |
| Windows |
| Debian |
| Ubuntu |
| Amazon Linux |
| CentOS/RedHat |
| Fedora |
| SUSE |
| CoreOS |
| Docker |
| Kubernetes |
| Openshift |
| Chef |
| Puppet |
| Ansible |
| Cloud Foundry |
| From Source |

Installing on Mac OS X

1 The Datadog Agent can be installed on OS X as easily as:

```
DD_API_KEY=278375898eee5adc594e6a49d58986d5 bash -c "$(curl -L https://raw.githut
```

You can also download the DMG package and install it (you will have to add your `api_key`: `278375898eee5adc594e6a49d58986d5` in /opt/datadog-agent/etc/datadog.yaml).

To update an already installed agent from version 5 to 6:

```
DD_UPGRADE=true bash -c "$(curl -L https://raw.githubusercontent.com/DataDog/data
```

2 Manage the Agent:

Use the Datadog Agent app in the system tray, or the command line `datadog-agent` (located in /usr/local/bin).

Enable/disable integrations in /opt/datadog-agent/etc/conf.d .

3 By default, the agent will run at login (you can disable it via the system tray). If you want to run it at boot time, execute these commands:

```
sudo cp '/opt/datadog-agent/etc/com.datadoghq.agent.plist.example' /Library/Launc
sudo launchctl load -w /Library/LaunchDaemons/com.datadoghq.agent.plist
```

A number of monitoring targets are compatible, including Apache, Microsoft IIS and SQL Server, VMware vSphere, and other such servers.

The primary environment to monitor through Datadog is its cloud services. A lot of common services can be used with Datadog, such as **Amazon Web Services** (**AWS**), Microsoft Azure, and Google Cloud.

Pros

The number one advantage of using Datadog is no doubt their customer service, which comes in handy with all of the documentation, tutorials, and web content. From the moment you open their website, everything is easy to use and you can start setting it up. Most people out there will be able to easily integrate and configure this with their databases and servers.

Another very interesting feature of their panel is the monitoring of RDS CPU, which may prove to be really helpful. Even in Datadog, you can create custom graphs and metrics with ease. The ability to create different dashboards according to requirements is also a plus, as demonstrated in the following screenshot:

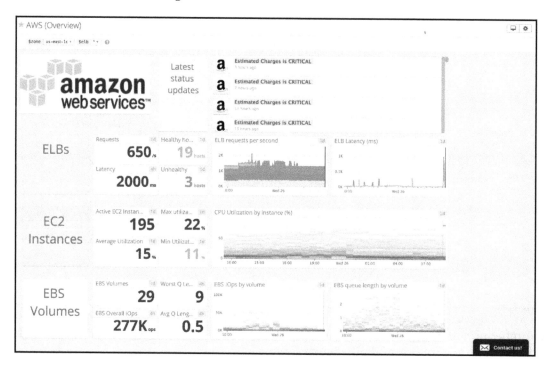

You can also create alarms or custom notifications when the metrics surpass any threshold. Multi-party support and flexible APIs make things work in a better way. It takes a lot less time to set up Datadog and get started as compared to the competitors out there.

Datadog also brings you the ability to analyze and explore log data in context. You can quickly search, filter, or analyze the logs whenever they run into any kind of trouble. Troubleshooting is made easy thanks to the automatic collection of logs from all services and platforms.

Cons

Although Datadog has been appreciated for its user interface, experience, and customizable dashboards, there are times that the dashboard can get too technical to understand and may cause complications in using Datadog. Another instance where you may encounter a lot of difficulties in monitoring their servers is when there are a lot of apps. These apps make it difficult to find what we're actually looking for in the dashboard.

The RDS health monitoring is an additional plus but it would have been more awesome if it could have worked without integrating it with the entire AWS. It takes time to get used to the dashboard or the monitoring screen, as there's a lot of information available at once on the screen, which can be quite overwhelming. There's scope to present the data in a better way. The pricing isn't excessive but not the best either. You can find similar services for substantially cheaper if you look carefully. Datadog also isn't suitable for all of the services on the cloud. If you're going to use it with Microsoft Azure, Azure's Log Analytics can easily beat Datadog in the case of monitoring. The free plan doesn't offer much to an enterprise.

Conclusion

Datadog is the ideal solution for smaller businesses with custom requirements due to the availability of the maximum number of platforms and the ability for customization. For companies that base their decisions or products on the basis of data being captured, Datadog is the way to go, as that's what Datadog is good at. Most of the companies in the market require traditional reporting and won't consider spending their time and resources on Datadog. Datadog has this brilliant ability to be tweaked according to personal requirements and preferences and it supports a large number of platforms, making it the ideal go-to tool for small and innovative companies.

Navicat

Initially released in 2002 by PremiumSoft CyberTech Ltd., Navicat is a series of graphical database management and development software. This tool can be used with MariaDB, SQLite, MySQL, Oracle, PostgreSQL, and Microsoft's SQL Server. Navicat supports connections across multiple databases and their monitoring.

The software has been designed so that it's able to cater for a large audience. The company wants it to be used not only by other enterprises but even by database administrators and programmers from businesses or companies of various sizes. Navicat for MySQL also offers a 14-day fully functional free trial and has pre-made packages available for Windows, macOS, and Linux. Navicat for MySQL installs with the help of installers, like any other software:

After installation, a window opens from which even an amateur can figure out what goes where. All that's left now is making connections with the database and you're good to go. Navicat is one of the oldest database monitoring tools in the market and has a premium product as well. Launched in 2009, Navicat Premium can perform everything combined. This means not only MySQL but PostgreSQL and Oracle also, simultaneously. The beauty of this product is that it allows users to migrate data between cross- databases:

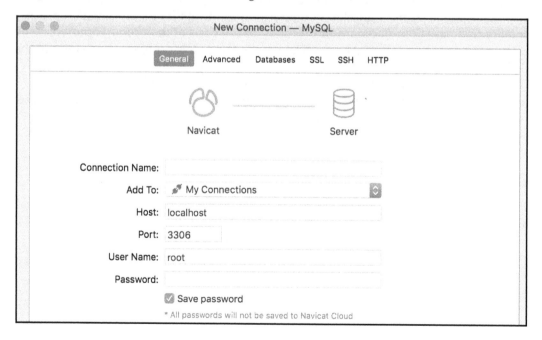

Pros

With Navicat, the ease of use and setup is a big plus. You can easily add or make connections and everything is right there on the screen. As the login information is set up only once, the process is speedy and smooth. Reviewing data is just like browsing through the original database but the data is presented in a better way. One double-click on the table and it'll open in the browse mode. Navicat also has built-in tools where you can write queries to pull the required data:

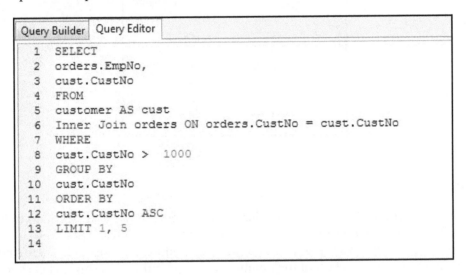

Some companies love Navicat just for the sole reason of the ability to export data to Excel. Often, these companies receive requests of data from a particular table in an Excel file. This is where the export wizard comes in really handy.

The ability to transfer data from one database to another or even to a different server makes the migration process much easier than it's generally. You can also store procedures and schedule tasks.

Navicat has some reasonable pricing as well and is being used by a large number of communities worldwide. Navicat is also compatible with cloud databases, such as Aurora, Amazon RDS, Microsoft Azure, Redshift, Alibaba, and Google Cloud, to name a few:

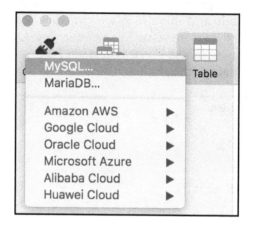

Cons

Navicat might respond a bit slowly when large queries are made. When it comes to Navicat Premium, the majority of consumers felt that the upgrade is expensive but they still proceed to buy it due to the cross-database migration options and support. There's no option present to make a backup of the database on the cloud with a single click, such as on Google Drive or Dropbox. A lot of purchasing options and packages are available from Navicat, which can be sometimes confusing and frustrating for the consumer. Another field Navicat lacks is tools that have extensive functionality with mobile devices. There's no way to receive notifications on the go if something goes wrong with your server.

Conclusion

Recent updates in Navicat added some very attractive tools and features to the platform. There are small features, such as displaying the most viewed tabs automatically when you open the Navicat window and an easy-to-use UI of the software. Data synchronization can be done across different databases and this alone is one factor influencing why enterprises might want to go with Navicat.

The interface is also usable with the Touch Bar in MacBook Pros, which shows the kind of support and thought constantly being put into the software to make it a better and more efficient product. Choosing an edition might be tough but once you do select the right one, you're good to go.

There are various guides available online that will help you make the right call. It may look like it's really expensive in the beginning, and it looked that way to us, but in the long run, it'll prove to be worth your money, as it packs in a hell of a lot of features. If you need to manage multiple databases in high availability environments, Navicat is the best solution you've got.

Comparison between monitoring tools

In this section, we'll look into the comparison between the monitoring tools, based on the pricing and top clients, and we'll look into the pros and cons.

The price

The following table compares each of the monitoring provider's prices:

MONyog	Starts from $199 (Professional version)—one-time cost per MySQL Server
Datadog	Starts from $15/host (Infrastructure version)—per month
Navicat	Starts from $1039.20 (Navicat Premium)—one-time cost

Pros

The following table illustrates some options that are available with each monitoring application, representing what's good value for you:

MONyog	• Real-time monitoring • Advanced query analyzer • Top five slow queries—identification • Replication monitoring • Deadlock monitoring • Security and attempts monitoring • Disk and locks monitoring • Metric graphs

Datadog	• Centralizes your monitoring of systems • 250 + integrations • Out-of-the-box dashboards • 15 months monitoring metrics retention • Full visibility of applications
Navicat	• Data modeler • Easy to use and intuitive user interface • Comprehensive file type (CSV, TXT, and so on) • Lightweight • Available on the cloud, macOS, Linux, and Windows • Metric graphs • Slack integration

Cons

The following table illustrates some options that are available with each monitoring application that might not suit you:

MONyog	• Web server that needs a lot of memory • Needs a lot of space when you enable the option of sniffer retention • It takes some time to learn the application
Datadog	• An overwhelming amount of information is offered to search through before starting the actual use of the product • Difficult to integrate the application with Amazon • Too many icons
Navicat	• Lot of bugs and releases • Tunnel not stable • Application not stable and sometime loses data

Top clients

The following table lists the most popular clients that use each application:

MONyog	• Netflix • Yahoo • Salesforce
Datadog	• Samsung • DreamWorks • Ferrari
Navicat	• Natixis SA • Redolent, Inc • Bay Shore Staffing

Tips and techniques

One of the best options available from the MONyog database monitoring tool is the easiest way to identify the top six slow queries via **QUERY ANALYZER**.

Here's an example:

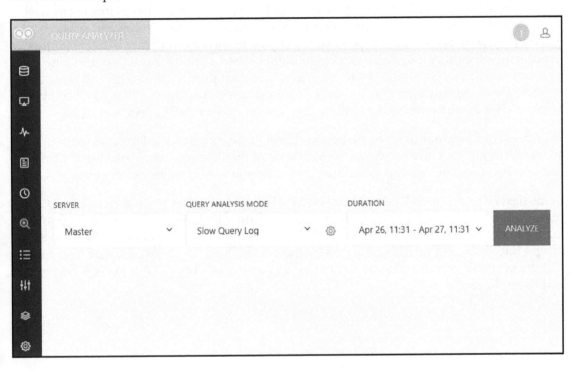

Summary

At the end of the day, out of thousands of database administration tools available out there, you can never declare a single one of them to be the best. It all depends on the requirements and the budget of the company/enterprise.

If you have multiple databases and you aren't only on MySQL but other platforms as well, then Navicat is your go-to platform. The simple reason is the ease of setup and cross-database support. It's the most expensive among the three but does bring a lot of features to the table that the other two don't. Datadog is another best option for small-to-medium companies. You can customize the tool according to your preference and get the best out of it. MONyog is the only agentless database monitoring tool and the fact that you'll be able to monitor your database without installing any kind of PHP or .NET agent is exciting.

All three tools are topmost in the market and provide a great service. Free trials are available for all of them, so make sure you use all of those demos before making the final decision because, after all, this investment can save you a lot of money in the future.

In the next chapter, we will cover the new MySQL 8.0 security features, such as MySQL roles, which is a new security and administrative feature that allows DBA to simplify user management and increases the security of their multi-user environments. You'll also get insight into the access privileges offered by the system, how the connections are encrypted, and the available security plugins and their effect on the security of your MySQL server and its applications.

10
Authentication and Security Management with MySQL 8.0

In this chapter, we will cover the new MySQL 8.0 security features, such as MySQL roles. This is a new security feature that allows DBAs or seniors developers to simplify user management and increase the security of their multi-user environments. You will also learn about the access privileges system, security plugins, and how they affect the security of your MySQL server and related applications.

We will explore the new security features in MySQL 8.0. Privileges provided by MySQL 8.0 also include the differences between dynamic and static security privileges, and an overview of the grant table, and we will also see how to troubleshoot a connection problem and share some tips and techniques.

We will cover the following topics:

- MySQL 8 security features
- Privileges provided by MySQL 8.0
- The differences between dynamic and static privileges
- Creating roles and users in MySQL 8.0
- Troubleshoot connection problems

MySQL 8.0 security features

MySQL 8.0 is continuing in the same vein as that set by MySQL 5.7—to be secure by default. The Oracle MySQL development team has added a number of interesting security features, including, SQL roles, making the ACL statements atomic, and also dynamic global privileges.

Another aspect that has been improved is the keyring API.

New MySQL 8.0 roles will give you better access controls:

- An easy way to manage user and application rights
- As compliant with standards as is feasible in practice
- Multiple default roles

MySQL 8.0 provides a better way to have administrative-level access controls with dynamic privileges:

- Too often, super privileges are given for tasks when fewer privileges are actually required.
- These are needed to allow the addition of administrative access controls.

Examples of the new components include the following:

- Replication
- HA
- Backup

Let's discover the new MySQL 8.0 security features together.

Privileges provided by MySQL 8.0

Privilege refers to the right or authorization that can be granted to a user account, and it defines which operations can be performed by that account. MySQL privileges are of three types. These types specify the context in which they apply and their scope and are as follows:

- **Administrative privileges**: These privileges are used to enable users to manage the operations of MySQL server. They are applied globally due to their inability to be applied to a single database.
- **Database privileges**: These privileges apply to an entire database and all of its objects. You can apply them to a particular database or they can be applied globally to affect all databases (scope).
- **Privileges for specific database objects**: These can be applied to the following:
  - Database objects such as tables, indexes, routines that are stored, and views.
  - They can also be applied to a particular object type in the database, for example, all tables in the database.
  - Globally for all the objects of a specified type in all the databases.

The privileges are also divided into two categories according to when they are defined, in other words, static privileges, which are built into the server, and dynamic privileges, which are defined at runtime.

Where are privileges stored in MySQL 8.0?

The privileges are stored in the following tables of the MySQL system database:

```
user, db, tables_priv, columns_priv, procs_priv, and global_grants
```

When the MySQL server starts, it reads all the grant table content into memory and the in-memory tables become effective for access control.

The grant tables can be modified using statements that belong to the account manager. For example, the SET PASSWORD, REVOKE, RENAME USER, and GRANT commands can be used. However, when they are used, the changes that they make, will be caught by the server and this leads to the grant tables being loaded into memory instantaneously.

However, if the grant tables are modified indirectly using commands such as INSERT, UPDATE, or DELETE, until such time as the server is restarted or the tables reloaded, your changes will have no effect. So always bear this in mind to ensure that your changes take effect.

Now, in order to reload the grant tables, you can provide this instruction to the server by doing the following:

- Using the FLUSH PRIVILEGES statement
- The mysqladmin reload or mysqladmin flush-privileges command

Now observe when the reloading of grant tables affects privileges for each client connection:

- The table and column level privileges will take effect after the next request by the client.
- Database privilege changes will be affected only after the execution of the USE database_name
- For a connected client, global privileges, and passwords will remain unaffected. They will take effect only after the next connections.

As we know, we can grant privileges using the GRANT command, and the privilege can be taken back using the REVOKE command.

The differences between dynamic and static privileges

Unlike the dynamic privileges that get defined at runtime, the static privileges are built within the server itself. The following are some of the static privileges available in MySQL and explanations thereof:

- ALL, or ALL PRIVILEGES: This privilege is a shorthand specifier. If we consider any privilege level, this specifier would refer to all the privileges that are present in the considered level.

Here is an example. If we grant ALL privileges for table-level or even global-level access, it indicates that the grants are applied to all global or all table-level privileges.

Maybe, on occasion, you need to give a user named (user_read) just the ability to read data (SELECT) from the table (teachers) of the database (school), rather than providing all privileges to the database as a whole. You can accomplish this by doing the following:

```
mysql> GRANT SELECT ON school.teachers TO 'user_read' @ 'localhost';
```

And then grant all privileges to user_super:

```
mysql> GRANT ALL (or ALL PRIVILEGES) ON school.teachers TO 'user_super';
```

And then grant privileges for INSERT, UPDATE, and DELETE to user_write:

```
mysql> GRANT INSERT, UPDATE, DELETE ON school.teachers TO 'user_write';
```

The following table lists a number of other useful static privileges for GRANT and REVOKE:

Privilege	Description	Context
ALTER	This grants privileges to use ALTER table commands to alter the structure of table.	Tables
ALTER ROUTINE	This grants privileges to alter or drop stored routines (including procedures and functions).	Stored routines
CREATE	This grants privileges to create new databases and tables.	Databases, tables, or indexes
CREATE ROLE	This facilitates the creation of new roles.	Server administration
CREATE ROUTINE	This grants privileges to create stored routines, in other words, stored procedures or functions.	Stored routines

CREATE TABLESPACE	This grants privileges to CREATE, ALTER, and DROP TABLESPACE.	Server administration
CREATE USER	This grants privileges to use user creation statements such as ALTER USER, CREATE ROLE, CREATE USER, DROP ROLE, DROP USER, RENAME USER, and REVOKE ALL PRIVILEGES.	Server administration
CREATE VIEW	This enables users to create views.	Views
DELETE	This grants privileges to delete rows from the tables in a database.	Tables
DROP	This grants privileges to drop tables, databases, and views. If this privilege is granted for the mysql database, then the user will be able to delete/drop the database that stores all the privileges!	Databases, tables, or views
DROP ROLE	If this privilege is granted, the user will be able to drop the roles.	Server administration
EXECUTE	This grants privileges to execute the stored routines.	Stored routines
FILE	This grants permission to read and write the files on the server host.	File access on server host

The following table lists some other useful dynamic privileges for GRANT and REVOKE:

Privilege	Description	Context
AUDIT_ADMIN	This grants privileges to audit the log configuration.	Audit log administration
BACKUP_ADMIN	This privilege, defined at server startup, enables execution of the LOCK INSTANCE FOR BACKUP statement along with access to the Performance Schema log_status table.	Backup administration

Creating roles and users in MySQL 8.0

Now, imagine that we need one user account with the developer role, one user account with read-only access, and two user accounts that can have read/write access.

To do this, first, we need to learn about creating roles. To create a role, use the following command:

```
CREATE ROLE privilege;
```

Let's create three roles for developer, read-only, and read-write rights:

```
mysql> CREATE ROLE user_dev, user_read, user_write;
```

Here, the role name is similar to the user account and it has both the user and host parts. Let's say role_name@host_name.

You can omit the host part to make it default to %, which means any hosts.

Now, we need to grant privileges to the roles we created, as follows:

```
mysql> GRANT ALL ON school.* TO 'user_dev';
```

```
mysql> GRANT SELECT ON school.* TO 'user_read';
```

```
mysql> GRANT INSERT, UPDATE, DELETE ON school.* TO 'user_write';
```

Next, we need to assign roles to the user accounts:

Now, let's assume that we need one account with developer rights (privileges), two accounts with read-only access, and two accounts with read-write privileges. We therefore need to create five users.

Now we will be creating users. As we know, the CREATE_USER statement will be used to create users. A password can be provided through the IDENTIFIED BY clause, as demonstrated in the following code block:

```
mysql> CREATE USER 'user_dev@localhost' IDENTIFIED BY 'pwd_dev';
```

```
mysql> CREATE USER 'user_read1@localhost' IDENTIFIED BY 'pwd_read1';
```

```
mysql> CREATE USER 'user_read2@localhost' IDENTIFIED BY 'pwd_read2';
```

```
mysql> CREATE USER 'user_write1@localhost' IDENTIFIED BY 'pwd_write1';
```

```
mysql> CREATE USER 'user_write2@localhost' IDENTIFIED BY 'pwd_write2';
```

Now, simply assign the roles using the GRANT command:

```
mysql> GRANT 'user_dev' to 'user_dev@localhost';
```

```
mysql> GRANT 'user_read' to 'user_read1@localhost', 'user_read2@
```

```
localhost'; //Assigning user_read role to both the users (user_read1 and
user_read2)

mysql> GRANT 'user_write', 'user_read' to 'user_write1@localhost',
'user_write1@localhost';
```

Here, you can note that we have assigned both the roles, in other words, `user_read` and `user_write` to the `user_write1` and `user_write2` users to enable them to have SELECT, INSERT, UPDATE, and DELETE privileges.

The `user_read1` and `user_read2` users will only have SELECT privileges, whereas the `user_dev` user will have ALL privileges.

Displaying assigned roles using SHOW GRANTS

If you want to see the roles assigned to a user, use the SHOW GRANTS statement as follows:

```
mysql> SHOW GRANTS FOR 'user_dev@localhost';
```

It will display the roles and usage granted to the user: `user_dev`. The following is the sample output:

```
+----------------------------------------------------+
| Grants for user_dev@localhost@% |
+----------------------------------------------------+
| GRANT USAGE ON *.* TO `user_dev@localhost`@`%` |
| GRANT `user_dev`@`%` TO `user_dev@localhost`@`%` |
+----------------------------------------------------+
```

This output specifies that it has usage granted on all the tables of all the databases (*.*).

The second row provides the name of the role assigned/granted to the user. So what if you want to see the privileges contained in that role?

You have to use the following statement, which includes the USING clause to show the privileges:

```
mysql> SHOW GRANTS FOR 'user_dev@localhost' USING 'user_dev';
```

The output will be as follows:

```
+---------------------------------------------------------------+
| Grants for user_dev@localhost@% |
```

```
+----------------------------------------------------------------------+
| GRANT USAGE ON *.* TO `user_dev@localhost`@`%` |
| GRANT ALL PRIVILEGES ON `school`.* TO `user_dev@localhost`@`%` |
| GRANT `user_dev`@`%` TO `user_dev@localhost`@`%` |
+----------------------------------------------------------------------+
3 rows in set (0.00 sec)
```

Troubleshooting connection problems

Sometimes, you may encounter a couple of problems while trying to connect to the MySQL server. In such situations, you can try some of the following actions to rectify the situation:

- Ensure that the server is working correctly. If it is not, clients cannot connect to it. Let's say that you are attempting to connect to the server, but that this operation fails. You may get an error message and, if that message is similar to one of the following messages, there is a very high chance that your server isn't running:

  ```
  $ mysql
  ERROR 2003: Can't connect to MySQL server on 'host_name' (111)
  $ mysql
  ERROR 2002: Can't connect to local MySQL server through socket
  '/tmp/mysql.sock' (111)
  ```

- Another scenario is where the server is up and running. However, you are attempting to connect to it via a named pipe. Or perhaps you are using a TCP/IP port or an incorrect Unix socket file, one that isn't being used by the server:

  ```
  $> netstat -ln | grep mysql
  ```

- MySQL might be blocked by some firewall software that needs to be checked.

- The server uses the grant tables for access control, and so it is important that they are set up properly.

- You can expect the following error message when you try to log in to the server without using the password for the first time:

  ```
  > mysql -u root
  ERROR 1045 (28000): Access denied for user 'root'@'localhost'
  (using password: NO)
  ```

This error indicates that the password for the root user has been set during installation and you are required to use that password while logging in.

- It is highly recommended that you run the scripts necessary after successfully updating the MySQL database. `mysql_upgrade` is one such script that has to be run.

Tips and techniques

We will cover the various tips and techniques for authentication and security management in MySQL 8.0.

Restricting or disabling remote access to the server

Determine whether MySQL would be accessed from its own server or over the network.

Make sure that there is a set of defined hosts and that only they have permission to remotely access the server. There are several ways to do this, such as by using a firewall software, or iptables, or even TCP wrappers. Hardware devices that are available on the market are a viable alternative as well.

You can restrict MySQL's ability to open network sockets. To achieve this, in the `my.cnf` or `my.ini` file, add the following parameter in the [`mysqld`] section:

```
skip-networking
```

Disabling LOCAL INFILE usage

Another modification to perform is to prevent the use of the `LOAD DATA LOCAL INFILE` statement. This will help prevent local files being accessed by unauthorized entities:

```
mysql> LOAD DATA LOCAL INFILE '/etc/passwd' INTO TABLE table1
```

Changing the username and password for root

MySQL server provides `root` as the default username for the administrator. Most hackers aim to get and access the permissions that are set to the `root` user.

A simple way to make it hard for hackers is to change the name from `root` to something different and then set a complex password by using a host of alphanumeric characters.

Using role-based access control increases the security of the database. This would mean there should be a lowering of the system privileges required.

Applying the generic advice given to any database to MySQL, it is highly recommended that you provide a low level of permissions to the various parties involved.

Summary

In this chapter, we covered the new MySQL 8.0 security features, including MySQL roles. This is a new security and administrative feature that allows DBAs to simplify user management and increases the security of their multi-user environments. You also learned about the access privileges system and security plugins. Finally, you learned about the security impact this has on the database server and all the other applications.

We introduced the new security features in MySQL 8.0, the privileges provided by MySQL 8.0, and also explored the differences between dynamic and static privileges. Finally, we looked briefly at the grant table, covered how to troubleshoot a connection problem, and shared some tips and techniques.

11

Advanced MySQL Performance Tips and Techniques

This chapter will cover some important tips/best practices to keep your critical data-reach to its full potential, and through our techniques section, we will answer questions that people often ask regarding large data performance with optimizations, along with the efficient resource utilization of MySQL database. Specifically, this chapter will cover the following topics:

- Tips/best practices
- Techniques

By the end of this chapter, you will understand what patterns and anti-pattern use cases that are used for MySQL are, as well as different ways to enhance and optimize the performance of a database, followed by solutions to commonly asked questions.

Tips/best practices

There are several features of the MySQL database that can be misinterpreted easily. To avoid this, next, we will cover a few of the tips/best practices recommended for building an efficient and optimized MySQL database as a source of truth. The assumption for this entire chapter is that you have access to a local or remote MySQL database.

Optimizing your queries for the query cache

Any database converts raw SQL query statement into an internal structure through which it will process and acknowledge clients accordingly; similarly, MySQL also converts any statement (SQL/stored procedures/functions/triggers/events) into an understandable structure by MySQL's engine. The majority of the queries by an application would be static, with only values changing; for example, during a login call, a SELECT query would be static with only query arguments changing, so MySQL caches that internal structure to eliminate the overhead of internal structure conversion, which, in turn, would utilize those resources for other purposes, resulting in an effective utilization of resources.

The following statements give details of query caching:

```
SHOW VARIABLES LIKE 'have_query_cache';
SHOW VARIABLES LIKE 'query_cache_size';
SET GLOBAL have_query_cache = <YES/NO>;
SET GLOBAL query_cache_size = <size in bytes>;
```

The following screenshot shows the values of the have_query_cache and query_cache_size query caching settings:

```
● ◎ ◉                    Terminal — docker
mysql> SHOW VARIABLES LIKE 'have_query_cache';
+------------------+-------+
| Variable_name    | Value |
+------------------+-------+
| have_query_cache | NO    |
+------------------+-------+
1 row in set (0.00 sec)

mysql> SHOW VARIABLES LIKE 'query_cache_size';
Empty set (0.00 sec)

mysql> _
```

The sizing of this cache depends on multiple parameters, such as the size of the database, query patterns, read and write operations, and hardware specifications. It is understandable that these features would lead to misconceptions concerning the selection of the query cache size; hence, it is recommended to start small and then increase it in small increments and find the static point, after which performance is not enhanced, even after increasing its size for effective resource utilization for the same workload.

The following diagram shows the flow chart of the query-caching process:

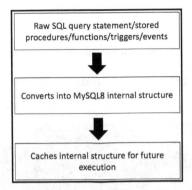

From the flow chart, you can clearly see the entire process of how a query would be processed on MySQL. If prepared statements are used, then it will be even more efficient, which is discussed in later sections of this chapter. This cache, which is maintained by MySQL, is specific to a session; for example, If S1 and S2 are two MySQL sessions, then the cached statements of session S1 will not be accessible by session S2. And when this session ends as its cache, it is cleared by the server.

There are some precautionary steps that need to be taken care of, such as that the schema shouldn't be outdated; if it is, then it will start throwing errors accordingly; hence, restarting all sessions during schema change is a recommended practice.

Refer to *8.10.3 Caching of Prepared Statements and Stored Programs* documentation by MySQL at https://dev.mysql.com/doc/refman/8.0/en/statement-caching.html for more information.

EXPLAIN your SELECT queries

EXPLAIN is a great utility statement in MySQL, which will help us understand the execution plan of the optimizer. This would require SELECT access to view those corresponding tables. With EXPLAIN, you get to know the options/hints for enhancing the performance of your query, such as by adding indexes accordingly to the columns, changing filter criteria for subqueries, the order of joins to be performed, and so on. The result would have all the information required for making decisions such as what kind of select, table name, partitions if they exist, type of columns being used in the where clause, the possible set of keys, the key being used for that query, the number of rows it would have scanned, and the percentage of filtering.

Run the following queries for getting the output:

```
USE mysql;
SELECT Host, Db FROM db;
EXPLAIN SELECT Host, Db FROM db;
EXPLAIN SELECT HOST, count(Db) FROM db GROUP BY Host;
```

The following screenshot displays EXPLAIN on different SELECT queries:

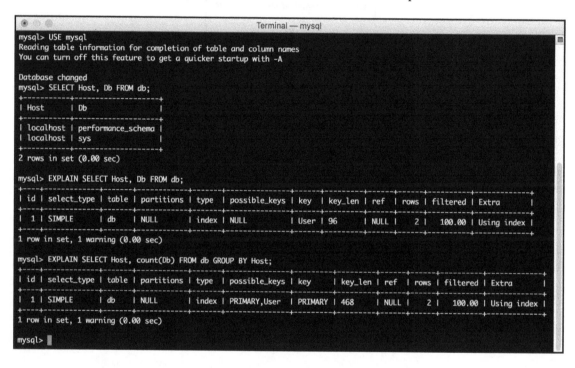

From this screenshot, you can see the amount of information provided for two SELECT statements and the complexity of aggregation queries with GROUP BY, even though both seem to be simple; as there are only two rows in the preceding example, it would increase complexity and degrade performance as the table grows if it has to do an entire table scan without indexes.

DESCRIBE and EXPLAIN are actually synonyms, but DESCRIBE is more widely used for knowing more about table schema, whereas EXPLAIN is used for SQL queries.

Refer to the *EXPLAIN Syntax* documentation by MySQL at https://dev.mysql.com/doc/refman/5.5/en/explain.html for more information.

LIMIT 1 when getting a unique row

LIMIT is another feature that restricts the result set's size based on the number of rows provided. When getting a unique row, it depends on what kind of column the where clause is filtering. For example, if the where clause is filtering on a constrained column (primary key/index), then it wouldn't have any improved performance, as it already knows the location of the filtered row, whereas, on the other hand, if it is used on a non-constrained column, then the overhead of the full table can be eliminated, as it would stop once that where clause is hit, thus resulting in better efficiency and reducing latency.

The following commands explain different select statements with and without LIMIT:

```
EXPLAIN SELECT Host, Db FROM db WHERE Select_priv = 'Y' LIMIT 1;
EXPLAIN SELECT Host, Db FROM db WHERE Select_priv = 'Y';
```

The following screenshot displays using LIMIT on unique rows:

```
                            Terminal — mysql
mysql> USE mysql
Database changed
mysql> EXPLAIN SELECT Host, Db FROM db WHERE Select_priv = 'Y' LIMIT 1;
+----+-------------+-------+------------+------+---------------+------+---------+------+------+----------+-------------+
| id | select_type | table | partitions | type | possible_keys | key  | key_len | ref  | rows | filtered | Extra       |
+----+-------------+-------+------------+------+---------------+------+---------+------+------+----------+-------------+
|  1 | SIMPLE      | db    | NULL       | ALL  | NULL          | NULL | NULL    | NULL |    2 |    50.00 | Using where |
+----+-------------+-------+------------+------+---------------+------+---------+------+------+----------+-------------+
1 row in set, 1 warning (0.00 sec)

mysql> EXPLAIN SELECT Host, Db FROM db WHERE Select_priv = 'Y';
+----+-------------+-------+------------+------+---------------+------+---------+------+------+----------+-------------+
| id | select_type | table | partitions | type | possible_keys | key  | key_len | ref  | rows | filtered | Extra       |
+----+-------------+-------+------------+------+---------------+------+---------+------+------+----------+-------------+
|  1 | SIMPLE      | db    | NULL       | ALL  | NULL          | NULL | NULL    | NULL |    2 |    50.00 | Using where |
+----+-------------+-------+------------+------+---------------+------+---------+------+------+----------+-------------+
1 row in set, 1 warning (0.00 sec)

mysql>
```

Here, the Select_priv column is not a constrained column; hence, an SQL query without LIMIT will have to do a full table scan, whereas LIMIT will stop a table scan at the first hit and acknowledge the client earlier, thus resulting in lower latency. There are a few exceptions that need a deeper analysis of using LIMIT with ORDER BY, which can be referred to from the documentation.

Refer to the *LIMIT Query Optimization* MySQL documentation for further information at https://dev.mysql.com/doc/refman/5.5/en/limit-optimization.html.

If LIMIT is used on constrained columns, then there might not be a significant improvement in latency; as for constrained columns, the MySQL database engine already knows where it is present, then fetches it and acknowledges the client accordingly.

Refer to the MySQL documents for further information on *PRIMARY KEY and UNIQUE Index Constraints* at https://dev.mysql.com/doc/refman/8.0/en/constraint-primary-key.html.

Indexing for search fields

Indexing is a great feature of MySQL database; it can be used wisely, and it is also a best practice to use it for regex filtering through where clauses for those frequently used columns. If indexing is not there, then it would result in a full table scan, which would deteriorate performance as the table grows, resulting in bad schema design. It would use little more disk space than without an index, but it's worth it for desired performance.

For example, consider a user's table that has the userId, firstName, and lastName columns, among which none of them have indexes. If a read query for filtering based on firstName, along with a regex or like pattern in the WHERE clause would definitely have to go through the entire table for getting the result set, which would take longer as the table size grows, resulting in performance degradation due to a full table scan.

The following screenshot shows an example table for search field indexing:

userId	firstName	lastName
uid1	aaaaa	bbbb
uid2	abcd	dcab
uid3	bbbd	dabbb
uid4	efgh	ijk
.	.	.
.	.	.
uidn	zzzz	xyz

If frequently used columns have an index such as `firstName`, then there would be a significant improvement in the performance of the MySQL database. Moreover, it's pretty simple to create an index that makes our regex queries more effective, resulting in lower latencies, even though the table is of multi-million rows.

The syntax for creating `index` is as follows:

```
CREATE INDEX <index name> ON <table name> (<column name>);
```

Hence, it is always recommended to index any kind of search fields for generating a higher performance yield with the same set of resources for the MySQL database.

Refer to the MySQL documentation for further information on *CREATE INDEX Syntax* at https://dev.mysql.com/doc/refman/8.0/en/create-index.html.

Indexing strategy for Joins

It is always recommended to use the same data type columns during joining, along with indexing, as those columns will significantly enhance the performance of the MySQL database without increasing the computational resource capacity of the MySQL database. If you do not follow this approach, you would still get results, but you would get degraded performance and deteriorate as the size of the table grows.

For example, consider two tables: `offers` (`offerID`, `itemId`) and `orders` (`userId`, `itemId`), where they are being joined on the `itemId` column in both tables, performance, and latency. The difference between 2 different strategies where one has different data types for joining columns without indexes and an other that has the same data types along with indexes for joining columns would be significant, even for smaller size of tables. Logically, MySQL would perform better.

The following screenshot shows joining two tables with different data types:

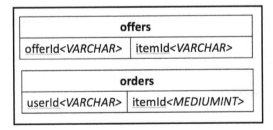

In strategy one, the `itemId` of the `offers` table has a VARCHAR data type, whereas in the `orders` table, it is MEDIUMINT, and both of them do not have any indexes for the `itemId` column.

The following screenshot shows joining two tables with the same data types, along with the indexes:

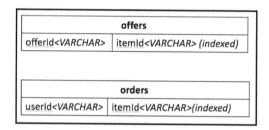

In strategy two, the `itemId` of the `offers` table and the `orders` table have the same data type, *VARCHAR*, along with indexing in both tables. Definitely, strategy 2 is highly recommended for efficient MySQL databases to yield higher performance and lower latency. Logically, MySQL would perform better, as it is indexed, and moreover, MySQL does not have the overhead of converting data from one data type to another for processing the join.

Refer to the MySQL *JOIN Syntax* documentation for further information at `https://dev.mysql.com/doc/refman/8.0/en/join.html`.

Avoiding SELECT * and COUNT *

Avoiding SELECT * and COUNT * is a kind of logical reasoning; for example, imagine you have a use case where you are need an entire table. In these instances, you don't have any option in the matter, but there are drawbacks by doing this, such as the majority of the database resources would be used only for that query, resulting in degraded performance, and thus resulting in higher latencies, as this data would be huge, so it would take a longer time to acknowledge clients.

The syntax is as follows:

```
SELECT * FROM <tableName>;
```

The following screenshot shows an example of the result set of SELECT on all rows and columns:

a11	a12	....	a1n
a21	a22	....	a2n
.	.	....	.
.	.	....	.
.	.	....	.
an1	an2	....	ann

Imagine you are querying an entire table that's 100 GB; an entire 100 GB of data needs be transmitted to the client, which would even block networks, resulting in higher latencies. The preceding screenshot shows a table of n columns and rows, so if SELECT * is used, then it has to fetch all n rows with all its n columns, which makes the resulting size pretty big, among which only desired rows are filtered at the client side.

The syntax is as follows:

```
SELECT * FROM <tableName> WHERE <columnName> = <stringToBeFiltered>;
```

The following shows an example of the result set of SELECT on all columns but restricted rows with the WHERE clause:

a21	a22	....	a2n

If only a specific set of rows are desired, then the WHERE clause can be used to fetch only those sets of rows, rather than the entire data of a table, as here only a particular row is fetched, which makes the result set pretty small, resulting in higher performance and lower latencies.

Refer to the MySQL *SELECT Syntax* documentation for further information at https://dev.mysql.com/doc/refman/8.0/en/select.html.

Similar to SELECT *, there are problems with COUNT * as well, because the MySQL database has to obtain an entire result set and then perform the aggregation on all the columns, which would also use a huge amount of resources, resulting in higher latencies and degraded performances. In fact, it would lock database resources for that query and might result in timeouts for subsequent queries.

The syntax is as follows:

```
SELECT count(*) FROM <tableName>;
```

The following shows an example of how COUNT would be applied to all rows and columns:

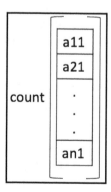

From the table itself, you can see the amount of computational power required for producing the result. This can also be achieved by counting only on a single column, which is a primary key. This is a more optimized way of getting the count of an entire table or subset of a table.

The syntax is as follows:

```
SELECT count(<columnName>) FROM <tableName>;
```

The following diagram shows an example of how COUNT would be applied to all rows and restricted columns:

Instead of counting across all columns, it would improve performance drastically just by counting on a unique column that may not be a primary key, but for this reason, it has to perform an entire table scan, and this can also be optimized by counting on a primary key that is also unique, resulting in higher performance and lower latencies. The more data is read from the tables, the slower the query will become.

Refer to the *Counting Rows* MySQL documentation for further information at `https://dev.mysql.com/doc/refman/8.0/en/counting-rows.html`.

Almost always have an ID field

It is always recommended to use an independent ID field, even though there is an existing unique field present. For example, consider an application that was launched only for mobile users; if you look at the following table, it has `mobileNumber` as the primary key; as long as this schema is static and there's business use cases as well, then you wouldn't have any issues with it, apart from different sizes of mobile numbers based on locality and country.

The following diagram shows an example table of `mobileNumber` as an ID field:

mobileNumber	firstName	lastName
mob1	mob1fName	mob1lName
mob2	mob2fName	mob2lName
.	.	.
.	.	.
mobn	mobnfName	mobnlName

Then, the business wanted to expand this application to email users as well, where the email ID can also be part of the primary key. At this point, you would have to rewrite the entire schema and table with this additional column. There are other ways to implement this feature, but there are more drawbacks than benefits of those implementations; hence, we will stick to rewriting the entire schema and data of this table, which would result in more resource effort, downtime, and so on. Moreover, it would take higher response times for the VARCHAR data type column than for the INT data type column.

The following shows an example table of `mobileNumber` and `email` as an ID field:

mobileNumberOrEmail	firstName	lastName
mob1	mob1fName	mob1lName
email1	email1fName	email1lName
. .	. .	. .
mobn	mobnfName	mobnlName

After all the rework, the business has asked you to expand to pager users and landline users as well. Therefore, you have to redo all the effort as it was done during the email user's expansion; however, this problem can be eliminated if there is a unique ID field that's independent of any feature data (mobile number/email ID/pager number/landline number) that was being used. In this case, if the `userIdentifier` column is of the `VARCHAR` data type, which has the compatibility of any kind of user identifier, then it would eliminate rework, resulting in an optimized schema and entire schema driven by `userId`.

The following diagram shows an example table of using an independent `userId` as the ID field:

userId	userIdentifier	firstName	lastName
id1	mob1	mob1fName	mob1lName
id2	email1	email1fName	email1lName
id3	pager1	pager1fName	pager1lName
. .	.	. .	. .
idn	mobn	mobnfName	mobnlName

Clearly, this independent ID column (`userID`) has solved the majority of the complexity; moreover, it is highly recommended to use auto-increment (`AUTO_INCREMENT`) for that column, as `INT` is more effective in operations and uses less resources for any computational tasks. Hence, it is always recommended to use an ID field that is independent of the feature data, along with `AUTO_INCREMENT`.

Refer to the *Using AUTO_INCREMENT* MySQL documentation for further information at `https://dev.mysql.com/doc/refman/8.0/en/example-auto-increment.html`.

Using ENUM over VARCHAR

Another recommended best practice is to use the ENUM data type for a limited number of static values for a column, rather than the VARCHAR data type. For example, consider a user profile table that contains userId, userIdentifier, firstName, lastName, and gender, among which gender has a limited number of values (male/female/other) that are also static; for this kind of use case, ENUM is more efficient than VARCHAR size-wise, as well as performance-wise.

Performance would also be based on the data type chosen for the data as it grows. It would be fine for smaller dataset sizes, but as it grows, if the right data type is chosen, then there would be degraded performance increasing to higher latencies, even though you are increasing the computational power of the MySQL database.

The size of the VARCHAR data type would be based on the length of the string; hence, it would be an average of 5 bytes per row and is occupied by the gender cell, which requires an amount of computational resource and disk capacity.

The following diagram shows an example table of a gender column in VARCHAR:

userId	userIdentifier	firstName	lastName	gender
id1	mob1	mob1fName	mob1lName	male
id2	email1	email1fName	email1lName	female
id3	pager1	pager1fName	pager1lName	other
.	.	.	.	.
.	.	.	.	.
idn	mobn	mobnfName	mobnlName	male

From the preceding table, it is clearly seen that gender can only be male/female/other and if this table has 100 million rows, then there would be a huge difference between using gender as an ENUM data type over a VARCHAR.

Refer to *The CHAR and VARCHAR Types* MySQL documentation for further information at https://dev.mysql.com/doc/refman/8.0/en/char.html.

On the other hand, with the ENUM data type, an actual skeleton/indexed data is stored in the meta of the table schema, and the actual cell of the gender column would store only the corresponding index that points to a value, which boosts the performance of the MySQL database significantly for the same amount of computational resources given to MySQL. Moreover, on the client side, it would display an actual value, rather than an index that makes it readable, and MySQL intelligently takes care of converting them while writing or reading the ENUM data type column.

The syntax for creating the ENUM data type during table creation is as follows:

```
gender ENUM('male', 'female', 'other')
```

The following diagram shows an example table of gender column in ENUM:

Value	Index
NULL	NULL
male	0
female	1
other	2

There are some limitations as well when using ENUM data types, such as it has to be predefined during table creation, which makes its options for a column limited, but it would increase performance significantly, and, moreover, it would have less disk footprint, as ENUM would store the only index in which only a byte per cell rather than a couple of byes in VARCHAR. Hence, it is recommended to use ENUM over VARCHAR in use cases such as this.

Refer to *The ENUM Type* MySQL documentation for further information at https://dev.mysql.com/doc/refman/8.0/en/enum.html.

Using prepared statements if and when possible

It is recommended to use prepared statements for all those queries that are frequently used for better performance. For example, as we discussed in earlier sections, for a login call, the read query is the same for any number of users, so even though caching increases the performance of turn-around latency, this prepared statement will enhance it further, because the payload size is smaller when the client is making that call to the MySQL database, thus reducing the network packet size indirectly, therefore enhancing performance and reducing latency.

The syntax of the prepared statement is as follows:

```
PREPARE <name of prepared statement> FROM '<SQL statement to be prepared>';
```

The following diagram shows a flow chart of the prepared statements process:

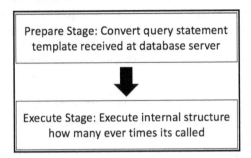

The process, which is involved in the end-to-end execution of a prepared statement, is clearly shown in the diagram, where it is divided into two stages: firstly, the preparation stage, where a raw SQL query statement is converted to a prepared statement like assigning a value to a variable, followed by the execution stage, where the prepared statement name is passed with corresponding arguments, which reduces payload size and increases the efficiency of a database. It would even have the added security of a table schema, without being exposed to threats.

Refer to the *Prepared SQL Statement Syntax* MySQL documentation for further information at https://dev.mysql.com/doc/refman/8.0/en/sql-syntax-prepared-statements.html.

Splitting the big DELETE or INSERT queries

There would be times when the cleaning of old data is a requirement from a business or data-retention perspective, and in those situations, it is always recommended to split them into multi-threaded so there is a smaller set of queries, rather than one big fat query. If the retention policy is well-built and maintained, then this situation may not exist at all. Or even if there is a batch process to perform these kinds of operations on a regular basis, such as daily, this also might cause an outage to your application.

For example, if a business wanted all of those 100K test accounts that are not being used in the production environment to be deleted, then, in that case, there are multiple options to write this query, such as combining an entire range of those test accounts into a single delete query and running it against a production database. If you run it in this way, then your table will be locked by your delete job until it is finished, and until then, all the other actual live user traffic would be waiting for this delete job to release the lock for processing live traffic. In these cases, your application would be facing an outage.

The following diagram shows the execution of the DELETE operation of multiple rows in a single big query:

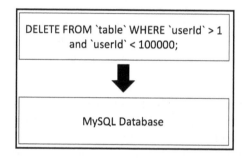

To overcome this outage, it is highly recommended to split your big fat query into multiple small queries on a multi-thread of a single thread based on the requirement that it would eliminate an outage to your application, resulting in 100% availability for user traffic. It is not hard to split them into multiple queries with a single delete job, either on a single thread or a multi-thread. This process would definitely split that lock time as per your splitting logic in the delete job.

The following diagram shows the execution of the DELETE operation of multiple rows in multiple small queries:

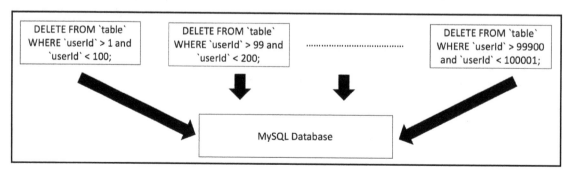

As we can see, if a big fat query takes 10 minutes to be executed, then, that whole time, all the queries depending on that table would have to sit and wait, resulting in time-outs, as generally it would be set to 3-5 seconds, resulting in lost business. On the other hand, if they are split, then there might be a performance impact such as slowness, but the outage would be mitigated; moreover, this slowness can even be reduced by splitting even further in a single delete job or running during the maintenance window.

Refer to the *DELETE Syntax* MySQL documentation for further information at `https://dev.mysql.com/doc/refman/8.0/en/delete.html`.

Similar to a big `DELETE`, even `INSERT` can also cause the locking of that table untill all the inserts of that query have been processed and acknowledged according to the client. Both are related to changing data in a table, resulting in an outage that can be mitigated by splitting them into multiple queries in a single insert job with single or multi-threaded.

Refer to the *INSERT Syntax* MySQL documentation for further information at `https://dev.mysql.com/doc/refman/8.0/en/insert.html`.

Avoiding the delete trigger

Using trigger is acceptable for any application, but when it comes to the delete trigger, I recommend you avoid it. One of the reasons is that it's very hard to regain data once it is deleted, as restoring a table from backup that has a set of stale data is not advisable at all, as it might incur data inconsistencies from that table with others. In this case, you would have to restore the entire MySQL database, which is stale, resulting in lost trust from users, and frustrating them.

For example, due to business requirements, if the corresponding data is deleted through a trigger that might have a dependency on a new feature, it would be really hard to regain that data. Moreover, new developers might miss this, as it is part of the database, and a new development might trigger this delete hence, resulting in losing that data.

The syntax of a trigger is as follows:

```
CREATE
    TRIGGER <trigger name>
    <trigger time> <trigger event>
    ON <table name> FOR EACH ROW
    [<trigger order>]
    trigger_body
```

```
trigger_time: { BEFORE | AFTER }
trigger_event: { INSERT | UPDATE | DELETE }
trigger_order: { FOLLOWS | PRECEDES } <other trigger name>
```

You need to be cautious when using a trigger itself, because it might result in degrading the performance if those events fall into an infinite loop. Alternatively, if there is a huge amount of load on the MySQL database, then having a trigger for certain set of events would degrade its performance even more and thus resulting in higher latencies.

If you need to delete something, even as part of a business's requirements, or a data retention process, then it should be formed as a batch process that can be run during a maintenance window, thus eliminating performance degradation of the database. Moreover, it would be a controlled way for the cleaning of that data, which needs to be deleted. Hence, it is highly recommended to avoid using delete triggers for any set of use cases.

Refer to the *CREATE TRIGGER Syntax* MySQL documentation for further information at `https://dev.mysql.com/doc/refman/8.0/en/create-trigger.html`.

Techniques

Apart from using features in the right way, there are certain parameters that can be tweaked based on use cases being solved by MySQL. These will be discussed in further sections, along with common reasoning for deteriorating performance for a large or small database.

Can MySQL perform queries on billions of rows?

MySQL can perform queries on many, many rows, but it also depends on the kind of query being executed. For example, if a read query contains filtering of only the primary key being equated, then that is a kind of golden query and, yes, it will perform well, but, at the same time, if it is a range/like/regex query for a primary key, then it will perform not quite as well as the previous query.

But if a query uses a non-constrained column, its performance would be worse, due to a full table scan. So, MySQL does have good performance for a table containing many rows, but it depends on the query pattern being used.

Is InnoDB the right choice for multi-billion rows?

If you have multi-billion rows, InnoDB is definitely the right choice, but, depending on the payload size of the response, it might or might not be the right choice. For example, if the average row size is around 10 MB, then it would definitely cause performance issues, which would lead to the misinterpretation of the multi-billion rows capability, but, at the same time, if an average row size is around 1 KB, then InnoDB is definitely the right choice for a multi-billion rows dataset.

How big can a MySQL database get before the performance starts to degrade?

This is debatable. Based on schema and query complexity performance, it can degrade or enhance, because there are MySQL databases that are optimized and efficient at having more than a billion rows due to proper implementation. On another hand, if they have deteriorating performance, even for a thousand rows, that is totally due to the schema and complexity of the MySQL database, along with the kind of query being performed on it.

Why MySQL could be slow with large tables

The primary reasons for degraded performance with larger tables is due to the query pattern/kind of query being performed. For example, querying on non-constrained/non-indexed columns would definitely result in higher response times because it has to perform an entire table scan, which is a resource-intensive process, leading to degraded performance. Another kind of query is range scans, which has a similar reasoning to non-constrained columns.

Is MySQL the best solution for handling blobs?

It would vary based on the kind of blob (TINYBLOB/BLOB/MEDIUMBLOB/LONGBLOB) being used, as they vary on capacity, which is from 1 byte to approximately 4.3 GB. Because MySQL is definitely the best solution to any kind of blob, it would depend on the size of the table and how frequently it would be used.

For example, `TINYBLOB/BLOB` types of blobs with millions of rows would definitely be the best solution, whereas `MEDIUMBLOB/LONGBLOB` with millions of rows and frequent operations would definitely result in degraded performance. Moreover, table-related operations such as `OPTIMIZE/ALTER` type of operations have longer execution times due to the size of the table.

Refer to the *Data Type Storage Requirements* MySQL docs at `https://dev.mysql.com/doc/refman/8.0/en/storage-requirements.html` for further information.

Summary

There are several SQL databases, among which MySQL is one; it has a number of unique features that are better than those of other databases due to its ease of implementation for enhancing efficiency and optimizing it. But due to this ease, many implementations land in an anti-pattern side, which results in the deterioration of performance.

This chapter provides different tips/best practices and techniques that help in overcoming these situations. We started with caching queries as shock absorbers for same query repetition, optimizing queries based on an execution plan using `EXPLAIN`, limiting the result set size with `LIMIT`, indexing search fields, the disadvantages of using `SELECT */COUNT *`, the recommended way of having an ID field along with other columns, optimization using prepared statements, splitting big `DELETE/INSERT` statements to avoid a deadlock state, and the reasons for avoiding delete implementation through trigger.

This was followed by a discussion on the billion rows performance of MySQL database, InnoDB with multi-billion rows, the limitations of the MySQL database before which it starts deteriorating, performance degradation on large tables, and the handling of the `BLOB` data type in the MySQL database.

Other Books You May Enjoy

If you enjoyed this book, you may be interested in these other books by Packt:

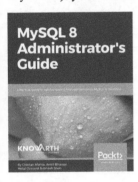

MySQL 8 Administrator's Guide
Chintan Mehta, Ankit K Bhavsar, Hetal Oza, Subhash Shah

ISBN: 978-1-78839-519-9

- Understanding different MySQL 8 data types based on type of contents and storage requirements
- Best practices for optimal use of features in MySQL 8
- Explore globalization configuration and caching techniques to improve performance
- Create custom storage engine as per system requirements
- Learn various ways of index implementation for flash memory storages
- Configure and implement replication along with approaches to use replication as solution
- Understand how to make your MySQL 8 solution highly available
- Troubleshoot common issues and identify error codes while using MySQL 8

MySQL 8 Cookbook
Karthik Appigatla

ISBN: 978-1-78839-580-9

- Install and configure your MySQL 8 instance without any hassle
- Get to grips with new features of MySQL 8 like CTE, Window functions and many more
- Perform backup tasks, recover data and set up various replication topologies for your database
- Maximize performance by using new features of MySQL 8 like descending indexes, controlling query optimizer and resource groups
- Learn how to use general table space to suit the SaaS or multi-tenant applications
- Analyze slow queries using performance schema, sys schema and third party tools
- Manage and monitor your MySQL instance and implement efficient performance-tuning tasks

Leave a review - let other readers know what you think

Please share your thoughts on this book with others by leaving a review on the site that you bought it from. If you purchased the book from Amazon, please leave us an honest review on this book's Amazon page. This is vital so that other potential readers can see and use your unbiased opinion to make purchasing decisions, we can understand what our customers think about our products, and our authors can see your feedback on the title that they have worked with Packt to create. It will only take a few minutes of your time, but is valuable to other potential customers, our authors, and Packt. Thank you!

Index

A

agentless monitoring 219
Amazon Web Services (AWS) 223
ARCHIVE storage engine 207
asynchronous replication 144
atomic DDL 18
atomicity consistency isolation and durability
    (ACID) 157, 208
auto-increment counter 17

B

B-tree type index 90
batch jobs 15
big data 18
binary log 143
BLACKHOLE storage engine 207
blobs
    handling 261

C

certification process, group replication
    about 151
    failure, detecting 152
    network, partitioning 153
    total order delivery 151
    traditional locking, versus optimistic locking 154
    tuple, modifying across primary 154
Classless Inter-Domain Routing (CIDR) 169
combined index 95, 104
commands, MySQL Shell
    AdminAPI 186
    Shell commands 186
    ShellAPI 186
common table expression (CTE) 6
connection problems
    troubleshooting 240, 241

CPU usage
    case study 130
    correcting 132
    detecting 131
    preventing 132
critical phase 7
CSV storage engine 206

D

data dictionary
    applications 119
    benefits 117
    limitations 121
    problems 116
    structure 115, 116
    transactional storage 118
data redundancy 138
database replication, MySQL
    asynchronous replication 144
    global transaction identifier (GTID)-based
        replication 145
    multi-source replication 146
    overview 142
    semi-synchronous replication 144
database
    size complexity 261
Datadog
    about 222
    conclusion 225
    cons 225
    installing 222, 223
    pros 224
declarative 29
delayed replication
    about 145
    use cases 145
dictionary object cache 117, 118

disk swapping 133
duplicate index
  avoiding 86, 87
dynamic privileges
  AUDIT_ADMIN 237
  BACKUP_ADMIN 237

E

EXPLAIN plan tool
  case study 57, 60, 62, 63, 65
  EXPLAIN options 58, 59, 60
  missing index, creating 65, 66, 67
EXPLAIN results, reading
  id() 44
  partitions() 45
  select_type() 44
  table() 45
  type() 45

F

FEDERATED storage engine 208
file-based storage metadata
  removing 119
full-scan indicators 74, 75, 76

G

global data dictionary 9, 10, 12
global transaction identifier (GTID)-based
    replication
  about 145
  generating 146
gray-zone phase 7
GROUP BY clause
  for query optimization 94, 95, 96
group communication system
  about 149, 151
  working 149, 151
group communication thread (GCT) 174
group replication, security
  IP address whitelist 169
  managing 169
  SSL 170
  VPN 171
group replication, use cases
  about 140

autonomic systems 142
elastic replication 140
highly available shards 141
master - slave replication, alternatives 142
group replication
  about 138, 139, 140
  architecture 147
  certification process 151
  configuring 158, 159, 160, 161, 163, 164, 166
  group 148
  limitations 168, 169
  modes 155
  monitoring 166
  multi-primary mode 157
  replication_applier_status 167
  replication_connection_status 167
  replication_group_member_stats 166
  replication_group_members 166
  requisites 157
  server, configuring 158
  server, state 167
  single primary mode 156
  writeset 148

H

HASH partitioning 82
high availability
  about 136
  requisites 136
  scaling 136, 137
horizontal partitioning 77

I

index
  columns, organizing 54, 55, 56
  creating 48, 49
  data type, considerations 30, 31
  for optimizing MySQL performance 33, 34
  strategy 32, 33
Indexed Sequential Access Method (ISM) 205
InnoDB cluster
  about 182, 184
  details, obtaining 202
  dissolving 203
  installing 188

installing, for sandbox environment 188, 189, 191, 192, 194

installing, in production environment 195, 196, 197, 199

instance states, checking 203

instances, adding 202

instances, removing 202

limitations 203

management 201

master-slave replication, migrating 209, 210, 212, 214

MySQL Shell, installing 184

rebooting 202

requisites 184

rescanning 202

restoring, after quorum loss 202

router, configuration 199

InnoDB engine

  about 208

  advantages 209

  features 208

InnoDB

  enhancements 18

  for multi-billion rows 261

invisible indexes 6

J

JSON

  enhancements 18, 19, 21

K

KEY partitioning 83

L

LIST partitioning 80, 81, 82

M

mass DELETE

  example 111, 112

Master 143

master-slave replication

  migrating, to InnoDB cluster 209, 210, 212, 214

MEMORY storage engine 206

MERGE storage engine 207

missing index

  handling 88, 89

monitoring tools, comparison

  clients 230

  cons 230

  pros 229

  with price 229

MONyog

  about 218

  conclusion 221

  cons 220

  pros 219

  tips 231

multi primary mode 157

multi-source replication

  about 146

  use cases 146

multiple column index

  versus multiple indexes 49, 51, 52, 54

multiple rows

  queries, performing 260

MyISAM storage engine 205

MySQL 8.0

  privileges 234

MySQL 8

  architecture design 7

  features 6, 24

  history 12, 13

  need for 6

  removed features 24, 25

  resource groups, creating 14, 15, 16, 17

  resource groups, managing 14, 15, 16, 17

  support roles 12, 13

MySQL optimizer

  improvements 28, 29, 30

  invisible indexes 21, 22, 23

  soft delete 22

  staged rollout 22

MySQL Shell, commands

  SQL syntax 186

  X DevAPI 186

MySQL Shell

  installing 184

  reference 184

  using 185, 186, 187, 188

MySQL
  database replication 142
  group replication, architecture 147
  reference 5, 21

N

Navicat
  about 225
  conclusion 228
  cons 228
  pros 227

O

online group
  flow control 175, 177
  group replication versions, combining 173
  message compression 174
  mode, modifying 172
  operations 171
  performance, tuning 174
  recovery, tuning 172
  server, setting as primary 171
optimistic locking
  drawbacks 155
  versus traditional locking 154
ORDER BY clause
  for query optimization 96, 97, 98

P

partitioning
  about 76
  HASH partitioning 82
  horizontal partitioning 77
  KEY partitioning 83
  LIST partitioning 80, 81, 82
  managing 77
  overview 76
  partition pruning 84, 85
  RANGE partitioning 78, 79, 80
  techniques 107
  tips 107
  types 77
  using 84
Paxos protocol 138
performance optimization, tips

delete trigger, avoiding 259
  INSERT queries, splitting 259
persisting configuration variables 6
privileges, MySQL 8.0
  administrative privileges 234
  database privileges 234
  dynamic privileges 237
  for specific database objects 234
  static privileges 236
  storing 235

Q

queries
  performing, on multiple rows 260
query execution plan
  EXPLAIN results, reading 41, 42, 44
  EXTRA column 46, 47
  reading 41
query optimization
  about 90
  case study 101, 102, 104
  techniques 108
  tips 108
  with GROUP BY clause 94, 95, 96
  with ORDER BY clause 96, 97, 98
  with WHERE clause 90, 91, 92, 93, 94

R

RANGE partitioning 78, 79, 80
ranges 19
redo log 17
relational database management system (RDBMS)
  7
reliable source 11
replication 137
replication topology
  elasticity 138
  fault tolerance 138
  high availability 138
resource groups
  creating 14, 15, 17
  limitations 14
  managing 14, 15, 17
roles
  creating 237, 238, 239

displaying, with SHOW GRANTS 239
routing strategy algorithms
  next-available 201
  round-robin-with-fallback 201
row-based logging 143

S

scaling 136
security, tips
  LOCAL INFILE usage, disabling 241
  password, modifying 242
  username, modifying 242
security
  features 233, 234
semi-synchronous replication 144
Serialized Dictionary Information (SDI)
  about 120
  advantages 120
server optimization
  about 125
  adaptive hash indexing function, enabling 125
  amount of InnoDB pre-loading, controlling 126
  data change operations, controlling 125
  InnoDB buffer pool 128, 129
  InnoDB input/output performance, controlling 127
  multicore processors, advantage 127
  number and size of instances, configuring 127
  number of background threads, increasing 126
  number of concurrent threads, limiting 126
  punctual operations, preventing 127
shard 137
shared center 11
shared-disk 136
shared-nothing 137
SHOW GRANTS
  assigned roles, displaying 239
single primary mode 156
slave server 15, 143
Software as a Service (SaaS) 222
sort indexes
  optimizing 105, 106
statement based logging 143
static privileges
  about 236

ALTER 236
ALTER ROUTINE 236
CREATE 236
CREATE ROLE 236
CREATE ROUTINE 236
CREATE TABLESPACE 237
CREATE USER 237
CREATE VIEW 237
DELETE 237
DROP 237
DROP ROLE 237
EXECUTE 237
FILE 237
storage engine
  about 204
  ARCHIVE storage engine 207
  BLACKHOLE storage engine 207
  CSV storage engine 206
  FEDERATED storage engine 208
  InnoDB engine 208
  MEMORY storage engine 206
  MERGE storage engine 207
  MyISAM storage engine 205
  setting 205
swap space 133

T

table structure
  analyzing 35, 37, 38, 39, 40, 41
  displaying 35, 37, 38, 39, 40, 41
tables
  impact on performance 261
  partitioning 76
temporary tables 98, 99, 100, 101
thread cache
  about 129, 130
  CPU usage, case study 130
threads 14
time series data
  use case 108, 109, 111
tips, performance optimization
  about 243
  COUNT *, avoiding 250, 252, 253
  DELETE queries, splitting 257, 258, 259
  ENUM, using over VARCHAR 255, 256

EXPLAIN, with SELECT queries 245, 246
ID field, using 253, 254
indexing strategy, for Joins 249, 250
indexing, for search fields 248, 249
INSERT queries, splitting 257, 258
LIMIT, using 247, 248
prepared statements, using 256, 257
queries, optimizing for query cache 244, 245
SELECT *, avoiding 250, 252, 253
tips, query execution plan
  about 67
  case study 70, 71, 72
  configuration 69
  material resources 68
  performance recommendations, of MySQL
    architecture 70
  queries, optimizing 68
  rules, for indexes 67
tips, security
  about 241
  remote access, disabling to server 241
  remote access, restricting to server 241
traditional locking
  versus optimistic locking 154
transactional data dictionary
  tips 121
transactional storage
  of data dictionary 118
type, EXPLAIN results
  all 46
  const 45
  eq_ref 45
  fulltext 45
  index 46

index_merge 46
index_subquery 46
range 46
ref 45
ref_or_null 45
unique_subquery 46

U

unused index
  avoiding 86, 87
user-defined functions (UDFs) 171
users
  creating 237, 238, 239

V

variables
  about 123
  innodb_buffer_pool_size 124
  innoDB_flush_method 124
  max_heap_table_size 124
  query_cache_limit 124
  query_cache_size 124
  query_cache_type 124
  table_open_cache 124
  techniques 133
  tips 133
  tmp_table_size 124
virtual private network (VPN) 169, 171

W

WHERE clause
  for query optimization 90, 91, 92, 93, 94
writeset 148

Lightning Source UK Ltd.
Milton Keynes UK
UKHW031806160622
404538UK00008B/703